RURAL
WOMAN
BATTERING
AND THE
JUSTICE
SYSTEM

SVAW

Sage Series on Violence Against Women

Series Editors

Claire M. Renzetti
St. Joseph's University

Jeffrey L. Edleson
University of Minnesota

In this series. . .

RURAL WOMAN BATTERING AND THE JUSTICE SYSTEM
An Ethnography

Neil Websdale

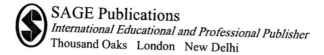

Sage Series on Violence Against Women

SAGE Publications
International Educational and Professional Publisher
Thousand Oaks   London   New Delhi

For information:

SAGE Publications, Inc.
2455 Teller Road
Thousand Oaks, California 91320
E-mail: order@sagepub.com

SAGE Publications Ltd.
6 Bonhill Street
London EC2A 4PU
United Kingdom

SAGE Publications India Pvt. Ltd.
M-32 Market
Greater Kailash I
New Delhi 110 048 India

Printed in the United States of America

Library of Congress Cataloging-in-Publication Data

Websdale, Neil.
   Rural woman battering and the justice system: An ethnography/
by Neil Websdale.
      p.   cm.—(Sage series on violence against women; v. 6)
   Includes bibliographical references and index.
   ISBN 0-7619-0852-8 (pbk.: acid-free paper).—ISBN 0-7619-0851-X
(cloth : acid-free paper)
   1. Abused women—Kentucky. 2. Rural women—Kentucky—
Social conditions. 3. Criminal justice, Administration of—Kentucky.
I. Title. II. Series.
HV6250.4.W65W453 1997
364.15'553'09769—dc21   97-33760

          00 01 02 03 04 10 9 8 7 6 5 4 3

Acquiring Editor:	C. Terry Hendrix
Editorial Assistant:	Dale Mary Grenfell
Production Editor:	Michele Lingre
Production Assistant:	Denise Santoyo
Typesetter/Designer:	Andrea D. Swanson
Indexer:	Julie Grayson
Cover Designer:	Candice Harman
Print Buyer:	Anna Chin

Cover photograph by John Websdale

For Amy and Mia

Contents

Acknowledgments

Andrew Bush helped turn me on to sociology and I thank him for that and a number of other dubious favors. I am also grateful to Eva Gamarnikow at the University of London, Institute of Education, and to historian and barrister-at-law, Margherita Rendel, who did much to nurture my early interest in gender and power. I commenced researching *Rural Woman Battering and the Justice System* while teaching Sociology and Criminology at Morehead State University in Kentucky. There I found a warm working environment and would like to acknowledge the helpful and varied contributions of Dave Rudy, Ed Reeves, Karl Kunkel, Jamie Dahlberg, Ric Karic, and George Ecklund. Since coming to Northern Arizona University I have benefited greatly from the insights of Ray Michalowski, with whom I discussed a number of the ideas about rural criminal justice that appear in the book. My conversations with Ralph Weisheit and Evelyn Zellerer about rural crime and justice issues have also been most helpful, as have my more general exchanges with my good friend and colleague, Alex Alvarez.

My research was generously supported by two research grants from Morehead State University and three from Northern Arizona University. Susanna Maxwell, Dean of the College of Social and Behavioral Sciences at Northern Arizona, has been especially supportive of my research endeavors. I thank her.

The backbone of this book derives from my lengthy conversations with 50 rural battered women, resident in various spouse abuse shelters in Kentucky. They offered up the connective tissue of rural patriarchy and I have benefited from that offering in ways they will not. I thank them.

I also want to recognize the important contributions of 46 other people whom I interviewed regarding rural woman battering. In addition, there are numerous other key informants, including judges, police officers, attorneys, and advocates, whose names I cannot make public but whose contribution to some of the finer details of the manuscript was crucial. Several judges spoke with me off the record about some very difficult decisions they made. Attacked by the press, these judges did not want their side of the story to appear in this book. I have respected their wishes and thank them for taking the time to explain their positions to me privately. In all cases, names have been changed or permission was obtained.

Material from the following publications was used with permission: the McCreary County Record, the Lexington Herald-Leader, Pulaski Week, and the Troublesome Creek Times.

I thank sociologist Laurie Garkovich at the University of Kentucky for providing me with useful data on the social condition of rural women in Kentucky. I am most grateful to Stan Swarts, Department of Geography, Northern Arizona University, for producing the regional map of Kentucky. At the Kentucky Commission On Women, former Executive Director Marsha Weinstein and current Executive Assistant Lindsay Campbell generously provided me with useful materials and information. Staff at the Kentucky Domestic Violence Association (KDVA) helped in many ways. Gil Thurman and Monique Parker-Knoll of the KDVA went out of their way to assist me. The Executive Director of the KDVA, Sherrie Currens, educated me about domestic violence and politics. This book could not have been written without the input of her sharp mind, her astute appreciation of political processes, and her numerous contacts. At the time of doing this research, shelter directors Peggy Payne, Ramon Walton, Connie Wagers, Melissa Kemp, Judi Elder, Becky Hagan, Debbie Stevens, Beverly Fenigstein, the late Marlice Pillow, and Helen Kinton helped to introduce me to women who wanted to tell their stories, and otherwise offered invaluable assistance as I tried to make sense of rural battering. Stephanie Hong, then a counselor at the Lexington YWCA spouse abuse shelter, also offered valuable insights. Of these women,

Helen Kinton, then president of the KDVA, was especially helpful. As director of Sanctuary Incorporated, Hopkinsville, Kentucky, Helen is a veritable gold mine of information about rural domestic violence. I thank her in particular.

In addition to my ethnographic research, Byron Johnson and I surveyed battered women in Kentucky shelters about their victimization and their experiences of policing and the judiciary. Together we traveled many thousands of miles in Kentucky and became much more than co-researchers. I thank Byron for his many insights into my work.

Claire Renzetti and Jeff Edleson read earlier drafts of the manuscript and offered many helpful suggestions concerning its development. I am grateful to them for their insights, kindness, and support. Diane Reese, Executive Director of the West Virginia Coalition Against Domestic Violence, critiqued a later draft and provided detailed feedback. I am very grateful to her. Likewise, the production staff at Sage have assisted me in numerous ways. In particular, I want to thank Dale Grenfell for her kindness.

The chapter titled "Policing Rural Woman Battering" was written at June Takenaka's house in Hawaii. I want to thank her for her hospitality and generosity over the years. Although the bulk of the manuscript was written in Flagstaff, Arizona, parts of it took shape at my parents' house in East Anglia, England. I am indebted to my parents, Molly and John Websdale, for their love and kindness toward me. Likewise, I want to thank my sisters, Jill Minter and Judy Flew, who have supported and helped me in many ways over the years. Finally, I'd like to thank my wife Amy and our daughter Mia for the countless ways they have contributed toward my work and enriched my life.

Introduction

Over the past decade or so, policymakers have increasingly come to realize the epidemic proportions of violence against women in the home. It is easy to see how one of the alternative pop/folk/rock icons of the past 30 years, Leonard Cohen in his song "Democracy," can wax lyrical about the "homicidal bitchin' " that occurs in the kitchens of family homes over "who will serve and who will eat."[1] Put simply, intimate gender relations in the United States are a lightning rod for assault and homicide. Likewise, these relationships are also marked by enormous psychological tension and antagonism, regardless of whether such hostilities manifest themselves as physical violence. At the same time, many families are the sites of love, intimacy of all kinds, and support for constituent members.

These observations are not new. The research literature on violence between intimates is massive, and continues to grow. My purpose in writing this book is to draw attention to a phenomenon that has received scant research attention: namely rural woman battering and the so-called justice system's response to that violence. One of the reasons for the neglect of woman battering in rural communities is that researchers have ignored rural communities. There may be any number of explanations for this neglect. It is not easy for researchers to study rural communities. Rural citizens tend to be suspicious of outsiders in general. Even conducting research through techniques such as telephone surveying is more problematic in rural communities because telephone subscription rates can be much lower than they are in cities. Another reason for the dearth of research into rural domestic violence may be the popular tendency to see rural communities as more tranquil than urban ones. This image of tranquillity is not mythical. Rather, it is supported by crime statistics that show much lower levels of violent crimes such as robbery and aggravated assault in rural regions. However, as research reveals, violence within families does not follow the same social patterns as street violence. As I go on to show, rural families seem just as prone to outbreaks of violence against women as their urban counterparts. Take for example the following murder-suicide that occurred in rural Eastern Kentucky.

Myrtle Whitaker survived her husband's attempt to murder her.[2] Myrtle had been victimized for many years by her husband, Allen Whitaker, Jr., prior to the abusive episode on December 15, 1990, when Allen Jr. tried to murder Myrtle and successfully murdered two of his sons and then killed himself. The couple started dating when he was 18 and she was 16. Myrtle noted that in the early days of their dating "he was good to me" (*Lexington Herald-Leader*, March 27, 1991, p. A6). They married on June 21, 1973 and Myrtle reported that "the next day he changed. . . . He was my boss. I had to do what he said" (*Lexington Herald-Leader*, March 27, 1991, p. A6). In 1981 she left him to live with her parents in a small house in Puncheon Camp hollow in Eastern Kentucky. He arrived at her parents' house a few days later and ordered his wife and children into his truck at gunpoint. As the family left, Allen held a gun to Myrtle's head. Fearing for her life, she told her parents not to call the Magoffin County sheriff. Allen Jr. continued to abuse his wife and children over the years. The family lived in a remote hollow known as Bear Branch. Their house, like other houses in the hollow, had no running water and no indoor toilet, and the nearest road was a mile away. Allen Jr. had a job as a Magoffin County school bus driver and Myrtle received $614 a month in disability and welfare payments. He controlled his family tightly. According to Myrtle's mother, Susie Prater, "He didn't allow them to talk to nobody . . . just whoever he wanted them to speak to. He wouldn't let her visit nobody" (*Lexington Herald-Leader*, December 30, 1990, p. A10). Arbie "Bubby" Sublett, whose sister married into the Prater family, commented that, "He kept them up in a hollow . . . like cattle" (*Lexington Herald-Leader*, December 30, 1990, p. A10).

Myrtle was ensnared in a network of deeply conflictual family relationships, ambushed by her poverty, and unable to break free in a community that was home to both her own and her abuser's parents and friends. At one point, Myrtle told her sister, Norma Cole, "I ain't got no place to go, no place to stay, no way to make it" (*Louisville Courier-Journal,* December 23, 1990, p. A7).

In spite of her desperate situation, Myrtle planned her escape. On January 19, 1990, she waited until Allen Jr. passed out drunk and then took her two sons and her daughter with her to walk to the mouth of the hollow to use a neighbor's telephone. She called her father, who collected her and the children and subsequently arranged a secret meeting with local police. As a result of this meeting, Allen Jr. was charged with sodomizing his daughter. He was later released on bail. Myrtle moved out to the spouse abuse shelter in the area and then into her sister's house. She obtained a restraining order from the court to limit Allen Jr.'s access to her and her children and began to live a new life. This new life included divorcing Allen Jr. The divorce was due to be finalized within a week or so after the murder-suicide.

On the day of the murder-suicide, Allen Jr. and Myrtle met so that he could take the youngest son to stay with him overnight. Their oldest son, Kermitt, reached for some food to hand to his father. Allen Jr. took the food and put it on the hood of Myrtle's car. He then told Myrtle and the kids that he had a better idea than eating food and started firing his .38 caliber revolver at his family. He killed the two boys and left Myrtle for dead. His daughter escaped. He then reloaded the revolver and shot himself in the head.

Events such as the Whitaker murder-suicide send shock waves through small Kentucky towns. These shock waves are often amplified through the urban presses in Louisville and Lexington. One of the discursive themes of these shock waves is the disturbance of the apparent rural idyll. These rural atrocity tales cast an ominous shadow over a way of life that is locally governed, that shuns outsiders, and in which people's families and friends are often intimately interconnected over generations. However, it is not my point that violence against women in rural communities takes different physical forms from that in urban areas. This book is not an attempt to provide hard quantitative data on the prevalence of battering in rural vis-à-vis urban areas. Rather, the book is a study of interpersonal violence against women within a number of intersecting contexts, one of them being the rural sociocultural milieu.

Rural phenomena are not easy to study using quantitative data sources such as police call data and arrest reports, court convictions, and the like. My use of ethnographic methods, including 96 focused interviews[3] and participant and nonparticipant observation is designed to overcome these difficulties and to produce a detailed study of the ways of life in rural areas. Although the details of the Whitaker case were gleaned largely from newspaper sources, in this book I attach central importance to the voices of rural women themselves. I rely on my conversations with criminal justice and other professionals to augment women's own words about their victimization, policing, the courts, and the state in general. In this way I hope to redress some of the imbalance in the research literature on woman battering and criminal justice that, as I will show in Chapter 3, often ignores battered women.

Part of the art of the ethnographer is to identify his or her place amid a labyrinth of social forces and to reflect upon how this locus affects the research. This "situated" stance raised important questions for my research on rural woman battering. By trading on my privilege as a white male college professor, do I invade the territory inhabited by rural battered women, and rural folk in general, as I re-present their words and deeds in text? Am I the ethnographer-invader reproducing the imperialist modus operandi of bygone Empires? Recent critiques of ethnographic research have leveled the charge that ethnographers interpret "other" cultures through the lens of the ethnographers' own cultural heritage, thereby engaging in what Michelle Fine calls "imperial translation."[4]

During my own ethnographic research I vacillated between seeing myself as a pro-feminist man researching a hitherto much ignored social problem and a colonizer invading an alien culture. I became what I call the "hesitant ethnographer." These feelings are not unusual, and other ethnographers have wrestled with similar problems. Pinpointing some of the anxieties of conducting ethnographic research in Cuba, Ray Michalowski (1996) shows how the geo-political vortex of U.S.-Cuban relations generates considerable anxiety for him as he negotiates the ebb and flow of political tensions at an interpersonal level.

For some, my ethnography may appear more noble if I assume the master status of activist-ethnographer. But this is not the case. My overwhelming feeling as I rode with police officers, talked with battered women, observed domestic cases in court, and lived in

Eastern Kentucky, was one of awe and bewilderment. I liken it to my 2 years living in Japan after having spent most of my life in England. In Japan the trees, the stores, people's attire and style, language, the color of food, the smell of culture, indeed the entire social fabric, seemed to me to have been inverted. These feelings of awe and bewilderment are doubtless similar to those experienced by the early cultural anthropologists and may not form the basis for writing good sociology. In fact, even reporting my childlike curiosity or voyeuristic tendencies may be seen as either a form of self-indulgence or a type of cynical insurrection by those who would tyrannize all ethnography by manacling it to the lofty goal of producing a just society.

Just as my sense of wonderment at cultural life in rural Kentucky may have been partially influenced by my childhood as a working-class Briton, so too must my curiosity about rural woman battering have been partially shaped by personal inexperience with such matters. Not having grown up in a battering family and not having been a batterer, I cannot speak from the unassailable pulpit of experience on these matters. Indeed, as one of my colleagues recently suggested, I may have been better able to write about battering had I been the perpetrator of such violence, at least at some point during my life.

Since woman battering seems to be as prevalent in rural families as it is in urban families, and because researchers and policymakers have not addressed this disturbing social problem, it is imperative we learn more about it. The search for such knowledge requires an understanding of rural cultural life and the social condition of women. I claim no special expertise in this area, except that I lived, worked, observed, and conversed with people in a small rural town in Eastern Kentucky from 1991 to 1993. It was in that small town and its beautiful hinterland that my ethnography began. By *ethnography* I refer to the "study of ways of life." Eventually, the ethnography spread across the lovely state of Kentucky to encompass a number of rural communities. Amid the green rolling hills of the Bluegrass, the derelict mining towns, the steep mountains of Eastern Kentucky, and the fertile farmland of Central and Western Kentucky, I went in search of intimate violence and the societal reaction to it.

In the fall of 1991, I made contact with and got to know the women who ran the "Washington" spouse abuse shelter. After outlining the broad scope of my research venture and receiving their detailed input, we jointly arranged for me to approach women who were the victims/survivors of interpersonal male violence. The shelter director told battered women of my research interests and asked if they might be interested in telling their story. Once my first few interviews were completed, women who had talked with me shared their experiences with other women in the shelter, some of whom in turn agreed to share their experiences with me. Having women pass on information about their conversations with me served to introduce me to new interviewees. This snowballing effect also raised trust and comfort levels for both myself and the women I talked with. It is my perception that when men interview women, it is helpful if they are introduced by women and that their research focus is relayed by those women who, ideally, have played an integral part in formulating the research vista.

One dark January night in 1992, I pulled up and parked my car in the trees close to the spouse abuse shelter in Washington. At that time the shelter was somewhat ramshackle. The entry was by a sidedoor and I could not help but think that this door was very easy to break down. The dead-bolt lock appeared insubstantial. I entered to be greeted by the shelter director who introduced me to Barbara, the first woman who expressed a desire to tell her story. I glanced into the administrative office where I saw a security screen that displayed the outside of the premises and particularly the back door, which one worker told me was "very flimsy." The inside furnishings were at best modest and reflected both the poverty of the region and the fact that woman battering was not seen as a particularly serious offense by local government. All of the women in shelter were poor.

The air was thick with cigarette smoke and the house alive with the sound of children playing and crying. One of the women who resided in the shelter bore the marks of physical abuse on her face in the form of a black eye, and on her leg in the form of softened blue/black bruises. Except for Barbara, whom I was about to interview, I was barely acknowledged by the other women residents. Barbara had a scar at the side of her forehead evidenced by streaks of whitish tissue that contrasted sharply with her regular skin color. This scar was the legacy of a stab wound inflicted by her abusive ex-husband. During this first visit to the Washington shelter I sensed I was standing at the feet of patriarchy. The very architecture of the shelter, with the security system, the drawn blinds so as to exclude the hostile world, and the residential language of injury and abuse, evidenced the "reality" of patriarchy. However, this was not a universal patriarchy, but rather a patriarchy nuanced by the silks and rags of class relations and the idiosyncrasies of the rural culture of Eastern Kentucky.

Certainly it was a patriarchy characterized by coercion, violence, and cruelty, but also a patriarchy distinguished by a profound sense of resistance and endurance on the part of battered women.

The centerpiece of my ethnography is the focused interviews I conducted with battered women, police officers, judges, attorneys, social workers, spouse abuse shelter employees and directors, and the leaders of the Kentucky Domestic Violence Association (KDVA). I also engaged in various forms of observation and participant observation that augmented my interview findings and my everyday cultural appreciation. I rode with police officers and observed their performance at domestics. For a year or so, I served on the advisory board of the local spouse abuse shelter and was involved in discussions about how to raise funds and how to alter the architecture of the shelter itself. In another capacity, I acted as an external evaluator of a federal program operating in seven Kentucky spouse abuse shelters. Through these various roles I became well acquainted with these shelters, their staff, and their problems.

In the spirit of ethnographic inquiry, I gathered a lot of raw, unstructured information about rural woman battering that was inextricably tied up with tales of rural life in general. Putting my findings together and interpreting their numerous possible meanings involved considerable subjective analysis. By piecing together my ethnographic data and combining it with other documentary sources, I hope to contribute to our understanding of rural women's lives and their victimization by their intimate partners. More than anything, my approach is designed to present rural woman battering through the eyes and words of the women who have experienced it. In this sense I am following the theoretical line taken by Dorothy Smith and other realist feminist researchers, who acknowledge the authenticity of women's everyday experiences.[5]

Due to the dangerous and highly privatized nature of violence against women, ethnographic research opportunities involving participant observation are limited. Researchers cannot easily reside in homes where battering takes place and, if they did, their presence would seriously affect behavior therein. An alternative strategy in developing a textured understanding of abuse is to have women or men who have been in battering relationships systematically reflect on past events. In a sense, my interviews were a way of doing this.

Most battered women do not enter spouse abuse shelters. In Kentucky, as in other states, many more women are served by shelters through outreach programs rather than through staying in shelters. At another level still, many abused women, for a variety of reasons, do not even have contact with shelters. The experiences I explore are therefore snapshots of a much larger social problem. It is not my argument that the experiences I report are somehow "representative" of all battering that goes on in rural communities.[6]

When two people undertake a personal interview, they may have many things in common. They may work at the same job, live in the same region, occupy the same social-class position, believe in the same religion, or be members of the same sex, race, or age group. Differing levels of shared experience produce varying degrees of congruence between the interviewer and the interviewee. The gendered experiential incongruence between myself and the women I talked with was perhaps compounded because interviewees were victims of male violence, not just "any" violence. Their experience of male violence, and my maleness, may have intensified the experiential incongruence between us. At times I wondered if I, as man, would be perceived as what Christine Delphy (1977) once called "the main enemy."[7] I shared these concerns with administrators of the KDVA and individual shelter directors and staff. Most told me that many battered women wanted to tell their stories to someone who would listen, regardless of whether the interviewer was male or female. This desire to tell their stories was, in some cases, heightened by the fact that as victims of violence, my interviewees had often been ignored by their abusers and criminal justice personnel, and their opinions and stories trivialized, met with disbelief or disdain, or, possibly, met with more violence. Indeed, several women told me they were glad that I was an "outsider" in the community. My outsider status meant that I was not part of the deeply entrenched gossip circuitry and was safer to trust with personal details.

There are other reasons for interviewers not to shy away from interviewing people with different social backgrounds. Human subjects stand at the juncture of a multitude of intersecting social forces and possess what Donna Haraway (1991) has called "fractured identities" (p. 155). Robert Merton (1972), using the different language of status sets, notes that "individuals have not a single status but a status set: a complement of variously interrelated statuses which interact to affect both their behavior and perspectives" (p. 22).

Merton notes that Insider and Outsider groups emerge at particular sociohistorical junctures characterized by the stress of acute social change. During these periods of acute social change, numerous tensions emerge surrounding the acquisition of knowledge about Insiders and Out-siders. In particular, Insiders (in Merton's original article, blacks) have claimed a special understanding of the condition and social world of "their" group. He calls this enjoyment of a special understanding, the "Insider doctrine," which, in its "strong form," constitutes an epis-temological principle that states "that particular groups in each moment of history have *monopolistic access* to particular kinds of knowledge" (Merton, 1972, p. 11; emphasis in original). In its "weaker, more empirical form, the claim holds that some groups have *privileged access,* with other groups also being able to acquire that knowledge for themsel-ves but at greater risk and cost" (p. 11; emphasis in original). The logic of the Insider doctrine is alarming to Merton because in its extreme form it denies that human beings are the possessors of multiple and intersecting sets of social statuses. Instead, the Insider doctrine argues that there is one overarching status determinant that signifies the essence of that particular human being's experience in the world.

If the interviewer is of the same class, gender, or race as the interviewee, then such compatibility or congruence may enhance dis-closure in different directions. However, in spite of the differences and similarities between myself and the battered women I interviewed, our conversations revealed rich details of women's lives and led me to believe that it is not necessary to "match up" all of the fractured identities (Haraway) or status sets (Merton) of the interviewer and interviewee. It is possible that if a woman interviewed my interviewees the conversation would have developed differently. However, after many long hours of interviewing and pawing over transcripts, I feel that it is inappropriate and contrary to the spirit of subjectivist methodologies to argue that gender congruence produces more "valuable" interview outcomes. Rather, we might usefully explore how the outcomes of interviews where there is gender congruence differ from those where there is not.

As we will see in the first and subsequent chapters, women disclosed much about their private lives, including details of their brutalization, and their dealings with the police, courts, and other arms of the state. Women reported their experiences in a variety of ways. Some balked at revealing certain intimate details. For example, Lynn openly reported extensive details of physical abuse but refused to discuss her sexual victimization.[8]

Websdale: Were there any times when you suffered injuries that required you to seek medical attention or go to the ER?

> *Lynn:* No, because Donny was very calculated in the way that he
> did his physical abuse. He knew if he hit me or hurt me, that
> I would have to go to the hospital and he'd have to answer
> for things. So the way he did it was, ah, bruising, ah, pinning
> me down, knocking me against the wall, stuff like that, but
> never hard enough. I would think well he's done this, he's lost
> his self-control. But he always had control the whole time.
>
> *Websdale:* Were there any times during your relationship when
> he sexually abused you?
>
> *Lynn:* I don't want to talk about that.

I weighed the pros and cons of asking direct questions about
sexual abuse very carefully. Cognizant of Helen Eigenberg's (1990)
critique of the National Crime Victimization Survey's (NCVS) failure
to access the magnitude of rape because NCVS questions shied away
from directly asking women if they'd been raped or had sex against
their will, I decided that a direct approach might be better.[9] My
decision to proceed in this direct manner on the question of sexual
abuse was also based on my understanding that battered women are
not helpless victims. My sense was that they would tell me if they did
not want to answer a question. Lynn confirmed my belief.

Katie typified those women who felt they could discuss their
sexual victimization.

> *Katie:* . . . When he wanted to have sexual intercourse, he did it,
> without my consent. . . . Or whenever he wanted me to give
> him a blow job, he would take my head and push it down
> toward him and I'm like, "No, I don't want to do this." But
> to get him to shut up, I did it anyway.

My interviews with women did not follow the typical conversa-
tional flow between men and women. In mixed-sex conversations,
men tend to talk more, their ideas are more readily taken up, women
typically ask more questions than men, and women do more work than
men to keep conversations going and to fill silences (see DeVault,
1990; Fishman, 1978; West & Zimmerman, 1983).[10] In our conversations, it was I who wanted to listen to their stories. On the rare
occasions when there was a lull in the conversation, it was I, as
interviewer, who kept the momentum going. It was interviewees who
provided the directions for the conversations, although those direc-

tions used women's personal biography, their victimization, and the criminal justice response to their victimization as broad frames of reference. Finally, women talked much more than I did during the interviews.

Women may have disclosed information because they perceived that I, as a white male college professor, may, for example, have the power to influence the future policing of their cases, judicial outcomes, or the provision of social services. Women may have had a similar feeling if interviewed by a white female college professor as well. A number of women asked me questions about their cases. Typical questions concerned police practices, judicial actions, and child custody issues. Like Oakley (1981), I answered whenever I could, and gave my opinions freely. Several women told me they shared because they hoped the information would reduce the victimization of other women. Hanna, a spouse abuse shelter director, referred to the tendency of battered women to see me as someone in authority who might help them or assist in the struggle against woman abuse, as the "Knight in Shining Armor Syndrome." The interviewer as "knight" raises some awkward issues.

First, if the interview setting is as nonhierarchical as possible, and I as interviewer am inverting traditional male stances in mixed-sex interactions, then how could some battered women still perceive me to be potentially heroic? If I am trying to subvert the posture of "man- or interviewer-as-dominant" in my approach to interviewing, then how might women see me in shining armor? The answer to these questions may lie in the point I made earlier: that battered women are not addicted to their victimization, or their abuser. They are not masochistic and are able to tell the difference between the violent domination of their abusers and the different kind of power that I perhaps exerted over them. Simply put: To perceive me as "knight," women did not have to see me as dominant in ways that their abusers were (violently) dominant.

Second, if the interviewer is seen as "knight," whether or not she or he eschews that role, is she or he not manipulating the interviewee at some level? Assuming the Knight in Shining Armor Syndrome, reported by a number of shelter workers, is real, what can the interviewer do, at an ethical level, to reduce the dangers of manipulating interviewees? In an attempt to address this ethical concern in my interviews, I told women that although I was interviewing criminal justice personnel, I did not know them personally and was not likely

to because I was essentially an outsider in the community. Consequently, I hoped interviewees would be less influenced by the fact that
I may have "connections."[11]

My analysis of my conversations with women have focused almost
exclusively upon linguistic interchanges between us. It seems to me
that whatever the sex makeup of the interviewer-interviewee dyad, we
are left with the very thorny epistemological issue of what aspects of
the presentation of the interviewee's self and the interviewer's self
should researchers incorporate into their broader understanding of a
social phenomenon? I noted, and in Chapter 1 will note in much more
detail, how women shared what I perceived to be a number of intimate
details of their lives. At times women refused to answer certain
questions or directed the flow of conversation to topics they appeared
more comfortable with. However, if there was substantial resistance
to answering my questions, or even to being in the interview situation,
we must not assume that we can map that locus of refusal merely by
using interview transcripts and meticulously dissecting the words they
(and I) used. If one of the main problems with men interviewing
women is experiential incongruence, we cannot assume that it is
overcome if women divulge information that appears to male interviewers to be sensitive and highly personal. If the interview exchange
between men and women is a microcosm of patriarchal relations and,
in a sense, a potential lightning rod for that social structural tension,
then we would do well to ask ourselves: "How is the resistance of
women to men expressed in interviews?"[12]

I will make a few rudimentary suggestions about possible directions to move in to begin to answer this question. If we accept that the
interview exchange between men and women is a potential lightning
rod for wider gender tensions, then we must look at what women
interviewees think as well as what they say in their conversations with
male interviewers. Since our conversations occurred in a relatively
unstructured setting, we ought to explore the silences, the things
women do not say and the leads they might have pursued but did not.
We must also be aware of the heavily nuanced and textured nature of
human interaction that cannot be mechanically read off of people's
position in a gender hierarchy. Put simply, battered women's words
and silences do not passively mirror their gendered disadvantage.

Angela McRobbie (1978) points to the way that adolescent working-
class girls see "romance" as a social lubricant that smoothes the
difficult transition to adulthood. Contrary to the notion that these

girls are duped into their interest in romance by a misunderstanding of marriage, McRobbie found that, given the limited choices of working-class girls, a little romance spruced up their lives before the realities of marriage set in. Could it be that battered women talked with me because it was a somewhat interesting diversion from the humdrum of shelter life? As much as I was using them as subjects in a research project, could they have been using me as a break from the routine? an opportunity for someone else to watch the children? Like McRobbie's working-class girls and their brief excursion into the world of romance, were the women I talked with somehow resisting by conversing with me?

Finally, it must be said that there is a whole terrain of human communication that I have not touched. This is the area Foucault (1977) calls the material body. I have not engaged in an analysis of the rich tapestry of symbolism and personal style evidenced through modes of eye contact, bodily postures and language, facial gestures, and the presentation of injuries. Such a tapestry may be too ethereal to tap. If it is the case that battered women I conversed with resisted me in subliminal ways that defy observation, then such elusive aspects of the interview exchange might be another reason for challenging the argument that only women can interview women. For it is likely that in woman-woman interviewing dyads, subliminal resistive forces, whether the same or different, may also operate.

I direct the reader to Appendix 1 for a detailed discussion of the other aspects of my ethnographic approach. There I discuss my interviews with criminal justice professionals, spouse abuse shelter directors and staff, social workers, journalists, and attorneys. There I also explore my role as "observer" and "participant observer."

Chapter 1 bears the title, "For Batter or For Worse." As I indicate, the institution of marriage seems to be more revered in rural communities and, as I will point out in subsequent chapters, marriage rates are higher there than in urban centers. Marriage and the family lie at the heart of rural patriarchy. In traditional marriage vows the participants swear an oath of allegiance to each other "for better or for worse." From my ethnographic findings, it seems as if we ought to be warning women at the altar that "for better or for worse" might be more aptly stated as "for batter or for worse." For some readers, the title of the lead chapter may seem cynical. If it does, then the subheadings for that chapter may create further discomfort. The first section, titled "For Batter," looks at rural woman battering through the experiences of rural women themselves. Since such an alarming number of Kentucky's rural women are murdered by their husbands and partners, the second part of Chapter 1 is titled "For Worse" and addresses homicides and homicide-suicides within rural families.

It is my contention throughout this book that violence between intimates, and violence in general, is best understood as a product of social conditions, not as a result of the genetic makeup of perpetrators and victims, their psychological characteristics, or both. In order to understand the social-structural backdrop to the violence, we must have a working appreciation of what "rural communities" are. Chapter 2 addresses this issue of what a rural community is. In talking about "rural" social phenomena, I do not mean to imply that all rural regions are the same. Instead of essentializing rural culture, I adopt the idea of a rural-urban continuum and explore both the seeming similarities and differences among rural communities. It is in this chapter that I introduce and define rural patriarchy and highlight the social condition of many rural women. In addition, I discuss rural crime and criminal justice, taking care to point out that rural woman battering and the criminal justice response to that battering, have received scant attention from researchers and policymakers.

Rural patriarchy is the conceptual tool that I find most useful in making sense of the phenomenon of rural woman battering. In Chapter 3, I delve into the research literature on familial violence in order to explain exactly why I find the concept of rural patriarchy such a useful explanatory tool. My purpose here is not to engage in an exhaustive review of this monumental literature. Rather, I hope to provide readers with the essential reasons for my argument that it is the gender struggle within rural families that lies at the root of the socially patterned battering of women in these communities. In Chapter 3, I also discuss the research on the reticent and often problematic response of criminal justice agencies to violence against women. This discussion lays the groundwork for my ensuing ethnographic assessment of the responses of the police, courts, and state agencies to battered women in rural Kentucky.

While recognizing the dearth of studies on rural battering and the criminal justice response to it, I also stress that many of the studies of the policing and judicial responses to woman battering have relied upon official data rather than women's own perspectives. This reliance reflects a political choice and not just a methodological concern with obtaining "clean data." It is profoundly ironic that in this age of "community policing" and its alleged concern to receive input from the community, the six National Institute of Justice (NIJ) studies on the role of arrest at domestics failed to publicize women's subjective experiences of police performance. Ascertaining the effectiveness of various criminal justice strategies without taking seriously the voices of those whom the strategies are purportedly designed to protect, makes little sense. I close Chapter 3 with a call to researchers to incorporate battered women's subjective experiences into their studies if we are to gain a more comprehensive understanding of the role of the "justice" system in supposedly protecting battered women.

Chapter 4 is the first of three chapters that explore the response of the patriarchal state to rural woman battering. In Chapter 4, I focus on the responses of various police agencies. The picture that emerges is a complex one. I do not find that all police agencies automatically and inevitably perpetuate the disadvantage of rural women by failing to take women's interpersonal victimization seriously. Local rural police (county sheriff's departments and municipal police) are more enmeshed in what I call the rural "ol' boys network" and, for a multitude of reasons, are less likely to enforce the law and protect battered women in ways that those women appreciate. Police agencies that are more detached from this rural political milieu (e.g., the Kentucky State Police) are more likely to be seen by women as doing a better job at domestics. Put simply, the police responses to woman battering seem to be linked, in many cases, to agencies' degree of enmeshment in local patriarchal culture. Nevertheless, the compromised response of some police agencies to the plight of battered women does not just stem from officers' involvement with the ol' boys network. Tax bases are much lower in rural communities, especially in some of the Eastern Kentucky counties where the bite of poverty is particularly severe. This means that resources for local police are few. If this low resource base is combined with the problems of negotiating often difficult and remote rural terrain, then there are real "physical" reasons that impede the delivery of police services to battered women.

Through interviews with battered women, rural judges, attorneys, and legal advocates for battered women, Chapter 5 weaves a complex picture of the judicial disposition of rural domestics. While the law itself clearly relegates domestics to the stigmatized status of "misdemeanor" offenses, battered women report that with the support of their legal advocates there are ways they can use the courts to their own advantage. However, using the words of women, I introduce incidents where rural judges humiliate and dismiss the victims of interpersonal violence. I also point to the connections between judicial decisions and patriarchal beliefs about the social place of rural women. In particular, I highlight the way some judges, like some police officers, engage in victim blaming. Given that judicial decisions in rural domestics can save women's lives, I scrutinize those cases where some parties to domestic cases feel that judicial mistakes have resulted in loss of life. Putting all of the ethnographic evidence together leads me to the conclusion that battered women court revictimization when they enter some rural courtrooms. A significant number of rural judges behave like the rural patriarchs women are beaten by in their own homes.

My ethnography is also devoted to understanding the complex role of the patriarchal state in both confronting and, paradoxically, reproducing the subordinate position of rural women vis-à-vis men. In Chapter 6, I explore the efforts of welfare and other agencies of the liberal-democratic state and juxtapose these responses alongside those of what Mazur and McBride-Stetson (1995) call the agencies of state feminism. From battered women's perspectives, a mosaic of problems exists when it comes to the state's delivering various services to rural women. Some of the difficulties stem from the remoteness of rural regions and the sociocultural and physical isolation of women. Other problems emerge because of the lack of privacy in rural areas or the interconnections between those who provide services and those who consume them. Still more problems arise from the generalized dearth of state services in rural communities brought about by a combination of factors including the inability of the state to infiltrate or access rural communities. When services are delivered, some women report them to be highly beneficial, others say they feel stigmatized or blamed as they claim what is rightfully theirs. All of these themes characterize the relationship between the state and the rural citizenry. In addition, I also explore the contradictory relationship between rural beliefs in self-sufficiency and the need for many rural dwellers to survive from meager state provisions.

The three chapters on the response of the "justice" system to rural woman battering invite certain specific policy suggestions as to how we might better confront the social problem of rural woman battering. In the final chapter (Chapter 7), I offer some policy proposals based on the recognition that rural battering is intimately associated with the disadvantaged social condition of women. Drawing upon the overall findings of the ethnography, I recommend a coordinated multiagency approach to rural battering that is spearheaded by the agencies of state feminism. These agencies include the Kentucky Domestic Violence Association (KDVA), the Kentucky Commission on Women, and of especial importance in rural communities, the spouse abuse shelters themselves. The shelters are the crucial grassroots agencies in rural communities and I recommend using them and their outreach services as the core agencies for strategizing and improving the overall delivery of state services in general. My logic here is that these agencies are more in tune with the needs and experiences of battered women themselves. Essentially this is an argument for the extension of the services of the agencies of state feminism. It may seem naive to point to such a direction in the formulation of state policy because such a policy may on the surface appear to "ask" the patriarchal state to turn against itself. However, I argue that the state does not operate in a monolithic manner with regard to the social regulation of women. Rather, there are democratic spaces and these spaces can be worked more effectively for battered women by state feminist organizations.

Notes

1. From the song "Democracy" on the album titled *The Future*, Columbia, 1992.
2. For details of this case see the *Louisville Courier-Journal*, December 23, 1990, pp. A1, A7; *Lexington Herald-Leader*, December 30, pp. A1, A10; and *Lexington Herald-Leader*, March 27, 1991, pp. A1, A6.
3. I interviewed 50 battered women, all of whom were residents of one of seven shelters; 17 police officers; 11 judges; nine advocates for battered women; four attorneys; three journalists; and two social workers.
4. See Appendix 1, where I engage in a lengthy discussion about the role of the ethnographer and the many problems with ethnographers contributing toward the "othering" of the cultures and ways of life they attempt to interpret.
5. I elect to validate and make use of the concept of "experience." I make this affirmation based on my (not unproblematic) observations that the word *experience* has meaning for battered women. Such an affirmation flies in the face of postmodernist feminist challenges to concepts like "experience" and places me closer to the standpoint feminism of Dorothy Smith (1987, 1990, 1993). Unlike feminist cultural theorists, and particularly feminist psychoanalytically oriented semiotic theorists, Smith (1990) insists that "there is an actual subject prior to the subject constituted in the text" (p. 5). The subject position of human beings is grounded in everyday life and exists prior to its construction, insertion, and embodiment in discourse. For Smith, people's lives represent a point of departure for sociological inquiry rather than a phenomenon that is textually bound and in endless need of being deconstructed (Smith, 1993, p. 183). See also Walby

(1990) and Delphy (1977). For a critique of the realist position, see Barrett (1980) and Clough (1993).

6. Indeed, many researchers argue that women who enter shelters are among the most severely abused battered women of all. For example, Straus and Gelles (1995), citing the research of Giles-Sims (1983) and Okun (1986), suggest that women in shelters are abused at roughly 11 times the annual rate of battered women in the population at large (p. 85). Schecter (1996) estimates that 43,000 married and cohabiting women in Massachusetts suffered severe domestic violence in 1991 (p. 54). A further 149,000 experienced other forms of abuse, such as slapping and punching. However, in the same year only 1,900 used shelters as a refuge, and only 8,700 attended support groups.

7. I explore this issue of incongruence at greater length in Appendix 1.

8. All victims of battering mentioned in the book appear under an alias. Likewise, the people they talk about and the communities they come from appear under pseudonyms.

9. In a roundabout attempt to obtain data on rape, the NCVS asked respondents "whether anyone had tried to attack them in another way?" or "whether anything else happened to them which they thought was a crime?" Respondents voluntarily communicated they had been the victims of rape or attempted rape. NCVS respondents' own classifications were then accepted and recorded. As Eigenberg notes, the actual number of rapes may be up to 15 times greater than that reported in the NCVS. The NCVS has now changed its way of accessing rape data. For further discussion of the need for a range of agencies to ask women about their experiences of marital rape, see Raquel Kennedy Bergen (1996, pp. 101-104). Kennedy Bergen points out that not to ask whether women have been raped by their husbands may be to perpetuate the notion that this form of abuse is shameful and beyond discussion.

10. Dale Spender (1985) argues that language is man-made and is not amenable to women expressing their own experiences. In a similar vein, Margorie DeVault (1990) points to the way in which words like *leisure* and *work* are problematic for many women (p. 97).

11. Clearly, Knight in Shining Armor Syndrome is not limited to men interviewing battered women. Rather, this "syndrome" may be present whenever the power differential between interviewer and interviewee is great.

12. We may of course ask similar questions of the interview exchange between people from different social classes, races, ethnic groups, and so on.

1

For Batter or For Worse

Introduction

In traditional marriage ceremonies partners take vows to support each other "for richer or for poorer," "in sickness and in health," and "for better or for worse." This chapter facetiously borrows from that part of the wedding vows where partners say they'll stay together "for better or for worse," and replaces it with "for batter or for worse." The chapter title goes to the heart of the argument of the book, namely, that when women enter intimate relationships with men, they risk experiencing battering or something "worse" such as lethal violence. Put simply, women are much more likely to experience violence from the men they are in intimate relationships with, than from men who are strangers.[1]

The chapter is arranged around the title. I introduce those aspects of rural social life that appear to be conducive to battering and that may make it more difficult for rural as opposed to urban women to leave battering relationships. The section titled "For Batter" addresses those physical, sexual, and emotional violations women report through our interview exchanges. The section titled "Or For Worse: Patriarchy and Pine Boxes" rather melodramatically draws upon those cases in which women have been murdered by their intimate male partners.

There is a value judgment here insofar as the language of the sections implies that being murdered is worse than living out a battering relationship. That some battered women told me there were times during their abusive relationships that they would rather be dead, casts doubt on the appropriateness of the dichotomy "for batter," "or for worse." However, many more women reported they feared death, both for themselves and for what it would mean for their children. For these very fearful women, death was a "worse" prospect than living out all the pain of a battering relationship.

For Batter

The Magnitude of Rural Woman Battering

Early research shows that woman battering is as likely to occur in urban as it is in rural areas (see Bachman, 1994; Bachman & Saltzman, 1995; Websdale & Johnson, 1997a). Survey research in Kentucky also demonstrates that there are few differences between urban and rural rates of woman battering, except that rural battered women report a statistically greater likelihood of being "shot at," "tortured," and having their "hair pulled" (see Websdale & Johnson, 1995). My ethnographic research constantly turned up information on the pervasiveness of rural woman battering. I offer excerpts from this information not to prove that rural woman battering is as big a problem as urban woman battering, but rather to illustrate the diversity of people who see rural woman battering as a social problem. These people range from spouse abuse shelter personnel who have a fine, if not precise, statistical grasp of the prevalence of rural versus urban battering; police officers who work rural areas and who respond to domestic calls; judges who dispose of domestic cases; and, most important, battered women themselves who have experienced violence in rural communities and who have talked with other women who have had like experiences.

Sally, like a number of other interviewees who had resided in rural communities for a long period, knew of other women who reported being battered. She lived in the small rural community of Sale.

Websdale: What do you mean, it [woman battering] goes on a lot?

Sally: There are a lot of people, my friends, that got married and
   I know their husbands beat them. And the law does nothin'.
Websdale: How do you know this? Through informal conversations?
Sally: Yeah, with them.

With Sally, we sense an underbelly to rural social life characterized by
systemic violence against women within families. This underbelly is
something well known to at least some women.

Tamara perceived a similar set of patriarchal ground rules from
her vantage point in Western Kentucky. She felt that her refusal to
play subordinate wife was one reason she was beaten.

Tamara: The man is the head of the household. The woman has no
   say. It doesn't matter about her morals and her feelings, nothing.
Websdale: Was your husband like that?
Tamara: He tried to be. That was our biggest problem. I talked
   back. I had an opinion and I wasn't allowed to have an
   opinion. And I'd say, "I don't care if you agree or not, honey,
   that's how I feel." That's one reason I was hit.

Judge Alder also recognized the existence of the patriarchally
ordained position of women in Kentucky's western counties.

Websdale: If poverty's a major factor with the violence, then how
   come most of the violence is heaped out by men on women
   and they both live in poverty?
Judge Alder: Well, the man, historically, is the breadwinner. We
   give the man that position. This is Bible Belt country and I am
   Southern Baptist. I have strong religious beliefs. My wife
   works. My wife is not my chattel. Unfortunately, you still have
   a lot of men who look upon females as a chattel, as a piece of
   property. Those women are not supposed to question the
   authority of the man in the household.
Websdale: Is that really common here, would you say?
Judge Alder: Well, I think so.

In fiscal year 1993 and 1994, the Kentucky Domestic Violence
Association (KDVA) housed 2,301 and 2,346 battered women, respec-
tively, for varying periods of time.[2] The rural outreach programs from

each of the 16 shelters in the state report that many rural battered women cannot or will not use the services of shelters. This suggests there is a potentially large number of rural battered women whose plight is either not known or not officially documented.

State police officer Davis, who patrols several remote rural counties in Eastern Kentucky, reports that fully half of all his assault calls are domestics.

> *Davis:* I'd say fifty percent of them are assaults associated with domestics.

Municipal police officer Rudy also pointed to the central place of domestic disorder in the small town of Lovelace in rural Eastern Kentucky.

> *Websdale:* Is domestic violence a thing that you deal with very often?
> *Rudy:* Yes. I'd say that probably it rates real high as one of our complaints goes. We have quite a few of those.

Municipal officer Hogan notes domestic violence is a deeply ingrained feature of social life in rural communities in Kentucky.

> *Hogan:* The urban and the rural settings are altogether different. And you've got things that we encounter that's almost an accepted way of life. I mean, you're combattin' something that's been goin' on in this part of the country for years and years and years.

In two central Kentucky counties, Circuit Judge Fonda reports a very high level of women battering.

> *Websdale:* Do you see many domestic cases in your court?
> *Judge Fonda:* I don't see as many now at circuit court level as I did in district court. But almost without exception, most of the women that I see at the circuit court level now, will offer in mitigation, or will want me to understand, that they have had a life involving domestic violence.
> *Websdale:* In a child custody issue perhaps over divorce?

Judge Fonda: That's nonstop. I hear that in at least half of the divorce cases we handle or subsequent custody.

Woman Battering and Rural Isolation

By their very nature, rural regions tend to be more physically isolated, cut off from centers of trade and industry, schooling, hospitals and transportation facilities. The degree of isolation differs among rural regions. Farms and ranches can be extremely isolated, with residents not having neighbors for miles around. In small towns, neighbors are people who may be seen and interacted with on a regular basis, and community cohesiveness can be very high. However, even small towns tend to be cut off from major urban centers and the multitude of facilities offered therein. Although the words of battered women will illustrate a number of these salient aspects of the rural milieu, it is worth laying out the key features of rural life that are particularly relevant to battered women's lives.

One of the most common complaints of rural battered women concerns the physical and geographical isolation they experience. Some battered women who live up what is locally called a "hollow" (a secluded dirt road cul-de-sac with a small number of houses on it) seem to live extraordinarily isolated lives. Several of these women report not having had any friends for years. With no public transportation and large distances between houses, they report that it is often physically difficult to engage in community life. Even if battered women live in small towns and work outside the home, they still report great isolation and loneliness. The irony here is that rural areas are often assumed to be more cohesive and neighborly, and to have a social climate that is more friendly.

It is important to bear in mind that the geographical isolation experienced by battered women may stem from their batterers' calculated decision to reside in the country. In other words, the isolation may be a product of abuse, as well as a physical setting conducive to abuse. This loneliness brought about, compounded, or both, by the isolation battered women feel because of the controlling behavior of their abusers, is all the more unsettling given the societal expectation that the marriage bond should be harmonious. This expectation, and the attendant disappointment or disillusionment, may be all the greater in rural communities where marriage rates are higher and the institution of marriage more revered.

Women report that abusers' violence tends to feed off of women's physical isolation and may be all the more effective because of it. Among control tactics used by rural abusers, women mentioned men removing the phone receiver (e.g., when he goes to work) so that she could not contact the outside world by phone; locking the thermostat, especially in winter, as a form of torture; disabling and/or destroying motor vehicles to limit her mobility; closely monitoring the odometer reading on motor vehicles (a simple yet effective form of control due to the lack of alternative means of transportation); driving recklessly in order to intimidate his partner; and discharging firearms in public (e.g., at a battered woman's pet) in a manner that intimidates, scares, or otherwise distresses her. All of these tactics are used in urban areas, too, but according to the battered women I interviewed, these tactics are likely to be more successful in rural regions because of the isolation. In urban areas, the greater visibility of the control strategy would tend to render it less effective.

Rural battered women report how difficult it is to leave an abusive home that is located several miles from the nearest paved road. Though it may be possible for her to walk to the paved road, the chances of her taking her children along makes the task much more difficult. If we add the lack of public transport, the act of leaving the violent home in an isolated rural area becomes more difficult than leaving a similar abode in an urban setting. We must also note that the extended length of time it might take a rural battered woman to leave her abuser adds to the danger to which she is exposed. The act of leaving is a form of resistance that can evoke extreme violence on the part of abusers. Many women who are murdered by their violent partners are murdered during or shortly after leaving them. There are numerous other geographical considerations in rural areas that vary by region. For example, weather conditions may influence the way battered women strategize against their abusive partners and negotiate geographical isolation.

Living in a rural area, Barbara relied heavily on her vehicle to transport her children to school and herself to work. One night her abusive ex-husband set her car on fire and destroyed it.

> *Barbara:* He did not want me to have a car. That way I would have to stay home. I would have no choice. And he knew I would have no choice.

The isolation of some rural settings does appear to put battered women at a considerable disadvantage. Some women report it is simply too difficult to leave a "hollow" or other isolated setting. Penny, who resided in the Pennyrile region, was typical of many of the rural women I interviewed. With four young children and a violent husband whom she felt kept her pregnant to keep her out of the reach of other men, Penny was isolated both socially and geographically. Her nuclear family lived "on top of a mountain" about 8 miles from the nearest small town. Penny's house was separated from others by several acres of woodland. Her husband, Billy, through a variety of controlling tactics, played an active part in maintaining her isolation.

> *Websdale:* Tell me a little bit about your involvement with the community? Were you involved with social groups, church groups, or stuff like that at all?
> *Penny:* No. Not really. It's mostly like farm land. I didn't really get involved in the groups. Billy really didn't let me get involved. He was the type that wanted you to stay home, didn't want you to associate, be anywhere around men. . . . Nobody was allowed up there on the hill.

As in Penny's case, the limiting effects of isolation are compounded if women have children to care for. In cases where the abuser's parents live next door or in the same house, it is especially difficult to get away. I make these points because the women who were the victims of this abuse did plan their escape. They devised strategies to resist the abuse of their partners. It is not the finding of these interviews that battered women in rural areas are backward or suffer from what some psychologists call learned helplessness. On the contrary, there are very real geographical, economic, and sociocultural constraints that amplify the controls exerted by the terroristic tactics of their partners.

June lived in a very remote rural area and had no vehicle. The victim of extreme physical abuse, including a shooting, she reported that she would have filed charges against her abusive husband if she had had a vehicle to get to the courthouse.

> *Websdale:* Did you ever bring charges against him?
> *June:* I never had no way to get over to do nothin'. I never had no vehicle.

Because telephone subscription rates are significantly lower in rural communities, it is likely to be more difficult for battered women to call the police when an act of violence is committed against them. In urban counties in Kentucky, subscription rates run as high as 98%. In the counties from which the women I interviewed came, roughly 2 to 3 households in 10 do not have a phone. In a similar vein, if there is a considerable distance to a neighbor's house, then calling police or a spouse abuse shelter from the neighbor's residence is also more problematic.

Since rural batterers often employ tactics that compound isolation (including disabling cars, checking the odometer, and forbidding women to drive), the chances of reaching a phone by car are lessened. Out of the 50 battered women I interviewed, 6 did not have telephones at their residence and another 6 reported being prevented from using the phone by the batterer. In other words, 76% had phones they could use to call the police.

Geographical isolation in rural areas amplifies the subordination and loneliness of many women in the home. As I will discuss in the forthcoming chapters, geographical isolation also cuts rural battered women off from the potentially beneficial services of the state: for example, health care and social services, public transportation, independent housing, educational opportunities, and licensed child care.

The categories of abuse that I report are not mutually exclusive. For example, rape is a form of physical abuse as well as sexual abuse. However, since I stress the significance of rural woman abuse as a largely unrecognized form of criminality, it is convenient to classify that abuse with respect to the criminal code. This code differentiates between physical assaults and sexual assaults, and may or may not recognize certain forms of emotional abuse as a crime. I do not suggest that emotional abuse, because it usually is not contrary to the criminal code, is any less serious or less worthy of study. In fact, the multitude of forms of emotional abuse may be particularly important in rural areas because they serve to intensify the isolation of rural women.

Physical Abuse

Barbara, who endured physical abuse for 4 years at the hands of her violent husband, recalled the first time she was physically abused.

> *Barbara:* We had a house. He'd come in, was drinkin' and I was
> at the kitchen stove cookin'. The next thing I knew he came

in there and just kicked me right between the legs. I turned around and I said, "What's wrong with you?" And he just started slappin' me and kickin' me and that's when he twisted my arm and broke it. I kept coverin' my face and he just kept kickin' it and kickin' and kickin'. He grabbed me by the hair and the head and he threw me in the living room. Then he just went on to the bed. All like it wasn't nothin'. Like he didn't do anything.

Barbara's words echo those of a number of women who talked of the way their abusers seemed to see their abusive behavior as culturally sanctioned or as insignificant. Again, such sentiments point to a subculture of acquiescence or tolerance on the part of some rural men when it comes to woman battering.

Intimate violence against women cannot be divorced from the broader rural sociocultural setting that includes a long-established tradition of gun ownership.[3] A gun can be used to threaten or shoot people. Although rates of gun ownership are higher in rural areas, research indicates that people in rural regions are more likely to use their guns for hunting and not crime (see Bordua & Lizotte, 1979; Bureau of Justice Statistics, 1990; Weisheit, Falcone, & Wells, 1994c, p. 6). The Bureau of Justice Statistics notes that the rate of crime commission with handguns is 5.9 per 100,000 in central cities compared with 1.7 per 100,000 in nonmetro areas. These figures probably do not get anywhere near reflecting the use of handguns in domestic altercations. In rural areas, perpetrators of woman abuse may not use their guns to rob strangers on the street, but from my ethnographic data it is clear that many of them think nothing of using guns to intimidate their wives or partners. It could be that rural isolation aggravates the tendency to use handguns against intimate others for purposes of intimidation.

Karen, her abusive husband, and their two children lived in the same house as his parents. Her abuser was jealous of his own father's relationship with Karen. On one occasion during Karen's first pregnancy, he beat her up for shaking his father's hand. Karen's abuse was punctuated with various threats by her husband. Her interpretation was that the cramped living arrangements with his family, an increasingly common feature of rural life, exacerbated her victimization. She also reported a form of abuse that is probably much more common in rural regions, namely the threatened use or discharge of guns to intimidate women.

Karen: Yeah. He'd shoot somethin'. He'd say, "that could be your head, you know." . . . Not in the house. We'd be out walkin' around and bein' normal and he'd shoot a bottle or a can and say "that could be your head."

Other interviewees, like Karen, reported that their abusers had threatened them with firearms and/or shot at them, or something near and dear to them, to terrify them. Rural culture, with its acceptance of firearms for hunting and self-protection, may include a code among certain men that accepts the casual use of firearms to intimidate wives and intimate partners. In urban areas it is more difficult for abusers to discharge their weapons and go undetected.[4] People in the country are more familiar with the sound of gunshots and often attribute the sound to legitimate uses such as hunting in the woods.

To her detriment, June found that guns can also be used as a bludgeoning instrument. June described how she was pistol-whipped by her abuser in a particularly gruesome ceremony of subordination.

June: He got drunk. He laid down and went to sleep, but I walked down the road and visited my neighbor. Me and her has been friends for a long time. When I come back he was sittin' in the dark in his bedroom. He was sittin' on the bed. Had this .357 Magnum. He said, "June, you get down on this floor right now. You crawl to me." And when I got to his feet he took that pistol and hit me right alongside of the head. I thought I was gonna die. I still got the knot from it. He said, "if you even act like you're gonna run I'll blow your brains all over this wall." I couldn't help it. I took off anyhow. And I run all the way up the road just screamin' and hollerin' cause there was blood all over me, my shoes, my clothes. It was runnin' down the side of my face. And I got to this neighbor's house and they didn't believe nothin' I was tellin' 'em. They just wasn't believin' me. But she did get a washrag and wash some of the blood off of me.

In this excerpt we witness two important and paradoxical themes about the social context within which physical violence against rural women is embedded. First, June is not entirely isolated since she returns to her abuser from visiting a friend and neighbor she had known for a long time. She walked to this friend's house. Second, other neighbors, even when presented with the specter of her injuries, did not believe that she had been abused. June's description of events is not unique. Her isolation was relative. She did have a female friend nearby, yet the response of unknown neighbors was one of disbelief.

Bernice, who lived in the small town of Graperise in the heart of rural Eastern Kentucky, endured continuous threats against her life. Many women like Bernice reported a multitude of different forms of physical abuse.

> *Websdale:* Can you describe the forms of physical abuse?
> *Bernice:* He slapped me, kicked me, choked me, pulled my hair, threw things at me. He hit me with a two by four, put a gun to my head, put a knife to my throat.

Likewise, Toni reported an extensive history of physical victimization at the hands of her sadistic husband.

> *Toni:* He would hit me with belts and he would say "don't you like that" and I would be cryin' and he would tell me to stop cryin' and quit bein' a baby.

Bernice and Toni's interviews reveal something of the range of physical abuse directed at rural women. While this range may not differ much from that experienced by women in urban areas, we must nevertheless continue to juxtapose the abuse alongside the geocultural context within which it occurs. Of particular importance here are women's reports of lack of transportation, geographical isolation that renders escape difficult, absence of effective social services intervention, and a cultural climate that fosters a view of women as subordinate. All of these factors tend to limit resistance and exacerbate abuse.

Sexual Abuse

Diana Russell's (1990) survey of 930 women in San Francisco found that respondents reported being the victims of 2,588 rapes or attempted rapes. Of these victimizations, 38% were perpetrated by husbands or ex-husbands and 13% by lovers or ex-lovers. Only 6% were perpetrated by strangers. Given that women in nonmetro areas, as opposed to metro or central city areas, are more likely to report experiencing rape at the hands of an acquaintance or relative (Bachman, 1992, table 4, p. 558), we might expect married rural women to be disproportionately vulnerable to marital as opposed to other forms of rape.

Russell (1990) argues for seeing "wife rape" at one end on a continuum of sexual relations within marriage, with "voluntary, mutually desired and satisfying sex at the other end" (p. xxvii). In between these two extremes she situates what she calls "coercive sex" (without physical force or the threat of physical force) and "unwanted sex." The continuum approach resituates marital rape within an overall context of sexual oppression and choice within marriage. Such a recontextualization moves us toward seeing rape in less sensationalistic and more routine terms. Her desire to theorize wife rape as part of a continuum of marital sexual relations, rather than "one more traumatic assault experienced by an already battered woman" (p. xxvii), is consistent with my interview findings. Most women I interviewed reported having had "unwanted sex" or sex "to keep him quiet." But they also acknowledged they had on occasions enjoyed sex with their partners.[5]

Roughly half of the women I interviewed reported being forcibly raped by their abusers. June was one woman who reported a variety of forms of sexual violence.

> *June:* One time he made me leave with this one guy, he said, "take her out and fuck her, I can't do nothin' for her." And that guy did. He took him up on it.
>
> *Websdale:* So he felt like you were his property or something?
>
> *June:* A piece of meat, I reckon.
>
> *Websdale:* Were there any other forced forms of sexual activity?
>
> *June:* Well, yeah, he did force me to do him blow jobs.

Connie is a typical example of a rural battered woman who engaged in nonconsensual sex with her abuser. Her participation kept him from "getting mad" and fulfilled his expectation that wives should service their husbands sexually.

> *Websdale:* Were there any times in the five years that you were with him, that he forced you to have sex or that you had sex against your will?

Connie: Not really forced. There was a lot of times that I really didn't want to and he thought a woman should. And that was real uncomfortable.

Websdale: So you just felt that it was something you should do because you are a wife or something?

Connie: I didn't want to make him mad.

Websdale: Did that happen very often?

Connie: Quite often. I got to the point where I could live my whole life without sex.

Toni talks about being assaulted while having sex. On occasions her abuser held a knife to her throat in the full knowledge that she had been sexually molested at knifepoint as a child.

Toni: When we went to bed. He put a knife to my throat.

Websdale: He held a knife to your throat? When you say he held a knife to your throat, was he forcing you to have sex with him or was he just doing that to be cruel, or what was the reason?

Toni: He wasn't forcin' me to have sex with him. But he just liked that. . . . I don't think he would have brought a knife or anything like that to bed, if I hadn't told him about my being sexually abused as a child. . . . He knew how I sat and cried over it and how it hurt.

Keanne, in common with at least half of the interviewees, reported that she had been forced to provide sexual services she explicitly told her abuser she did not want to provide.

Websdale: And, when you say the sexual abuse was constant what do you mean?

Keanne: Um, he would force me. This is gross but I'm going to say it. He would force me to give him head. He would force me to do things that I didn't want to do. That I was totally against.

Sabrina lived in a small town in Western Kentucky and had known her neighbors for years. However, she reported that the neighbors never had an inkling of her husband's abusiveness. Sabrina notes that her husband engaged in a daily ritual of what I will call "gynecological surveillance."

> *Sabrina:* I hate the thought of him even touching me. He has this little thing that he does to me every morning. I have to let him check my "oil." And I, I don't know if you know what I'm talking about?
>
> *Websdale:* Tell me . . . elaborate.
>
> *Sabrina:* He sticks his finger up and I have to walk over there and let him check my oil.
>
> *Websdale:* Really.
>
> *Sabrina:* Every morning. From about 20 minutes after we get up there's talk about he wants to do this or he wants to do that. Ah, he wants me to bend over, um, or go to bed or give him oral sex. And sometimes three and four times a day we have sex. Always at least twice.
>
> *Websdale:* Yeah.
>
> *Sabrina:* Um, he, ah, has turned me against it, I have no feelings whatsoever, you know, concerning sex, other than it disgusts me.

These case illustrations do not tell us anything about sexual abuse that has not already been reported from urban areas. However, the sexual abuse of battered women in rural areas is not addressed by the extant research literature on either domestic violence or rural social life in general. The empirical evidence from my interviews shows that the rural family in Kentucky is not the idyllic and tranquil locus of social activity that, as we will see, the statistics on public sphere violent crime may imply.

Emotional Abuse

Every woman I interviewed reported experiencing emotional abuse. Most reported this form of abuse in tandem with physical or sexual abuse or both. The effectiveness of emotional abuse as a means of controlling women is often enhanced by the rural geo-cultural milieu. As noted, within this milieu many battered women live extremely isolated lives. Those women who report living in physical isolation talk of the way that isolation amplifies their abuser's ability to control them. Women who live in smaller communities or within the earshot of neighbors, tell how rural sociocultural mores dictate a certain place for women vis-à-vis men. Whether battered women's isolation be geographical, sociocultural, or both, many women find themselves without the emotional support of friends, neighbors, social services, and family. This lack of support makes it more difficult for victims of abuse to summon their psychological resources against the controlling behaviors of their abusers.

Just as the rural geo-cultural context provides men ample opportunities to control women, we must also remember that the individual control maneuvers of abusers may, in and of themselves, be the root of women's sociocultural and geographical isolation. As in Penny's case noted above, other women report that abusers sought housing in isolated places to keep them away from the community and especially other men. Many women report that abusers discourage them or, less often, forbid them from having close relationships with their family and friends. Still others note that abusers have a generalized hostility toward agents of the state, be they social workers, police, health professionals, or others, and that this too makes women more reluctant to seek professional help.

The emotional abuse of rural women, especially that designed to limit their physical and social mobility, forms a central part of an overall strategy of social control, even though it does not necessarily break the law. We can now examine some examples of the constraining effects of such abuse.

Typical examples of this emotional abuse include: continuous attacks on women's self-esteem, angry verbal outbursts, withholding money, extreme jealousy, false accusations of infidelity, control over women's physical movement, isolation from friends and family, and threats of violence and other adverse consequences. Some women report the emotional abuse is worse than the physical or sexual abuse, insofar as it leaves deep-seated psychological scars. Others express confusion about the disjuncture between woman abuse and the ideals of harmonious family life, which tend to be more powerful in rural areas where traditional marriage is more common and fundamentalist religious influences are stronger.

Ariel told of how her husband controlled her presentation of self and her bodily movement.

> *Ariel:* I'm not allowed to go anywhere. I'm not allowed to cut my hair. I'm not allowed to wear makeup.

Websdale: So when you say not go anywhere, you mean like go to the mailbox or go to the store or . . . ?

Ariel: Out. Like one day this past week there was nothin' there to eat. There's no refrigerator. So I told him, "I'm hungry and I want to go to town and get me somethin' to eat." He said, "okay." He said "well, I'm going. I'll see you this evenin' about 5:00." And this is like 6:00 in the mornin'. Well, he got up and he went and turned my car ignition on. So it run my battery down. When I went out there at 11:00 to start it up to go get somethin' to eat, my battery was dead. There are little things that he would do to make sure that he knew where I was at. I wasn't allowed to go to my friends unless he went. Or to the store unless he went.

Jill reported the following:

Jill: He has destroyed photos of my family, ripped my clothing and destroyed a few important papers [birth certificate, social security card].

Judy recounted:

Judy: My husband destroyed a dresser which belonged to my great grandmother.

Sonia reported that her husband ripped the shower unit out of their house because she took too long in the shower.

Sonia: I didn't have the luxury of hot water whenever I wanted it. He would hook the hot water up if anybody needed to take a bath. And then after he took his bath, I had to use his water.

Nancy's abuser had a generalized contempt for anything that reminded him of her relationships with other people. Given the significance of long-standing relationships in rural communities, the abuse experienced by Nancy dislocated her from her biography.

Nancy: He tore up my high school graduation pictures and destroyed anything that related to other people outside of the home.

The process of erasure is often directed at familial links with the past that erode the biography of women. Since self-identity is built, checked, and transformed on an ongoing basis through social interaction, we find emotional abuse serves to isolate women and lower their self-esteem. This can happen in other ways, for example, by the abuser harming or killing other living things that women hold dear. A number of women reported that abusers harmed their pets. The below comments are typical:

> *Lily:* He cut up my dog in a bunch of pieces and put the pieces in the freezer.
> *Renate:* He took my dog and hung it over the clothesline with a chain.

Another form of emotional abuse reported by women was the abuser's attempts to control the temperature of the family home, even if the abuser was not present in the home. Some men did this by disabling the thermostat and others refused to provide money to heat the house. Serena talked of her husband's behavior around heating their home.

> *Serena:* He would follow me and turn the heat down. He refused to give me money for the gas.

Such tactics have also been reported by women in urban areas. However, I suggest that the consequences of such emotional abuse may be different in rural areas because rural women have few other places to go and limited means of getting there, especially in cold weather.

In many of these abuse cases, for example Sabrina's sexual abuse, Sonia bathing in her husband's bathwater, and the cruel refusal of Serena's abuser to heat the house, we witness what Garfinkel (1956) once called a "degradation ceremony." In the communicative interplay between abuser and victim, we witness a process that transforms and devalues the identity of women.

Women are also connected to the social world through their paid work. Many abusers emotionally abuse women by undermining their performance in the workplace, controlling their attendance at work, threatening them while they are at work, or by damaging equipment women need for work. Pamela reported that:

Pamela: He burned holes in my uniform for work. Then broke the desk into pieces and smashed the screen of the computer.

The few rural battered women I talked with who had reentered the education system found that abusers often derided their efforts, destroyed their curricular materials, or both. Given the difficulty all these women had accessing further education, this form of emotional abuse is especially damaging. For example, Carly, who was in college at the time of our conversation, told me her husband was threatened by her educational advancement. In this excerpt her husband abusively, and without foundation, implies Carly's educational journey was moving her toward a different sexual orientation.

Carly: He calls me an educated bitch and resents my education. He overheard me talking to my friend about a film on homosexuality I had seen in a sociology class. He accused me of being homosexual.

The symbolic erasure of women's identities, the limiting of women's personal development, and the degradation ceremonies rural battered women endure constitute the central ironies of what I will later discuss as the supposedly more "personalized" rural sociocultural milieu. In many ways these emotionally abusive practices resemble what Goffman calls the mortification process. Goffman (1961) showed how total institutions such as prisons, monasteries, and mental hospitals force inmates to lead a rigid and ritualized lifestyle that robs them of much of their autonomy and tends to erode their sense of self. The removal of personal items upon entry to the institution and the forcing of inmates to wear standardized clothing and to adhere to schedules beyond their control are all part of the mortification process. Goffman defines the total institution as "a place of residence and work where a large number of like-situated individuals, cut off from the wider society for an appreciable period of time, together lead an enclosed, formally administered round of life" (p. 11).

There are clear parallels between batterers' treatment of rural women and what Goffman describes as the mortification process. Men's emotional abuse of women is often directed at the erasure of women's prior (often premarital) identity. The destruction of things of meaning to women also resembles the disrobing process in total institutions where inmates lose many of their personal belongings. My interviews with rural battered women suggest strongly that abusers attempt to ensure their intimate partners develop few new ideas, values, and beliefs of their own. Of especial importance here is the desire of batterers to ensure women adhere to the tenets of the collective (patriarchal) conscience as each perceives it and constructs it to be. Again we see a parallel here with Goffman's observation that staff in total institutions attempt to redefine or reconstruct the persona of the inmate to fit the institutional label. The drug addict who enters a treatment facility is seen to be in "denial" until he or she adopts the staff's definition of him- or herself. Likewise, the rural battered woman who wants to tread a path beyond that preordained by the strictures of rural patriarchal life will be made aware of her foolishness and her failure to accept the "reality" of her biological calling. The control of women's movement and behavior is also like the surveillance of inmates in total institutions. The gynecological surveillance experienced by Sabrina recalls the pelvic exams experienced by girls who enter some drug treatment programs.

However, I do not want to carry this comparison between violent families and total institutions too far. Inmates who enter prisons, patients who enter mental hospitals, and people who enter religious retreats all have some sense of the austerity of their future. On the contrary, many of the rural battered women I talked with expressed genuine surprise at the abuse they experienced. While inmates in total institutions are cut off from wider society, they are not cut off from each other. It is in the isolation of the rural battered woman from other women who share her predicament that the comparison between the battering family and the total institution breaks down.

Resistance

Rural women I talked with did not acquiesce in their victimization. Rather, they actively sought out a variety of resistive strategies. The fact that women shared their stories with me was in itself an act of resistance. Several women told me that if their abusers ever knew they had shared their lives with me on tape they would be in grave danger. Likewise, living in the spouse abuse shelter was also a profound act of resistance. There women met other women from like situations and shared their stories and often felt empowered through the sharing. A significant number said that if their stories could somehow lead to an alleviation of the plight of other battered women then they would be well satisfied. Most women strategized about how to change their abusive relationship, protect themselves and their children, live apart from their abusers, and, at times, how to exact revenge. The following excerpts document some of these resistive strategies.

Patricia surprised herself one night when she came close to killing her abusive husband. Notice the way the thought of what would happen to her children restrained her from taking his life.

Websdale: Did you ever think about shooting him?
Patricia: Yeah. I almost killed him one night.
Websdale: Yeah.
Patricia: And it really surprised him. It surprised me because I
    didn't think I had it in me. He was losing his temper and he
    had me in the kitchen and he kept pushing me into the
    counter, over and over and over. And he was calling me names
    and, ah, he'd throw things every now and then, um, it just,
    it's like my mind just snapped. And I came after him. I reached
    behind me on the counter and I grabbed a knife. And, ah, I
    went at him. I ripped his shirt right off his back and everything
    he was doing to me the whole time I felt nothing. I was numb.
    It was like I wasn't there but I was there. I tackled him to the
    floor. I had him down on his stomach. I was sitting on his
    back. And, ah, I had my knees on his arms where he couldn't
    move. And I grabbed his hair and I pulled his head back and
    I put that knife up to his throat. And I thought, "What am I
    doing? I can't do this." You know I've got four kids back here,
    what would happen to them you know.
Websdale: Yeah.
Patricia: But it, it shocked him. I'll never forget the look on his
    face when he come up off that floor. He didn't come at me.
    He was just in total shock.

Tamara's thoughts of killing her husband were also checked by her feelings for her children.

Tamara: I slept one night with a gun under the pillow. I was trying
    to decide whether or not I should just put the gun in his mouth
    (cause he sleeps with his mouth open), pull the trigger and

make it look like a suicide. And the only thing that kept me from doing it was that I didn't want to wake the kids up with the gunshot and for them to walk in and see their daddy just dead.

Michelle was chastised by police for using the only weapon she found to be effective against her husband.

Michelle: I called the police because he had busted my nose. And we'd both been fighting. I, I fought him back that time. And I think I really hurt him and they told me that if I used what I'd used on him the next time, I was going to jail. I used a poker and they said that was considered as a deadly weapon and that I shouldn't have done that. And I said, "Well, ah, he's taller than I am and stronger," and I said, "I had to do something."

Roxy was especially angry about her husband's propensity for spending large amounts of their income on cocaine. She reported how she had strategized to shoot her husband if he hurt her again.

Roxy: I'm gonna tell you what I did. I didn't actually do it, I just thought about it. He had come home, he was with a friend of his named Steven. And they were doin' cocaine. And I just got really mad. I was sittin' there watchin' TV, I didn't say anything. It was on a Saturday and he had his little ol' pistol, just a .25. I guess that could kill somebody. And he was tellin' me he just went and spent $100 for some cocaine. Well, I got mad. I couldn't take it. So he started cussin' me and stuff. So he left with his friend, Steven. I was sittin' there and I thought to myself I should go in, get this little pistol and if he comes in and even acts like he's gonna put his hands on me, I'm gonna blow his leg off. I would never shoot to kill, but I'd hurt him.

Bonita schemed her escape from her abuser while he was away hunting. Notice Bonita's use of language as she asks his permission to go over to her mother's while he is away. Here, as in other cases, the tiny ripples of resistance make possible a decisive break from the seemingly frozen certainty of women's subordination. At one level

Bonita recognizes her subordinate position, but is still able to use it to her advantage. Her escape was planned in conjunction with her mother and social service workers. Without this support, Bonita may well have not managed to get away.

> *Bonita:* Well, my father-in-law's a coon hunter and my husband went with him the other night and I told him, "Can I go stay with Mom, can I visit with Mom while you go huntin'?" And he said, "Yeah." So my sister-in-law took me over there. When he come to get me I was gone.

Angela decided to leave her abusive husband after the nature of his abuse changed. Her husband wanted to start having sex with her daughter-in-law and also to force her daughter-in-law to have sex with other men.

> *Angela:* My daughter-in-law told me, "he is gonna have me too, he is gonna force me to go to bed with another man." I said, "no, no way." I said, "I'm out of here." . . . I packed my suitcase, put it in the back of the car and I left.

Brenda was threatened with a butcher's knife by her violent husband. She broke free, called the police, and went to the shelter with her children.

> *Brenda:* We had got into it because he was messing around with [old] ladies and stuff like that. And so I called him. I told him he had to move out. He refused to move out and he took a butcher knife and was gonna stab me in my side. But I broke loose from him. I ran out the door. I went to my neighbor's house and I called police. . . . The police brought me here and we've stayed here maybe two weeks.

Women's resistance to battering is also dependent upon support from various state agencies. That support in rural areas forms the focus of Chapters 4, 5, and 6. Without adequate support, a small number of women are pushed into a corner where they are forced to use lethal violence against their abusers. As Angela Brown (1987) puts it, lack of effective legal intervention in cases of wife abuse, and the lack of adequate and established alternatives to protect victims from further aggression, leaves many of these women alone with a danger from which they cannot escape. . . . A society that allows violence against wives to continue by forcing the individual woman to stop the perpetrator's behavior runs the risk that victims may eventually take action that the society does not condone. (p. 180)

One such rural woman who felt unprotected by the criminal justice system was Karen Stout. She told the Kentucky Legislative Task Force on Domestic Violence: "When are they going to start protecting women? We are people too" (see *Lexington Herald-Leader,* August 23, 1995).

Karen from Hardin County, endured 20 years of brutal battering and torture at the hands of her violent husband (see *Lexington Herald-Leader,* August 23, 1995). Eventually, her husband began sexually abusing their daughter and two sons. Karen was convicted of manslaughter in 1994 for encouraging her son to find someone to kill her abusive husband James. She was later paroled. In the summer of 1995, the parole board began examining the cases of some Kentucky women who had killed, or tried to kill, or played a role in killing their abusers. Just before leaving office, Governor Jones commuted the sentences of 11 of these women, effectively releasing them from prison.[6]

Focusing on rural women's resistance to battering is important because it serves to remind us that they are not the helpless, passive victims they are so often portrayed as. However, we must not lose sight of the fact that when homicides occur in domestic relationships, it is more often the man who perpetrates them, usually after many years of battering his partner (see Dobash & Dobash, 1992; Stark & Flitcraft, 1996). In the next section of this chapter I highlight the killing of rural women by their intimate partners. The extent of rural women's own use of lethal violence as the ultimate and only form of self-preservation pales in comparison to the extent of lethal violence directed at them by their male partners, who often kill as the ultimate assertion of their power and control.

Or For Worse: Patriarchy and Pine Boxes

I have documented the everyday violence and abuse experienced by rural battered women. However, in rural Kentucky a large number of women lose their lives every year because of the extreme violence of their abusers. In fact, a cursory glance at the modified crime index for domestic homicide and suicide reveals the highest rates of these offenses per capita in rural communities.[7] In the following accounts I draw upon newspaper reports and information provided by the KDVA to tell the stories of those women who can no longer speak for themselves. These reports are divided into two sections. The first deals with the murder of women by their abusers. The second deals with the rarer phenomenon of murder-suicide, in which the abuser murders his partner or ex-partner or other family members/friends and then shortly after commits suicide.

Murder

Men tend to kill their female partners after an extended period of abuse, whereas females usually kill male partners in self-defense or at least to preempt what they perceive to be inevitable further victimization. In Chapter 3, I note that in the United States, interspousal homicide data reveal that for every 100 women killed by their husbands, 75 husbands are killed by their wives. While it is not the focus of my ethnography to compare national domestic fatality statistics with those in rural Kentucky, it must be said that in rural Kentucky, many more husbands kill wives than wives kill husbands.

Gender roles in rural communities tend to be more stereotypical, with women being chained to their "biology" much more so than in urban centers where they have moved into the workforce in larger numbers and taken a more active part in formal politics (see Walby, 1990). Kalmuss and Straus (1982) argue that the more dependent a woman is on her abuser, the more likely she is to suffer extreme battering. Given the degree of dependence on men reported by some rural battered women because of the more traditional gender role expectations in rural Kentucky, it is conceivable that these rural battered women may be more prone to extreme violence. Indeed, this may be one of the reasons for our survey finding that rural battered women report experiencing significantly higher levels of "torture" and being "shot at" (Websdale & Johnson, 1995). This possibility is also supported by the research of Michael Smith (1990), who found that when husbands articulated various forms of patriarchal ideology in the home, then their wives were more likely to report being assaulted (p. 268). Arguably, the most extreme form of battering is murder.

Total Mutilation

McCreary County is located in southeastern Kentucky on the Tennessee border. According to the 1990 census, 45.5% of its residents live in poverty, making it one of the poorest counties in Kentucky and in the United States. In July 1995, in the small community of Pine Knot in McCreary County, Patricia Taylor was murdered by her live-in boyfriend James Naegele. According to the local newspaper, "Every part of Taylor's body from the top of her head to her feet had been severely traumatized" (*McCreary County Record,* July 11, 1995).

The *Lexington Herald-Leader* reported the fatal injuries differently: "McCreary deputy David Morrow made a circle with his thumb and forefinger yesterday to show how little of Taylor's body was not injured" (*Lexington Herald-Leader,* July 11, 1995).

In a conversation with a key informant who is still involved in the death of Patricia Taylor in Knott County, I was told that Patricia Taylor's body was brutalized beyond recognition.[8] To quote my informant, "the mutilation was the worst I have ever seen in my life. There was not one part of her body that was not touched by his violence."

No weapon was used to kill Taylor. David Morrow noted that Naegele was "wearing heavy work boots" (*Lexington Herald-Leader,* July 11, 1995) and that Naegele had also used his fists. As if in an attempt to erase all memory of Taylor, Naegele augmented the killing by slashing most of her clothes and tossing them into the trash bin.

A neighbor reported the beating to the local sheriff after hearing a loud disturbance at the Naegele-Taylor mobile home. Another neighbor who was a close friend of Taylor became concerned when she did not see Taylor the morning of the killing. She went to the mobile home and was greeted by Naegele. When the friend inquired about Taylor, Naegele walked off down the hallway toward a bedroom. The friend, unbeknownst to Naegele, followed him toward the bedroom. When Naegele realized Taylor's friend had followed him to the bedroom he quickly turned off the bedroom light, pushed her out of the bedroom, and shut the door. Although Taylor's friend did not see Taylor's corpse, she became suspicious because the bedroom had multiple tarp-like coverings over the window. Taylor's friend reported her suspicions to the sheriff who then investigated. A sheriff's deputy and Taylor's friend returned to the residence and were greeted by Naegele, who gave the deputy permission to enter and talk to Taylor. Taylor's friend commented: "The minute I touched her I knew she was dead" (*McCreary County Record*, July 11, 1995).

While the sheriff's deputy and Taylor's friend were establishing that Taylor was dead, Naegele escaped into the woods. However, he was spotted by yet another neighbor who informed sheriff's deputies of Naegele's whereabouts. As the search for Naegele continued, we learn that angry neighbors, friends, and family gathered at the scene of the crime. Sheriff Swain remarked that because of local hostility toward Naegele that Naegele would be safer in his custody. We will return to this case when I discuss the policing of rural woman battering in Kentucky. My reason for describing these events is to highlight the extensive involvement of neighbors at every stage of this murderous episode. This degree of neighborly involvement often characterizes domestic homicides in rural areas in Kentucky because of the close-knit nature of those communities.

Marijuana and the Smoke Residues of Death

Hindman is located in Knott County where, in 1990, 40.4% of the population lived in poverty. As in many other Eastern Kentucky counties where poverty rates are extremely high, there is also an active and illegal marijuana growing industry.[9] The presence of marijuana growers was of particular relevance in this case. The killing of Claudia Jacobs in January 1991, in Hindman, is one of the most controversial rural spousal killings in Kentucky. Her husband Johnny Jacobs killed her at close range by shooting her in the face.[10] According to press reports, the gun was so close to her when it discharged that it left smoke residues on her cheek and nose. Johnny Jacobs told state police that he only intended to scare Claudia by placing the gun to her face and that it was Claudia who caused the gun to discharge accidentally as she moved forward. His attorney, Larry Webster, told the press that the Jacobs marriage was a stormy one and that, "When they got into an argument, they both pulled pistols out. It was just part of it" (*Lexington Herald-Leader*, February 8, 1994). Webster added that the night of the fatal shooting both Claudia and Johnny had been drinking heavily and that Johnny had pulled his gun and cocked it in an attempt to scare Claudia as she approached him. However, she kept coming and bumped into him, and the gun discharged.

In the aftermath of the killing there was a polarization of portions of the community around this case. The controversy in the case stemmed in part from the fact that it took 4 years to dispose of it. Johnny Jacobs was arrested the day of his wife's death but was released on bail in February 1991. He was indicted for murdering his wife on March 6, 1991 by a grand jury. In the ensuing years, the slain woman's sisters complained bitterly that they would see Johnny Jacobs out shopping at the Wal-Mart in Prestonsburg. Jami Cook, Claudia's sister, commented, "I think it's a disgrace that somebody is walking around, and my sister is dead" (*Lexington Herald-Leader,* February 8, 1994).

The time taken to bring this case to trial was only part of the controversy. In the months after Claudia's death a much more "timely" form of federal criminal justice visited her parents and brother. During the brief period that Johnny Jacobs was jailed on the murder charge, he offered the FBI evidence against Claudia's parents, Donna and Claude Hall, and her brother, Claude Hall, Jr., that led to them being charged with possessing dynamite booby traps and conspiring to grow and sell marijuana. Within 5 months of Claudia's death the Hall family had been tried and convicted in federal court. Claude Hall was convicted on charges of possessing dynamite and conspiracy to grow marijuana and received a sentence of 27 years. His son was convicted on the same charges and received 28 years. Donna Hall was acquitted on the dynamite charges, but convicted of conspiracy to grow marijuana and was sentenced to 27 years. At their sentencing, U.S. District Judge Joseph Hood issued a clear message: "I want the people of Eastern Kentucky to know that pot growing in Eastern Kentucky will not be countenanced by this court" (*Lexington Herald-Leader,* February 8, 1994).

The juxtaposition of the swift and punitive federal "justice" handed down in the Hall's case, against the 4 years it took to bring Jacobs to trial, galvanized the community. Ned Pillersdorf, the Hall's attorney, commented on the discrepancy in the time taken to deal with the two cases: "In essence, the victim's family is in prison. . . . It sounds like if you kill the child of people whom you believe are drug dealers, then it's OK" (*Lexington Herald-Leader,* February 8, 1994).

For some people in the community, and particularly workers in the region's spouse abuse shelter, the differential sentencing of Johnny Jacobs and the Halls reflects the differential importance of wife killing and marijuana growing. We will return to this case.

Pillars of the Rural Community

A Rockcastle County murder reminds us that not all of these interspousal killings occur against the backdrop of abject poverty and drug dealing. Ginny Gilpatrick was a well-liked community volunteer who also taught part-time at Eastern Kentucky University.[11] She worked at a teen center run by the Christian Appalachian Project in Mount Vernon and wrote articles on parenting. In addition, she started a school antidrug program and joined a number of civic groups. According to press reports, her husband helped her in these projects. On the night she was killed she was sitting at her kitchen counter preparing for class, when her husband, Allen, struck her on the head with a wood-and-metal club. According to the pathologist's report she was struck 16 times. Blood was found in several bedrooms in the house and police reported that there were obvious signs of a struggle and no evidence of forced entry to the residence. As in the Patricia Taylor case, Ginny Gilpatrick was unrecognizable.[12] She was found laying on the floor covered with blood. At first, Allen Gilpatrick called Mount Vernon police on the night of the killing and told them that an intruder had broken into the house and committed the murder. Later Allen Gilpatrick recanted and confessed to the killing. He was also well known to the community because he worked for the Department of Social Services. Since the Gilpatricks were so well known to county residents, the subsequent trial of Allen Gilpatrick was moved to neighboring Pulaski County.

The Burning Bed

The role of neighbors and people who knew the parties was also evident in the murder of Elizabeth Thompson in the small Oldham County town of Orchard Grass Hills.[13] Donald Thompson, a counseling and treatment officer who worked for the state Corrections Cabinet, suddenly turned up on his neighbor's doorstep at 11:30 p.m. saying that his house was on fire. The neighbor, Fay Cartledge, asked where Elizabeth was and Donald replied that he did not know. Within minutes another neighbor who just happened to be driving by the Thompson residence saw the fire and rushed inside. There he found Elizabeth Thompson upstairs on a burning bed. Within a short period police arrived and determined that she had been shot several times with a .22 caliber Magnum handgun and then doused with gasoline and set on fire. Once again we witness a not unfamiliar theme in these rural homicides whereby the identity of the victim is almost completely erased as part of the ultimate act of domination. This bodily erasure and final disfigurement during the actual mortification process is the logical extension of the symbolic mortifying processes and degradation ceremonies I noted in cases of sublethal violence. Also, as in so many of these cases, Elizabeth Thompson had filed for divorce just prior to being murdered. For Donald Thompson, as for a number of other abusers who use lethal violence, the only way Elizabeth was going to leave the institution of rural patriarchy was in a pine box.

The Burial Dress

Loretta Colwell married her husband Tony when she was 14 years old. They lived in the small mountain community of Busy, in Leslie County. The press noted that many people in the community knew both families involved.[14] Loretta predicted she would be killed by her abuser and made certain contingency plans, including letting her family know which dress she wanted to be buried in. She modeled the dress for her friend Genevieve Davidson. The dress was white with a deep V in the back. The sleeves were trimmed in gold braid and pearls. Davidson reassured her friend that she was not going to be killed. On March 30, 1995, Loretta gave the burial dress to her mother for safekeeping. Within 2 days Loretta, at age 26, was killed by two gunshot wounds in the back.

In the month prior to her murder, Loretta sought and received help at the Perry County spouse abuse shelter. According to Lois Valentine, the shelter director, Loretta was "a very scared, hurt, mixed-up girl" (*Lexington Herald-Leader*, April 25, 1995, p. A8). During that month she secured a domestic violence order against Tony. In that order she stated, "I lefted Tony and he threated if I came and got my clothes or my baby he would kill me. I lefted him because he beats me and drinks a lot, and he call me hore and bitch and he was drinking at the time" (*Lexington Herald-Leader*, April 25, 1995, p. A8).

Loretta asked for the domestic violence order to be withdrawn after Tony promised to go to couple's counseling. Friends and family urged Loretta not to return to him, but she did. Prior to her death, friends said she had begun to make "progress." She had sought psychiatric help for some of her past demons, including a rape that occurred at the hands of strangers a number of years earlier. She had even acquired a driving permit for the first time in her life. But she wrote a letter, which she said she wanted read out at her funeral, that documented how hard it had been going back to Tony. In the letter she also stated that she loved her children so much. Tony Colwell was charged with the murder and was held in Leslie County jail without bond. According to Tony, it was Loretta who attacked him that night with a knife, inflicting serious wounds on his face, stomach, back, and arm.

Self-Defense Is No Defense

Finally, for those who argue that women should learn to defend themselves against violent men, I present the murder of Ella Hunter who, along with her new boyfriend Darrell Blackburn, was shot dead by her estranged husband, Phillip Hunter. Ella was a karate instructor. On the day she arrived at a Floyd County high school to teach a martial arts class, her husband arrived and killed her and her boyfriend. Both were killed by blasts from a 12-gauge shotgun. At the time of her death, Ella had a copy of the domestic violence order issued through Floyd County court prohibiting her husband from having contact with her. We will return to the enforcement of this order in Chapters 4 and 5, but it is worth noting that in the order Ella Hunter comments that, "He physically beat me and I have left home and he is constantly following me to where I live now and he also comes to my work place" (*Lexington Herald-Leader,* February 3, 1993). It appears from the contents of the domestic violence order that Ella's skills as a karate teacher did little to protect her from either the sublethal or lethal violence of her husband. As for Phillip Hunter, he pleaded guilty to both killings and was sentenced to two life terms in prison.[15]

Murder-Suicide

Most murder-suicides occur within families or between people who are or have been intimate partners. In nearly all cases the perpetrator is a male and the event is preceded by a breaking off of the relationship, a history of woman battering, or both. According to Marzuk, Tardiff, and Hirsch (1992), "While some murder-suicides occur shortly after the onset of 'malignant jealousy,' more often there has been a chronically chaotic relationship fraught with jealous suspicions, verbal abuse, and sublethal violence" (p. 3180).[16]

A Kentucky study also reveals that many murder-suicides are preceded by a history of woman abuse. Currens (1991) notes that,

> In 15 (41%) of the 37 cases in which the current husband was the perpetrator, the couple had previously filed for divorce (12) or was separated (3). In seven of these 15, the wife had obtained a domestic violence protective order or restraining order from a court. . . . The typical perpetrator is a man married or living with a woman in a relationship marked by physical abuse. (p. 653)[17]

The murder-suicide rate is low compared with the frequency of either murder or suicide.[18] Murder-suicides are also unusual crimes in that the perpetrator of the homicide also plays out the role of the victim of suicide as well (see Berman, 1979). Given that the media disproportionately report rare and particularly violent crime,[19] murder-suicides seem to be very newsworthy.[20] Rural Kentucky is no exception here and murder-suicides tend to send shock waves through tiny communities.

Fire, Feuding, and Rural Calm

A murder-suicide in Toddspoint, in which Wayne Miller killed his ex-wife Wilma Miller, revealed some of these discursive themes and was described as follows in the *Louisville Courier-Journal* of February 3, 1989:

> The calm of the small community of Toddspoint in rural Shelby County was shattered yesterday morning when a man shot and killed his former wife, wounded his son, then set fire to his house then took his own life.
>
> After shooting dead his ex-wife and wounding his son, we learn that Wayne Miller drove away from the crime to his farm several miles away. There he set fire to his farmhouse, went upstairs and shot himself in the heart. Friends and town officials knew that for several years after their divorce the Millers had been feuding. One friend of the Millers who had known them for more than 30 years, said Wayne had shot his wife before. But it seems that Faye Miller fought back against her husband and resisted his violence in a number of ways. Shelby District Judge William Stewart commented that Faye Miller was a "nice, straightforward woman, a real take-charge type, who had

fired shots into her ex-husband's truck several years ago. Still, Stewart said, Faye Miller was afraid of her husband" (*Louisville Courier-Journal,* February 3, 1989).

"There was not a divorce"

Themes of rural life regularly punctuate the media accounts of a murder-suicide in Waynesburg, where Shannon Greer of Waynesburg walked into the local elementary school where his wife, Glenda Greer, worked as the school secretary (see *Lexington Herald-Leader,* May 11, 1990). As in many murder-suicide cases, Glenda Greer was in the process of terminating her relationship with her husband by divorcing him. Armed with a 12-gauge shotgun, Shannon killed Glenda. He then drove to a remote logging road in eastern Casey County where he killed himself. Police found the divorce papers on the dashboard of his car. Scribbled on the papers was a note written by Shannon Greer that said, "there was not a divorce."

In this newspaper account of the Greer murder-suicide we witness the juxtaposition of a number of themes about rural life. We learn that Glenda Greer had worked as the school secretary for 11 years and was much loved by the schoolchildren. She was well known in the small farming community in the southern tip of Lincoln County. Alongside these themes of community cohesion, the agricultural setting, and the innocence of a small rural elementary school, we learn that Glenda Greer was killed by a shotgun blast to the face and another to the back as she tried in vain to escape. She had also been brutally beaten about the head with the gun prior to being shot. The themes of rurality and death coalesce in the photographic accompaniments to the news coverage. We see pictures not only of the murdered woman but also of the car in which Shannon Greer committed suicide on a logging road amid thick forest.

Conclusion

I contend that these reports of sublethal and lethal violence against women in rural families are best understood as part of the terror of rural patriarchy. Men are more likely to injure or kill women when their supremacy as patriarchs is somehow threatened. The social and physical mobility of rural women is often more restricted than it is for their urban peers. In the next chapter I highlight the distinctive qualities of rural patriarchy and argue these provide a way for understanding the levels and intensity of interpersonal violence against women and, at the same time, the sense of loss, shock, and tragedy that seem to permeate rural communities when these (somewhat predictable) events take place.

Notes

1. I will explore the gendered nature of intrafamilial violence in Chapter 3.

2. These figures are unduplicated for the fiscal year. A woman may come to shelter several times over the course of a year (July 1 through June 30) but these figures reflect only the first time she enters shelter. I am grateful to Monique Dalka-Noll of the KDVA for providing these figures.

3. Citing Wright, Rossi, and Daly (1983), Patricia Gagne (1992) points out, "the cultural acceptance and use of firearms in rural America has been well established" (p. 406).

4. However, in urban areas where gun ownership rates are lower, abusers can still threaten with guns even if they do not go off.

5. According to the research literature, there is a clear connection between marital rape and wife battering. Finkelhor and Yllo (1985) found that 50% of wife rape victims had also been battered. In addition, they note that battered women were roughly twice as likely to be the victims of multiple marital rapes (pp. 23-24).

6. For a discussion of the feminist political maneuvers which helped facilitate these commutations, see Chapter 6.

7. See *Attorney General's Task Force on Domestic Violence Crime: Domestic Violence Fatalities, A Statistical Report*, October 1993. The 3-year average modified crime index for domestic homicides and suicides (for the period 1991-1993) is 2.0 for the entire state. A county-by-county breakdown reveals that rural counties have far and away the highest indices. For example, the four biggest urban counties in Kentucky have relatively low indices: Fayette County (Lexington area, county population in 1993, 232,562) 1.5; Jefferson County (Louisville area, county population in 1993, 670,837) 2.0; Kenton County (county population in 1993, 143,550) 1.4; Campbell County (county population in 1993, 85,034) 1.6. However, some rural counties with very low populations have very high indices. For example, the Knott County (county population in 1993, 18,233) index is 7.3 and Hart County's (county population in 1993, 15,478) is 6.5.

8. This key informant must remain anonymous. A civil suit is pending against the McCreary County Sheriff's Department for its failure to respond in this case. James Naegele received 10 years for manslaughter.

9. See *Lexington Herald-Leader*, December 13, 1992 for a county-by-county listing of the number of marijuana plant seizures by the Governor's Marijuana Strike Task Force.

10. Johnny Jacobs had already been arrested on August 11, 1990 for fourth-degree assault on Claudia.

11. See *Lexington Herald-Leader*, March 10, 1993 and April 30, 1994.

12. See comments by Kentucky Commonwealth's Attorney Ray Carmichael in the *Lexington Herald-Leader*, April 30, 1994.

13. See *Louisville Courier-Journal,* December 23, 1992, pp. A1, A8.

14. For press coverage of this case see *Lexington Herald-Leader,* April 25, 1995, pp. A1 and A8, and the *Louisville Courier-Journal,* April, 1, 1995.

15. See the *Louisville Courier-Journal,* October 10, 1993 and October 23, 1993.

16. Marzuk refers to the research of Allen (1983), Berman (1979), and Dorpat (1966) to support his argument.

17. Studies cited in support of a prior history of domestic violence include Rosenbaum (1990) and West (1967).

18. Marzuk et al. (1992) suggest there are about 1,000 to 1,500 homicide-suicides annually in the United States. Research studies report a range of homicide-suicide rates including 0.21 per 100,000 for Philadelphia (Wolfgang, 1958), 1.5 per 100,000 for Philadelphia, Baltimore, and Washington, D.C. (Berman, 1979), 0.19 per 100,000 for North Carolina (Palmer & Humphrey, 1980), and 0.18 per 100,000 for the United States as a whole (West, 1967). In contrast, for the years from 1987 to 1993 the average U.S. murder rate has been 9.1 per 100,000 (Federal Bureau of Investigation, 1993). The homicide-suicide rate also differs from the suicide rate, which, for the years between 1987 and 1990, averaged 13.6 per 100,000 (National Center for Health Statistics, 1990).

19. For example, Esterle (1986, p. 5) found that murder, the rarest form of violent crime, is reported most often. Likewise, Graber (1980, pp. 39-40) notes that though murder constitutes only 0.2% of crime known to the police, it makes up 26.2% of crime news stories.

20. See Websdale and Alvarez (1998) for a discussion of the media portrayal of homicide-suicide.

2

Rural Patriarchy, Crime, and Criminal Justice

Introduction

In the preceding chapter, I identified some of the interconnections between the victimization of battered women and the rural geographical and sociocultural milieu. There are those who would argue that modern urban life has so deeply impacted "the countryside" that it is practically meaningless to use the term *rural* in a social scientific sense today. I am not one of those who believe the term *rural* is redundant. Rather, I concur with Weisheit, Falcone, and Wells (1996) that for those researchers who have actually spent time doing field research in rural communities, there is a considerable range of characteristics of rural regions that distinguish them from urban ones. I attempt to make sense of the term *rural* and proceed to use my flexible working definition as a touchstone for the framing of the concept of "rural patriarchy." Finally I accentuate the distinctiveness of rural areas by documenting the vast differences in rates of violent crime between rural and urban communities. These disparities may lead one to believe that if rural areas are more "tranquil" they would experience significantly less woman battering. However, as I have already documented, rural woman battering is an immense social problem that transcends the apparently "violence-reducing" effects of the rural collective conscience.

Defining "Rural"

The term *rural* is commonly understood to refer to the countryside or small towns as opposed to cities. The debate about the nature of rural social life has been central to sociology. However, whether sociologists employ the notion of a rural urban dichotomy or a rural-urban continuum, the term *rural* and the images it invokes are somewhat problematic. The discourse on rurality typically addresses the following: demographic factors; the rural economy and the division of labor; and sociocultural considerations.

Demographic Factors

The U.S. Census Bureau adopts a dichotomous rural-urban model by defining rural communities as those with populations of less than 2,500, and all others as urban. As Weisheit et al. (1996) point out, population thresholds below which a community is considered rural differ for various government programs and agencies (p. 142). For example, the Farmer's Home Administration uses a population threshold of 20,000 people; the Rural Electrification Act, 1,500; and community development block grant programs count cities as rural (nonurban) if they have fewer than 50,000 people. These authors argue: "when it comes to . . . collecting data, practical constraints often require that the content of rural be greatly narrowed" (p. 141).

Using a simple demographic measure of rurality such as population level, population density, or the number of households per unit of land area, provides an absolute definition of rurality that has a certain practical utility, especially when it comes to conducting quantitative research. As Bealer, Willits, and Kuvlesky (1965) note,

> Rural has . . . been used as an ecological concept to refer to the distribution of people in space. The most common usage of the term here has been to designate as "rural," regions of small population size or low density. . . . "Rural" defined in terms of size is precise, convenient, and easily operationalized. (p. 260)

However, using numerical thresholds to demarcate rural from urban is problematic. Communities of less than 2,500 that are within a readily commutable distance from a major metropolitan area are not usually considered rural. Neither are distinctive communities of less than 2,500 people that come within the political boundaries of a metropolis. In other words, in both everyday and more formal sociological parlance, "rural communities" usually invoke images of settlements in relative isolation from larger centers of population. This relatively simple definitional difficulty is one of the reasons why most sociologists favor the use of a rural-urban continuum model over a rural/urban dichotomy. On the supposed "isolation" of rural communities, Bealer et al. (1965) ask, "For instance, should isolation be construed in terms of physical distance, commuting costs, availability of communication media, some other factors or combination of factors?" (p. 263).

Seemingly absolute definitions are also problematic because they ignore or marginalize social, economic, and cultural factors. We can only begin to approach the essence of an ethereal term such as *rurality* when we combine demographic measures with information on both the rural economy and patterns of human interaction.

The Rural Economy and the Division of Labor

Emile Durkheim (1964) argued that the division of labor was simpler in "traditional primitive" societies. In such societies there is less occupational specialization. As urban industrial societies develop, the division of labor becomes more complex and occupational specialization increases. In smaller (rural) communities the interests of the individual are, according to Durkheim, more in tune with those of the collective whole. As urban industrial centers evolve, the cult of the individual emerges and egoism increases. In such settings, anomie (normlessness) develops and the traditional "collective conscience" begins to decay. This decay has particular implications for the regulation of social behavior.

In Durkheim's original formulation, traditional primitive societies were primarily agricultural, and people lived off of the land. The traditional notion that rural areas have primarily agricultural economies is still popular today, even although it is now no longer accurate. As Deavers (1992) points out, less than a fifth of what can be considered "rural counties" depend substantially on farming for their survival (p. 184). Today, fewer than 10% of rural dwellers are employed full-time in agricultural work (Weisheit, Falcone, & Wells, 1994b, p. 6).

There was a clear link between rural occupational structures and the natural resources of rural regions. In addition to farming, rural dwellers also fished, hunted, logged, and mined. However, there has been a shift from these kinds of extractive occupations. For example, during the 1980s coal mining jobs decreased by 47% (Bishop, 1993, p. D4, citing Deavers). Nowadays, as Deavers (1992) points out, "Manufacturing is the major source of export earnings for rural economies, and the service sector provides the largest share of income and employment" (p. 184). However, Deavers also acknowledges that manufacturing declined substantially in rural regions during the 1980s (cited in Bishop, 1993, p. D4). While companies invested in factories in rural areas to take advantage of lower wages, they soon realized they could cut their wage bills even more substantially by moving overseas. Indeed, during the early 1980s, rural counties in the United States lost more than 550,000 manufacturing jobs.

While Durkheim's work on the decline of the collective conscience constitutes a stinging critique of industrialization, others theorize the rise of cities differently. Rather than focusing on values and the diminution of collective sentiments that have traditionally exerted a powerful social control influence, Marx and Engels (1970) theorized the growth of cities as part of the rise of capitalism. For Marx, the divisions of capitalist society are primarily "material" and it is the exploitative nature of the capitalist wage relation that provides the motive force for modern urban disorder. Engels (1984), too, maps the correlation between the rise of capitalist factory production in Lancashire and Middlesex in England, and the rise of crimes such as theft, robbery, and burglary (pp. 159-162). For Marx and Engels, this social malaise was reproduced in part by the emergence of a set of dominant values that celebrated individual freedoms and democracy, and obscured the naked cash nexus that slowly replaced more traditional feudal community ties.

Sociocultural Considerations

Sociologist Ferdinand Tonnies (1940) contrasted rural and urban life using two concepts that became part of the iconography of sociology: Gemeinschaft and Gesellschaft. He used the term *Gemeinschaft* to describe those forms of social organization characterized by the central importance of kinship ties and a deep sense of preindustrial tradition. Typically, rural villages and small towns exhibit a greater homogeneity of values and less tolerance of diversity. Religion is a key component of their social cement. For a number of researchers, the rural community is characterized by patterns of social interaction involving an appreciable number of community members who are either related to each other, know each other, or know of each other, and are more likely than urban dwellers to know each others' business (Redfield, 1947; Simmel, 1950; Sorokin & Zimmerman, 1929; Wirth, 1938). Due to the primacy of kinship and other personal relationships in rural communities, "outsiders" attract considerable attention and suspicion. In a number of studies of rural and urban differences in both Great Britain and the United States, the polarities between insiders and outsiders have been shown to be more significant in rural areas (Chamberlain, 1975; Frankenberg, 1957; Littlejohn, 1964; Williams, 1956). The homogeneity of rural versus urban areas is evidenced by a higher level of value consensus, less tolerance of diversity, a greater reliance on informal social control such as gossip and shaming; and a distrust of government.

Some researchers have challenged the view that there are more "substantive" community ties in rural areas (see Avila, 1969; Connell, 1978; Dewey, 1960; Friedland, 1982; Gans, 1962; Pahl, 1965, 1966; Vidich & Bensman, 1968). For example, Dewey (1960) points to the disagreement among sociologists about those factors that best highlight the differences between rural and urban communities. The only factor that Dewey identifies as appearing consistently in sociologists' accounts of the rural urban dichotomy or continuum is the existence of "heterogeneity" in urban areas (p. 60). With regard to language and religion, two key components of the sociocultural cement, Dewey comments that "variety in language and religion may be greater in some rural areas than in certain large cities" (p. 63).

Vidich and Bensman's (1968) ethnographic study of the small rural community of Springdale in upstate New York argued that Springdale's claims to a small town-communitarian lifestyle were part of a bygone era and that Springdale was imbricated with many of the characteristics of mass urban societies. These characteristics included the growth of a new middle class that altered the face of small town America. In reflecting on this earlier work, Vidich and Lyman comment, "government, business, religious and educational super-bureaucracies far distant from the rural town formulate policies to which the rural world can respond only with resentment" (Vidich & Bensman, 1994, p. 35).

In contrast, *Gesellschaft* describes larger masses of population concentrated in cities. These impersonal urban-industrialized societies are bureaucratized to varying degrees. Human interactions are based more on "contract" than "honor." Cities exhibit greater diversity and a greater tolerance of diversity. Here, as Durkheim noted, the division of labor is more complex. Privacy and anonymity are more prevalent because most people do not know each other or each other's business. Religion is less important and religious diversity greater. The economy is based on factory production, and the criminal justice system and the state in general play a much more significant role in the regulation of social life.

Studies that emphasize the sociocultural homogeneity of rural communities tend to ignore the fact there is still a sense of community in urban areas. For example, Fischer (1981) stresses that urbanism does not result in a reduction in family ties or a distrust of neighbors. If divisions and rifts develop in cities, they take the form of a distrust of strangers or alternative subcultures. While Karp, Yoels, and Stone (1989) acknowledge that rural communities are more homogeneous, they also note,

> The relative disappearance of the "village" community type should not make us leap to the immediate conclusion that urbanites live "non social" existences. . . . If the essence of any community lies in patterns of warm, intimate interactions, then communities are to be found in cities. (p. 73)

From the interactionist perspective of Karp et al. (1989), there are as many communities in urban areas as there are individuals with inter-action networks. According to these authors, social actors in urban space create communities, in part, through the (paradoxical) construction of "anonymity."

While remaining cognizant of some of the problems associated with labeling communities rural and urban, I nevertheless argue, based in large part on the perceptions of rural citizens themselves, that there are discernible and meaningful differences between rural and urban communities. Ultimately, the definition of rural communities is arbitrary and open to debate. As Weisheit et al. (1996) put it, "Like such concepts as 'truth,' 'beauty,' or 'justice,' everyone knows the term rural, but no one can define the term very precisely" (p. 135).

Perhaps the most important point of caution implicit in the above discussion is that rural areas are not all alike. They will have different populations and population densities and they will have differing levels of sociocultural homogeneity, and varying economies. This diversity among rural communities may also be perceived as such by the residents of those areas. Weisheit et al. (1996) observe, "Many 'rural' areas of Delaware and New Jersey would be considered urban by residents of Wyoming or Montana" (p. 139).

For the purposes of this book, I use a composite definition of *rural*. Nearly all of the battered women I interviewed came from isolated communities of less than 5,000 people.[1] Those who came from slightly larger communities still self-identified themselves as coming from a rural community. None of the women were from communities with populations of more than 10,000 people. All of the communities were isolated insofar as they did not have easy access to metropolitan centers with populations of more than 250,000 (essentially, only Louisville) or the small number of cities in Kentucky with populations between 50,000 and 250,000 (Lexington, Covington, Owensboro, Paducah). It was clear from my interviews and observations that I was studying woman battering, and the criminal justice response to it, in relatively homogeneous rural communities with most, if not all, of the demographic, economic, and sociocultural qualities that I described above. This is not to say that there is not considerable variation among the communities I researched. These variations warrant mention.

Regional Diversity in the
Primarily Rural State of Kentucky

Kentucky is the most northern of the southern states and the most southern of the northern states.[2] Six major regions make up its geo-cultural fabric. The major urban centers consist of the metropolitan areas of Lexington, Louisville, and the southern Cincinnati area (Covington). Here we find what Miller (1994) calls a much more individualistic culture. In the cities, the role of government is more developed and better accepted than it is in rural areas.

There is tremendous diversity within the state. My research began in Eastern Kentucky, a region characterized by a declining economy, originally devoted to the mining of coal. Growing unemployment in these eastern counties has brought untold poverty and immiseration. According to the 1990 census, a large proportion of the counties in this region had more than 30% of their populations living below the federal poverty line ($12,695 per annum for a family of four; cited by Stewart & Payne, 1991). Of the 28 poorest counties in Kentucky, 27 are in Eastern Kentucky. The 19 counties in this region that had more than one third of their residents living in poverty were the main reason Kentucky ranked as the fifth poorest state in the nation in 1990. All these 19 counties were among the 100 poorest in the country. Owsley County, with an official poverty rate of 52.1%, ranked sixth poorest in the nation. This grinding poverty is associated with a tension in the community around the acquisition of scarce resources. Available resources in the Appalachian coal mining communities, including jobs, welfare benefits, and social programs, have become part of a corrupt system of patronage politics. As Duncan (1992) notes,

> there are no "good jobs" for the unskilled and barely literate from poor schools and poor communities. They stay home, piecing together incomes from "odd jobs," part-time work, illicit activities, and whatever welfare benefits they can qualify for. As economic conditions deteriorate, communities and schools become more violent and the social context itself deteriorates. (pp. 131-132)

Some have labeled this a culture of dependency and disenchantment, in which people have become historically dependent on welfare and unable or unwilling to pull themselves up by their own bootstraps (see Caudill, 1963; Weller, 1966). Others have sought more structural explanations of individual "failure" (see Coles, 1971; Waller, 1988). For example, Waller (1988) emphasizes the role of the coal corporations in creating a cultural hegemony in Eastern Kentucky. Central to this hegemony was the portrayal of the arrival of the railroads and the rise of the coal economy as "civilizing" influences. These influences downplayed the violence created by capitalist exploitation and exaggerated the historical significance of the legendary feuding in Eastern Kentucky between rival families such as the Hatfields and the McCoys.

Like Waller, I argue that social structural factors lay at the root of the historically enduring prevalence of local corruption and that this corruption, although not unique by any means to Eastern Kentucky, sometimes militates against the diligent policing of woman battering. In addition, such economic decline limits the job opportunities for women and limits their options for exiting violent relationships.

The central bluegrass area of Kentucky is the home of the tobacco and horse farms that punctuate the verdant and fertile landscape. Miller (1994) notes the presence of a landed gentry that constitutes an enduring elite. Poverty levels are lowest in the bluegrass area, where, perhaps not coincidentally, we find the political and cultural hub of the state.

The very conservative western counties of Kentucky attach considerable importance to "rural lifestyles" and are typically southern Democrat enclaves. As Miller (1994) notes, this region is the most hostile of all the regions to taxation (p. 69). Even the cities in the western counties (e.g., Paducah and Owensboro, both on the Ohio river) are different from the major urban areas in Kentucky in that they are expanded market towns and trading centers rather full-blown metropolitan centers (see Miller, 1994, p. 60). The western counties can be divided into three areas: the Jackson-Purchase area, the Pennyrile region, and the Western Kentucky Coalfield.

The Jackson-Purchase area is nestled in between the Kentucky-Tennessee border and the Ohio River. Of the three areas, it is the most southern in a cultural sense.

The Pennyrile region is blessed with very rich land and a thriving culture that Miller describes as a "yeoman agrarian culture" (p. 65). Even in this region there is considerable cultural variation within and between counties. For example, Christian County, the second largest county in Kentucky, is divided into distinctive northern and southern sectors. The southern end is flat and possesses very fertile soil. The northern sector undulates and is more heavily timbered. Two different types of agriculture arose at opposite ends of the county. The southern end engaged in plantation-type farming, principally dark-tobacco. Prior to the Civil War there were some very large tobacco plantations with typical antebellum-type farmhouses and slaves. The southern sector was settled by people from North Carolina and Virginia who were well acquainted with plantation agriculture. The northern sector was settled more by people of Irish, Scotch, and Scotch-Irish ancestry who migrated into the county a little later. They engaged in subsistence-type farming. These differences in cultural legacy are still evident in Christian County today. For example, it is in the northern sector, particularly in heavily timbered areas, that marijuana growing operations continue and subterranean economies flourish.

The Western Kentucky Coalfield, like its Eastern Kentucky counterpart, is in a state of decline. Coal producing areas such as Hopkins
County and Muhlenburg County have economies that are mere shad-
ows of what they were 30 years ago. Prior to this decline, miners
provided well for their children. Formal education was not valued in
the same way as in neighboring Christian County (to the south),
because young men could make as much money in the mines as they
could from entering a profession. With the decline of the coalfields,
however, the tax base has shrunk, social services have declined, and
frustrations have grown. According to my interviewees, the degradation and demoralization brought about by the decay of the coal
economy has exacerbated violence within families.

Rural Patriarchy

The Concept of Patriarchy

Throughout this book I contend the social, rather than biological
or psychological, condition of women provides the most accurate
touchstone for understanding violence directed at them by their male
partners. Consequently, one of the central contextual foci of this book
is the social condition of women in rural areas and particularly rural
Kentucky. In this section, I argue that the social condition of women
in rural America can be informed by Sylvia Walby's (1990) notion of
"private patriarchy."

In order to define private patriarchy and distinguish it from what
Walby calls "public patriarchy," we must first examine Walby's use of
the term *patriarchy*. By *patriarchy* she is referring to a "system of social
structures and practices in which men dominate, oppress and exploit
women" (p. 20).

Her use of the term *system* informs us that not all men engage in
oppressive practices, but that rather there is an overall pattern of
domination. This system of oppression intersects with other exploitative sets of social relations such as class and race relations. Walby
identifies six relatively autonomous structures: the patriarchal mode
of production in the household, paid work, the patriarchal state,
patriarchal culture, patriarchal relations in sexuality, and male violence against women. Husbands or cohabitees expropriate the labor

of their partners. Women receive their maintenance in return for their household labor, especially if those women do not work for wages in the socialized labor market. If women work as full-time homemakers, then they work just as long hours as they did a century ago. While many women, both married and unmarried, now work for wages, they still engage in disproportionate amounts of unpaid household labor (housework, child care) compared to the men they cohabit with (see Hartmann, 1981). For Walby, the patriarchal mode of production in the household is oppressive because of women's more limited opportunities for survival in the wage labor market. Even with the advent of divorce rights, women, especially those who leave with their children, face the prospect of poverty or at least a substantial drop in their material standard of living.

There have been a number of objections to the notion that the patriarchal household is a universal site of oppression for women. Black feminists have argued that black women's family life can be a refuge from racism (see Carby, 1982; hooks, 1982, 1984). From another angle, Hazel Carby (1982) comments,

> In questioning the application of the concepts of "the family" and "patriarchy" we also need to problematize the use of the concept of "reproduction." In using this concept in relation to the domestic labor of black women we find that in spite of its apparent simplicity it must be dismantled. What does the concept of reproduction mean in a situation where black women have done domestic labor outside of their own homes in the servicing of white families? (p. 218)

White wage working women have better jobs than black women. For this reason, black women may have found household labor less alienating. Nevertheless, Walby (1990) still argues that even if the black household has been a site of resistance to racism and been less alienating for black women, "this does not mean that the household is not also a site in which men oppress women, in that men benefit from women's domestic labor" (p. 87).

Women's wage work has always been less well paid and regarded as less skilled. Here Walby points particularly to the intersection between class and gender in referring to the disadvantaged position of women in the gendered capitalist economy. Although during the course of the 20th century more women, particularly married women, have entered the public sphere of paid work, their occupational loci have been heavily segregated, and in the workplace they have been dominated by men. Walby (1990) argues that the entry of women into the paid labor force was driven by two key forces: (a) the demand for cheaper sources of labor and (b) feminist pressure to end exclusionary practices in employment (p. 59).

Walby notes that the patriarchal state is also capitalist and racist. In the field of gender relations, the effects of the state are not monolithic. For Walby, and a number of other feminist theorists, the role of the patriarchal state is complex, contradictory, relational, and as such the state is a major site of struggle and social change. As Walby (1990) notes, there have been many changes in state policy over the past 150 years in both the United States and Great Britain. These changes have confronted legal discrimination, improved the availability of contraception and abortion services for women, and increased women's legal ability to leave violent men (pp. 150-172). Other theorists concur with Walby on, for example, the contradictory nature of the state (see, e.g., Ehrenreich & Fox Piven, 1983). Fox Piven (1990) sees the patriarchal state as potentially beneficial for women. Likewise, Connell (1987) sees the state at the confluence of a number of structural antagonisms: "The patriarchal state can be seen, then, not as the manifestation of a patriarchal essence, but as the center of a reverberating set of power relations and political processes in which patriarchy is both constructed and contested" (p. 130).

Patriarchal culture includes among other institutions, religion, the educational system, and the media. According to Walby (1990), discourses on femininity and masculinity have been fractured through the prism of both class and race. She also points to numerous points of intersection between the social construction of gendered identities and social phenomena such as pornography and the partial construction of masculinity through the ability of men to earn a "family wage" (pp. 104-108).

Radical feminists (Millett, 1977; Rich, 1980) argued that "heterosexuality" is not something that women entered through "free choice" or because of their "biological leanings," but is rather a system of sexual relations forced upon them as part of the general subordination of women under patriarchy. MacKinnon (1979), for example, accentuates the part played by sexual harassment in the workplace as a means of ensuring women's subordination. Radical feminist analyses of pornography also contribute to the overall argument that the terrain of sexuality is central to the objectification of women. According to

Dworkin (1981), pornography is part of the mechanism through which women are controlled. In addition, Walby notes the pivotal historical role of the sexual double standard, whereby patriarchal society allows men to engage in certain forms of sexual behavior (e.g., using the services of a prostitute) that are largely unavailable to women. Walby also locates rape within this nexus of sexual subordination, being careful to point out that the historic failure of the patriarchal state to pass marital rape laws has also made it difficult for married women ever to consent fully to sexual intercourse within marriage.

Of central importance to the arguments that I will make in this book is Walby's contention that there is a pattern of male violence against women that runs throughout British and American society. This violence is not confined to a few "abnormal" men, but is rather symptomatic of a social structure of subordination. She argues that woman battering and rape, which have been popularly seen as discrete phenomena often attributable in part to behavior of victims themselves, are best contextualized amid the structure of patriarchy. In the case of rape, there is much research to show that rapists are not typically strange men who are mentally deranged in some way (Smart & Smart, 1978). Rather, rapists are most often known to victims and are frequently in, or have been in, intimate relationships with victims (see Finkelhor & Yllo, 1985; Russell, 1990). It is toward this connection between intimacy and the violent victimization of women that my analysis of rural woman battering is directed.

In recent years there have been a number of criticisms leveled at the concept of patriarchy. Foremost among these criticisms is that patriarchy has been used to denote a universal condition of women's subordination. This universalism denies the cultural idiosyncrasies of the societies in which patriarchy is alleged to operate. Butler (1990) puts it as follows:

> The political assumption that there must be a universal basis for feminism, one which must be found in an identity assumed to exist cross-culturally, often accompanies the notion that the oppression of women has some singular form discernible in the universal or hegemonic structure of patriarchy or masculine domination. The notion of a universal patriarchy has been widely criticized in recent years, for its failure to account for the workings of gender oppression in the concrete cultural contexts in which it exists. (p. 3)

In the context of colonialism, Hazel Carby (1982) comments, "If we take patriarchy and apply it to various colonial situations it is equally unsatisfactory because it is unable to explain why black males have not enjoyed the benefits of white patriarchy" (p. 218).

Notwithstanding these perceptive criticisms of the notion of patriarchy, I follow realist feminists such as Walby (1990, 1992) and Bell and Klein (1996) in arguing for the explanatory power of the concept of patriarchy. To be sure, the issues may differ by country/culture. As Robin Morgan (1996, pp. 6-7) points out, the issues for radical feminists might be the nation's debt in Brazil, combating sex tourism in Thailand, winning suffrage rights in Kuwait, ending the practice of female genital mutilation in the Sudan, gaining inheritance rights in Nepal, or halting nuclear testing by the French government in the Pacific Islands because it produces "jellyfish babies" (children born with no spines). Nevertheless, the domination of women by men across cultures is a consistent international trend and if there is one unifying theme, one seemingly universal thread of patriarchy that inhabits most cultures, it is that of male violence. This unifying theme of male violence emerged crystal clear at the recent World Conference on Women, held in Beijing and Huairou, China. Of all the issues discussed—including women's poverty, education, health, decision-making power, the media portrayal of women—Rita Maran (1996) notes that, "Violence against women constituted a top priority, . . . it garnered the greatest consensus and served . . . as a unifying element" (p. 354). Indeed, one of the main platforms to emerge out of the conference was "the prevention and elimination of violence against women and girls" (Maran, 1996, p. 354).

The Concept of Rural Patriarchy

By *rural patriarchy* I am referring to that articulation of patriarchy found distinctively in rural areas. Put specifically, the relatively autonomous structures referred to by Walby (the patriarchal household; paid work; the patriarchal state; patriarchal culture; patriarchal sexuality; and male violence) manifest themselves differently in rural areas, although these structures still constitute a readily discernible set of gender power relations. While the ethnographic evidence I presented on rural woman abuse shows it to be similar to that already documented in urban areas, these experiences of abuse are embedded within a rural social context. This social context embodies a specific historical crystallization of the six aforementioned bases of oppression.[3]

Walby's (1992) theoretical distinction between private and public forms of patriarchy is helpful in attempting to define rural patriarchy. She notes:

> In private patriarchy the dominant structure is household production, while in the public form it is employment and the state, though in each case the remainder of the six structures is significant. In the private form the dominant mode of expropriation is individual, by the husband or father; in the public it is collective, by men. In the private form the strategy is exclusionary; in the public it is segregationist. (p. 36)

Rural patriarchy exhibits more of the historical vestiges of private patriarchy than does urban patriarchy. However, it is not my point that rural patriarchy is a form of private patriarchy or that it has not been heavily influenced by more public forms of patriarchy. It would be folly to suggest that rural patriarchy is not impacted by urban life, wage work, the state, and the media.

As Walby's definition of patriarchy notes, the disadvantaged position of women vis-à-vis men is particularly evidenced through the marriage contract. The key social locus of women's oppression and exploitation under private patriarchy is the household. Both historical and contemporary studies reveal that rural women have been more involved in household production and less involved in the public sphere of wage work and formal politics than urban women. In rural areas for example, the rates of marriage continue to be higher (Bushy, 1993, p. 188). In rural areas there is a much more traditional division of labor between men and women (Fassinger & Schwarzweller, 1984; Gagne, 1992). This is bolstered by a patriarchal ideology in rural areas in which men are seen as providers and women have an intense and highly privatized relationship with domestic production. As both Gagne (1992, pp. 395-398) and Bushy (1993, p. 191) note, rural women seem to be more strongly associated with domestic activities such as child rearing and housework.

We find examples of these rural gender power relations in the work of various researchers. Sociologist Patricia Gagne's (1992) ethnographic study of Raven Ridge, a small rural central Appalachian community, revealed a strong gendering in family life. She notes, "When men worked, they tended to commute shorter distances and rarely traveled with children. Few prepared meals, did housework, or took care of children after work" (p. 394).

In Raven Ridge the authority of men was maintained and reproduced by a number of strategies including violence. However, what Gagne (1992) calls "persuasive control" was a very important nonviolent form of regulation that fed off of what she calls the "norm of women's deference to men" (p. 398). The persuasive control of women consisted of men "repeatedly issuing verbal requests and arguments, withholding transportation, isolating them from family and friends . . . and forcing them to bear children against their will" (p. 398).

Deborah Fink (1986), in her history of farm women in *Open Country, Iowa,* argues that most studies of rural life assume that rurality is concerned with farming and that farming is performed by men. Consequently, women have often been written out of rural historical studies. This leads to inaccuracies because, as Fink points out, work performed by farm women was an integral part of the family economy, even if census enumerators did not see women as being "gainfully employed." She notes,

> there were many farm women who were maintaining substantial poultry enterprises, marketing butter and other produce, working in the farm fields, or tending animals for the purpose of making money, yet who were not listed in the census as being workers. (p. 74)

It is not my intention to depict rural patriarchy as an iron grid of oppression. Fink, for example, reminds us that the women in *Open Country,* while geographically isolated, still got together. Their socializing and networking was understandably shaped by the rhythms of the seasons, work, and family responsibilities (p. 100). Neither is it my intention to imply that rural patriarchy is only associated with farming. The gradual drift of Iowa's married farm women into jobs and education has not brought the kind of progress predicted by earlier research on married women in rural communities (see Bescher-Donnelly & Whitener-Smith, 1981; Vidich & Bensman, 1968). Fink (1986) notes,

> Although women have received more education in recent years, this has not helped many of them to earn a living wage. Iowa has one of the highest literacy rates in the country: women's low income has not been caused by their educational deficiencies. (p. 201)

Recent empirical evidence supports Fink's suggestion that education, or lack of education, is not the reason for the subordinate social position of women under rural patriarchy. Tolbert and Lyson's (1992) analysis of income inequality between metropolitan and non-metropolitan areas in the United States from 1968 to 1991, found that gender and college education were the two most influential variables. While gender was the most important variable in nonmetro regions, college education was the most influential in metro areas. These findings imply that it may be more difficult to undo the subordinate social status of women in rural communities, as opposed to urban communities, by introducing educational reforms alone.

Throughout her history of women in *Open Country*, Fink (1986) alludes to the ideological practices designed to keep women in subordinate positions. For example, she notes that in the 1970s and 1980s, land sales were negotiated through an inner circle of men who often purchased land and property. If these men did not want the property, then it would become available for others to buy. According to Fink, it did not occur to this inner circle of men to even consider selling land and property to women so that women could farm it. Indeed the inheritance of farmland was largely a patrilineal process that excluded daughters (p. 203). This practice, rooted in 19th-century patriarchal traditions, meant that if women wanted to be involved in farming, they had to gain access to land by marrying men. Given that there were few if any other viable means of women making a living, Fink presents rural marriage less in terms of "choice" and more in terms of women weighing economic necessities.

We see the operation of patriarchal ideology in other settings, including those gearing up for industrialization. The flow of unmarried women into the first manufacturing jobs in the Lowell, Massachusetts, textile mills relied upon mill owners assuring New England farmers that their daughters would be kept in strict "all female" dormitories and be prepared for marriage and motherhood in a manner consistent with the prevailing patriarchal ethos of New England's agrarian culture (see Kessler-Harris, 1982, p. 33). Marriage was the socially acceptable framework within which to develop family life in 19th-century rural Oregon. McFarland (1984) notes that in smaller communities the few single or unmarried women who attempted to support themselves were the subjects of gossip, ridicule, and scandal (p. 39). Lockley (1971) reports how Matilda Delaney told him of being whipped by her father at age 13 for merely going out with Mary Allen who had been born out of wedlock (pp. 8-10). Moynihan's (1983) biography of Oregon suffragist Abigail Scott Duniway reports Duniway opining that many wives in rural Oregon lived in a state of "enforced maternity" (p. 115). The birthrate in Oregon in 1850 was 50% higher than the national average. In rural Oregon, it was 30% higher than in Oregon's towns. Duniway reported that rural women's reproductive rights concerning their own control over abortion, birth control, and childbirth became a rallying cry for the nascent Women's Movement (see Moynihan, 1983, pp. 63-64).

While rural women have traditionally been limited to the private sphere of domestic production, many have moved into the public sphere of wage labor. When this has happened, rural women have earned roughly 50% of the wage made by rural men. This compares unfavorably with urban women, who have earned roughly two thirds of the urban male wage (Bushy, 1993, p. 189). Bushy suggests that rural women, more than urban women, may experience greater conflict with their partners over seeking employment outside the home. This fits with rural patriarchal ideology that emphasizes women's place in the home. The limited earning potential of rural women also negatively impacts their ability to leave violent, partners.

Fink's (1992) research in Nebraska rejects the notion that rural women were somehow liberated by life on the farm. She calls this the "agrarian ideology" (p. 2). Instead, Fink argues, rural women were in the same bind as nonrural women, although the nature of the bind was fractured through the prism of rurality. In mentioning the links between family violence and the lives of farming women, she comments,

> Although modern agrarians tend to dismiss incidents of breakdown and violence in rural homes as recent urban intrusions, I believe that rural women's difficulties have had a more fundamental basis in the structure of farming and rural communities. (p. 3)

My own research into gender relations in 19th-century Oregon concludes that the offering of unique land-owning rights to married (but not unmarried) women (Donation Land Acts of 1850) effected the patriarchal settlement of the region (Websdale, 1992; see also Chused, 1984). In addition, I point out the intimate connections between the social condition of rural women in 19th-century Lane County, Oregon, and woman battering. My research in Oregon (see Websdale, 1991, 1992) concurs with Fink (1992), who argues that,

"The establishment of the infrastructure that enabled these farms to survive was a joint venture of government and private capital, as was the printing and distribution of texts that proclaimed the superiority of family farming" (p. 3).

Elizabeth Pleck (1987) acknowledges the significance of "family privacy" in the early Puritan colonies as an obstacle to confronting family violence:

> One crucial element of the Family Ideal was belief in domestic privacy. . . . The family, it was held, should be separate from the public world. . . . In the sixteenth century, Luther and Calvin's emphasis on the individual's direct relationship to God, unmediated by church ritual, affected the view of the family. The home became a more important center of worship and began to appear as a more distinct and separate institution from the rest of society. (pp. 7-8)

Although the Puritans introduced the first laws against domestic violence, these laws were rarely enforced because of the way in which the family was seen as a private and untouchable domain. It was only when domestic violence took the form of "wicked behavior" and spilled out more into the community that such deviance threatened the divinely ordained fabric of Puritan social life. At the heart of this social life was the patriarchal family.

While the private sphere of the household is the key site of rural patriarchy, other "relatively autonomous structures" are still important. For example, there has been a steady decline in rural women's wages compared with urban women's, and an accompanying reduction in their options for independent survival. This decline is particularly significant for rural battered women who weigh the possibility of leaving violent men against their chances in the gendered capitalist labor market. Lucy Gorham (1992) observes that between 1979 and 1987 the gap between low wage earning rural men and women increased, whereas in urban areas the gap diminished (pp. 25-26). Between these years, Gorham notes that

> whereas the share of low earners rose from 22.2 percent to 31.6 percent for men, it rose from 43.7 to 53.9 percent for women. Thus in 1987 less than a third of rural men workers were low earners, compared with over half of all women workers. . . . Not only did the gap between rural men and women widen between 1979 and 1987, but so did the gap between rural and urban men and between rural

and urban women. . . . For men, the gap increased from 6 to 9 percentage points, whereas for women it increased from 11.5 to 17.9 percentage points. In 1979 only 2.9 percent of rural women were high-wage earners, compared with 5 percent of urban women. By 1987 the share of women high-wage earners had dropped to 2.3 percent in rural areas, but had risen to 6.3 percent in urban areas. (pp. 25-26)

Although little research has been published on the social condition of women in rural Kentucky, Miller (1994) observes that in Kentucky a highly traditionalistic culture prescribes stereotypical family roles for men and women. This traditionalism, particularly acute in rural regions, places women in sociocultural settings where it may be more difficult for them to resist battering, leave with their children, use the telephone to summon help, be supported by other women, or get help from the criminal justice system or the state.

In a recent survey of 510 battered women resident in shelters in Kentucky, 75% of the women were married and 22% reported they were in a cohabiting relationship. When broken down by rural and urban settings, rates of marriage were significantly higher in rural (182 out of 219 respondents, 83%) than urban areas (120 out of 182, 66%). This is consistent with the aforementioned literature pointing to higher rates of marriage in rural areas. Rates of cohabitation were also much lower in rural areas (36 out of 219, i.e., 16.4%) compared with urban areas (48 out of 182, i.e., 26.4%), suggesting that cohabiting relationships are less well tolerated in rural communities (see Websdale & Johnson, 1997a).

While I have argued that rural, more so than urban, patriarchy comes closer to what Walby calls "private patriarchy," it is not my argument that rural and urban patriarchy should be seen as distinctive types. Such an argument would be inconsistent with my aforementioned "subjective" understanding of rural and urban areas being on a continuum. Rather, I argue that the struggle between men and women in rural areas, while still comprehensible through the six bases used by Walby, exhibits consistent patterns of difference that warrant our attention. Indeed, these patterns of difference vary by rural region and are also fractured along local class and racial lines. Of prime importance for the substance of this book, is how rural patriarchy in Kentucky appears to influence the levels of intervention, support, and protection afforded women by the criminal justice system. It is in the direction of the foci of rural criminal justice systems that I now turn.

Crime and Criminal Justice in Rural Communities

Crime in Rural Areas

Crime and violence are popularly conceived of as being less prevalent in rural regions (see Willits, Bealer, & Timbers, 1990). However, rural citizens share many of the concerns of urban citizens about crime and violence. Although earlier studies show that people in rural areas have less fear of crime (e.g., see Baumer, 1978; Boggs, 1971; Conklin, 1971, 1976; Dinitz, 1973; Gibbons, 1972), later studies are mixed and tend to show the only difference is that rural citizens are less likely than urban dwellers to fear violent street crime (Weisheit et al., 1996, pp. 26-27). The literature on fear of crime is silent on rural women's fear about being battered by their partners. We should not be surprised by this silence. As Stanko (1995) notes, the fear-of-crime literature with its focus on the danger posed by strangers, is ill-suited to examining women's fears of being victimized. This is because those fears are derived in significant part from the men women live with, know, and work with.[4]

Historically, cities emerged as centers of trade, and later, as the industrial revolution got under way, workers left the land and moved into manufacturing centers. Engels (1984, pp. 159-162) describes in rich detail the demoralization and immiseration of English factory workers and the intimate connection between these social conditions and the rise of property crime and violence. He notes that Lancashire and Middlesex in England, two major manufacturing counties with large proletarian populations, "produced one-fourth of the total amount of crime, though their population is far from forming one-fourth of the whole" (p. 160).

More contemporary studies of reported violent crime rates in rural and urban areas attest to the increased frequency of violent crime in urban centers (see, e.g., Carter, 1982; Dinitz, 1973; Gardner & Shoemaker, 1989; Gibbons, 1972; Laub, 1983; Lyerly & Skipper, 1981; Sampson, 1986; Smith, 1980; Weisheit et al., 1996). The *Uniform Crime Reports* (UCR) shows that reported urban crime is higher than its rural counterpart in all offense categories. While we need not dwell on the detailed differences, a couple of examples of the magnitude of the difference between rural and urban public sphere violent crime warrant inclusion.

Robbery is the classic urban crime and according to the *UCR* is 46 times more likely to occur in cities with populations of over 250,000 than it is in rural counties. Murder and aggravated assault are both

4.5 times more likely to occur in cities (*UCR,* 1993, table 16). Data on rural and urban crime in general also tell us that the differences between the two areas are most acute in the case of violent crime, as opposed to property crime (see Weisheit et al., 1996, pp. 27-30). Nevertheless, the *UCR* shows that total property crime is four times higher in cities than in rural counties.

However, the *UCR* report only what the government deems to be "serious" crime. Woman battering is not tracked. As Ann Jones (1994) points out, the government has never collected data on the victims of aggravated assault, many of whom are women who are beaten by men they know and/or live with (p. 157). If batterers are arrested, it is usually for misdemeanor assault. Daniel Bell (1986, 1989), using data from police jurisdictions in Ohio, found that domestic violence disputes were more frequent in areas of Ohio with the lowest populations. Using National Crime Victimization Survey data[5] and the population threshold of under 50,000 for her definition of rural, Bachman (1994) finds that women in central cities, suburban counties, and rural areas are all equally likely to report being the victims of intimate violence (p. 7). This early research into the phenomenon of rural domestic violence seems to suggest that violence within families does not exhibit the same patterned difference between rural and urban areas as violence in general. Such work is a useful starting point because it alerts researchers to the fact that the social generation of domestic violence, or as I prefer to call it, woman battering, probably does not follow the same sociological ground rules as the social generation of violence in general. It is in the direction of those sociological ground rules that my analysis now turns.

Sociological Explanations of the Low Levels of Rural Crime

The greater presence of violent crime in urban areas fits with the argument that rural social life is governed by a stronger collective conscience that acts as an informal social control mechanism. These informal social controls seem to operate in spite of the grinding poverty of rural regions, which in 1986 was 50% higher than in urban centers (Garkovich, 1991). While numerous studies point to the association between poverty and violent crime in urban areas, few have shown a similar association in rural areas.

There are a number of theoretical paradigms that attempt to explain the phenomenon of violent crime. For functionalist theorists, the collective conscience decays in larger cities and moral regulation is weakened. Informal controls such as gossip, shame, and guilt play less of a social control role and in the anonymity of urban space, violent criminals run amok. As Durkheim put it, the "cult of the individual" and "egoism" are far more prevalent in urban/industrial society than in traditional/primitive society. A current version of Durkheim's thesis is articulated in the work of Kowalski and Duffield (1990), who find a positive correlation between urbanization and the homicide rate.[6] They report:

> Apparently, a rural residence does place some restraint upon violent acts like homicide. This provides a partial confirmation of Durkheim's notion that less developed areas facilitate more traditional bonds within a society. Thus, in rural areas, individualism is reduced, group identification is strengthened, and the potential for violence is diminished. (p. 86)

Neither social constructionists nor Marxists have a lot to say about rural crime and violence. For some social constructionists, urban growth is accompanied by the emergence of criminal justice and social service agencies that by their very existence and organizational net, catch and process more crime and criminals (see Becker, 1963; Lemert, 1972). Marxist criminologists explain crime not as a product of urban or industrial society per se, but rather as a product of the dehumanizing, alienating, and competitive conditions of industrial capitalism, which provided the motive force for the rise of cities in the first place. The rural-urban dimension of analysis is less important for Marxists than their analysis of the criminogenic social relations of production (see Spitzer, 1975; Taylor, Walton, & Young, 1973, 1975).

The bulk of the literature on rural crime and criminal justice accepts that rural crime rates, especially those involving violent crime, are lower than in urban areas. In numerous studies there is at least the implication that it is the rural collective conscience and its social control effects that are at least in part responsible for lower crime. These studies raise an important question: If the "crime prevention effects" of the more intense rural collective conscience operate to constrain or discourage violent crime, is such logic applicable to the private sphere of violence against women in rural families? In other words, does the rural collective conscience also limit the incidence of woman battering in families? Alternatively one might ask whether rural patriarchy subsumes the rural collective conscience to the point that to talk of the rural collective conscience as somehow distinct from rural patriarchy is meaningless? The empirical work of Bachman (1994) and Bachman and Saltzman (1995) suggests that the violence-reducing effects of the rural collective conscience, if they indeed operate at all, do not appear to pass beyond the closed doors of rural families. The ethnographic accounts that I laid out in the opening chapter support this argument. Indeed, the accounts of woman battering presented in Chapter 1 strongly suggest that the rural collective is a part of rural patriarchal relations.

Criminal Justice in Rural Communities

A number of studies emphasize that rural police, more so than urban police, tend to know, and be known by, residents of the smaller communities and isolated houses, farms, and ranches they police. This fact, together with the apparent homogeneity of their communities, means that rural police have more of a connection to the policed public. This "connectedness" has traditionally been interpreted to mean that rural police enjoy the seal of community approval to a greater degree than police in urban areas. While this may be true with regard to policing "public" sphere crime and disorder, it should not be assumed to be the case with private sphere violence and particularly woman battering (see Websdale & Johnson, 1997a).

Esselstyn's (1953) study of the social role of the county sheriff in Star County, Illinois, from 1946 to 1950, found that citizens wanted a sheriff who had a reputation for " 'fairness and good judgment.' He should know the county intimately and should be fairly mature. He should know 'how to get along with people' " (p. 179). The sheriff's power stems in part from his ability to give out jobs. In this sense the sheriff, and the political regime he represents, functions rather like the 19th-century system of patronage policing. According to Esselstyn, the allocation of jobs as a result of people performing certain favors is a self-limiting process:

> Obligations incurred during the campaign are discharged by appointments as deputies or jailers, court house jobs, and other types of patronage. Yet curiously, the spoils system is self-limiting. There is a

recognized point beyond which these preferential agreements violate the central values of personal worth and individualism, and thus constitute a threat to party survival. (p. 179)

According to Esselstyn (1953, p. 180), the power of the sheriff also derives from the degree of discretion written into the fabric of his occupational role by both the nature of law and the value prescriptions of local custom. The sheriff's use of discretion will mean that public perceptions of him will range from him being anything from "wise" to "arbitrary" to "corrupt." The latter perception is more likely to emerge because of the way the sheriff selectively polices phenomena such as gambling and prostitution. In more recent research, Potter and Gaines (1992) point out that drug dealers, bootleggers, prostitutes, gamblers, loan sharks, auto thieves, fences, and other "organized criminals" are alive and well in rural regions. Like Esselstyn, Potter and Gaines point to the way in which local politicians, businesspeople, and police officers accommodate and negotiate the presence of these illegalities and the way these illegalities are "functional for" the community.

Decker's (1979) observational study of the Pine County Sheriff's Department in rural Indiana affirmed many of Esselstyn's arguments about the manner in which the sheriff blends in with community sentiments in acting more as a "peace officer" than a "law enforcement officer." Decker comments,

> In communities with greatest consensus on the nature of social control—small, homogenous and stable—there will be even more peace work which conforms to the standards of the community than in areas characterized by cultural diversity, change and conflict. Police in areas characterized by a great degree of social cohesion will be judged more in terms of their responsiveness to the community they serve, than in their role strictly as law enforcers. (p. 101)

The rural-urban difference in policing is not restricted to the United States. Maureen Cain's (1973) influential analysis of the police role in rural and urban England informs us that for the rural police officer "members of the community defined for him what was trivial and what was important, what was real police work and what was not" (p. 32).

In his symbolic role as a bastion against the incursions of the central state, the American sheriff in many ways represents the political and cultural legacy of Jeffersonian self-sufficiency. Though rural citizens may not agree with all of the discretionary decisions taken by the county sheriff, there is usually a much higher degree of consensus about keeping the centralized state out of local affairs. The sheriff's role and responsibilities vary considerably, but, as chief law enforcement officer in the county, the sheriff usually has wide-ranging responsibilities. This diversity means that sheriffs fulfill a large number of administrative tasks in the county as well as serving as often the primary law enforcement body in the unincorporated areas of the county.

Insofar as the sheriff's position remains elected in all but two states, the pivotal political character of the sheriff's role has changed little since Esselstyn's pioneering work. Herein lies the central contradiction of the job. On the one hand, the sheriff, much more so than other law enforcement agencies that police rural communities (e.g., municipal police and the state police), depends upon the voting public for reelection. On the other hand, his (or rarely her) connections with the local community, and in particular, with certain power blocks in the community, stifle his or her objectivity and increase the likelihood of the selective enforcement of law and outright corruption. The synergistic relationship between sheriffs and the community also characterizes the relationship between sheriffs and the personnel they appoint. Since the majority of sheriffs' offices in the United States still rely on discretionary appointments rather than merit-based procedures, the election of a new sheriff often results in a changing of the guard among deputies, jail employees, and so on. This is not the case with either local municipal police or the state police, who tend to be much better insulated from the formal voting process.

The need to maintain a sense of "connectedness" is seen in the requirement that sheriff's deputies reside within the community in which they serve. For Decker (1979), the residency requirement ensures that the integration of police officers into the communities they serve will be more complete (p. 101).[7] Eighty-seven percent of sheriffs require that deputies be residents of the legal jurisdiction that they serve, compared with only 50% of municipal departments that make comparable residency demands of their officers (see Bureau of Justice Statistics, 1990b).

Compared with the state police, who in general are seen as more distanced from the communities they police (see Weisheit, Falcone, & Wells, 1994a, p. 564), the role of local small town police chiefs also turns, to a much lesser degree than in the case of sheriffs, upon their ability to use discretion and massage the community with the law. In their research on 74 Missouri communities of less than 50,000 people, Galliher, Donavan, and Adams (1975) attribute the popularity of small town police chiefs to their social worker/philosopher role and their reluctance to make arrests. These chiefs drew considerable support from local businessmen, fraternal orders, and local government bodies. Likewise, Marenin and Copus (1991) identify the newly emerging Village Public Safety Officer (VPSO) in rural Alaska as more of "social worker kind of job" (p. 16). The "successful" VPSO is able to use his or her discretion to negotiate the manner in which the law is applied to people the officer often knows. As Marenin and Copus report, "Officers are faced with situations in which their relatives are the suspects and offenders, and they often choose to do nothing. 'Clan members can't be expected to police kin effectively' (Interview with local politician)" (p. 16).

Contemporary research, including my own (see Websdale, 1995a, 1995c), concurs with the earlier studies in noting the essential ties between sheriffs and small town police and the communities they serve. This contemporary research traces a line back to Esselstyn (1953), who stressed the role of the sheriff was to maintain "public safety."[8] According to Weisheit et al. (1994a), rural police departments offer an "ideal type example of community policing" (p. 566). In particular, they argue that

> as a result of close social ties between police and community in rural settings and in the absence of organizational buffers in small rural departments, rural police are more accountable and responsive to local citizens than are urban police. . . . Rural sheriffs with whom we spoke were emphatic that, as elected officials, they were compelled to be much more sensitive to citizen concerns than were municipal chiefs. (pp. 563-564)

We must not take this notion of the "connectedness" of rural police to their communities too far, however. There are some forms of disorder that inhabit the private as opposed to the public domain of social life that they may not be able or willing to confront. Among these forms of disorder, the phenomenon of rural woman battering results in substantial social harm (see Websdale, 1995a, 1995c). As I will detail in Chapter 3, with rare exceptions (Bell, 1986, 1989; Brown, 1984; Decker, 1979; Gagne, 1992; Weisheit et al.,

1994c, pp. 4-5; Websdale, 1995a; Websdale & Johnson, 1997a), studies on the policing of domestic violence have traditionally dwelt upon urban contexts and ignored rural areas.

There is very little written about the operation of rural courts and even less about the way rural courts handle woman battering. That which has been written about rural courts emphasizes the "connectedness" of the court to the community. Fahnestock and Geiger (1993) note, "To rural judges, parties are not just docket numbers and fact patterns. They are known individuals, with families and problems, whose actions are viewed in the context of community values" (p. 258). For these authors, the rural judge, attorneys, court administrators, and staff work closely together and strive to make decisions that are in accordance with the values of the community. This puts the rural court at the center of local dispute resolution. Fahnestock and Geiger comment, "Rural courts are frequently at the center of the web of cooperation and accommodation that allows small communities to function" (p. 262).

This awareness of community concerns includes a sensitivity to the needs of local police. Rural prosecutors, for example, tend to be less willing than their urban counterparts to screen out "weak" cases for fear of offending local law enforcement officers (Fahnestock & Geiger, 1993, p. 258). Bartol (1996) observes that although rural courts may suffer from a lack of resources and a general isolation, compared with urban and suburban courts they have potential to be more effective because a "lower volume of cases and closer ties to the community may help rural judges fashion more just and relevant solutions to disputes than can urban judges" (p. 79).[9]

Given that rural judges tend to see "people" rather than "case numbers" in front of them, we might expect that extralegal considerations (factors such as age, race, sex, socioeconomic status) will play a greater role in the disposition of rural cases compared with urban cases. Austin's (1981) analysis of rural and urban courts in Iowa confirms earlier research conducted by Pope (1976) and Hagan (1977) showing indeed that extralegal considerations are more important in the dispositions rendered in rural court cases.

More recent research by Myers and Talarico (1986) finds that urbanization independently impacts sentencing decisions. They comment,

> Whatever the source of these differences, there is consistent evidence that urbanization strongly conditions the relevance of both social

> background and offense factors . . . urbanization tends to further disadvantage offenders who are members of less powerful groups in society. (p. 384)

At the same time, these authors also argue that once rural-urban differences in crime, inequality, and bureaucratization are controlled for, "rural judges do not appear more particularistic than their urban counterparts. If anything, urban rather than rural judges draw sharper distinctions based on the social background factors of sex, race, and age" (p. 385).

The research of Myers and Talarico (1986) conflicts with the popular view of rural judicial decision making and earlier research (Austin, 1981; Hagan, 1977; Pope, 1976) that showed that rural judges are more likely than urban judges to use extralegal factors in disposing of cases. However, all of this research ignores the disposition of rural domestics. If we accept that rural judges are closer to their communities (whether they use extralegal criteria as the basis of their courtroom decisions or not), we are still left, as we are in the case of rural policing, with a vacuum when it comes to examining how this "judicial connectedness" impacts the court handling of woman battering. As in the case of rural policing, we must not assume that connectedness translates into a more sensitive handling of domestic cases than we might see in more impersonal urban centers.

Conclusion

In this chapter I defined my use of the term *rural* and distinguished between rural and urban communities. Although I used the demographic cutoff of 5,000 population, my understanding is that rural and urban communities exist on a continuum, the polarities of which also depend upon sociocultural and economic characteristics. For the purposes of this book, rural communities are not only small in size and population, they are also more culturally homogeneous, and their economy is characterized by a relatively simple division of labor. Having argued for the efficacy and conceptual worth of describing communities as "rural," I stress that rural communities are not all the same. I illustrated the regional diversity of rural communities with examples of rural regional differences in Kentucky.

We should not assume that because rural communities tend to be more homogeneous than urban centers, and that because of the higher level of moral regulation effected by a rural collective conscience, that rural communities are not conflictual. The ethnographic materials presented in Chapter 1 and the studies of rural women mentioned in this chapter both demonstrate how rural patriarchy is highly conflictual.

My working definition of rural communities accepts in large part the greater homogeneity of those communities in the "public sphere" of social life. This homogeneity is borne out by crime statistics that demonstrate that rural areas, in spite of their higher levels of poverty, tend to be less criminogenic. Public sphere violent crime is much lower in rural regions. Most explanations of this low violent crime rate rely upon the greater regulating effects of the more intense rural collective conscience. While feminist criminology has yet to extend to the rural domain and deconstruct the implicit assumption that all violent crime is lower in rural communities, I drew attention to research showing that private sphere woman battering is likely as high in rural as it is in urban areas.

Finally, I explored the nature of rural policing and judicial agencies. Both are portrayed in the research literature as being more sensitive to the needs of the citizenry than are urban police and courts. While concurring that this may be true in regard to the enforcement of public sphere offenses where crimes and disputes are settled more with respect to community standards, I noted that the policing and judicial response to rural woman battering has barely received any attention and should not be assumed to be more sensitive to the needs of battered women.

Notes

1. Using the Census Bureau's definition of *rural*, Kentucky ranks 8th out of the 50 states and the District of Columbia, with 48.2% of its population being rural. Of those states with a higher percentage of rural dwellers than Kentucky (Vermont, West Virginia, Maine, Mississippi, South Dakota, North Carolina, and New Hampshire), only North Carolina has a higher rural population. I am grateful to Mike Ratcliffe, Geographic Area Branch, Bureau of Census, January 25, 1994 for providing me with these data.

2. See Appendix 2, "Regional Map of Kentucky."

3. It would serve us well to collect more empirical data on the social condition of rural women in order to provide a better context for understanding rural woman abuse.

4. See my analysis of "Predator Laws" (Websdale, 1996), which shows these draconian laws also heightening awareness about the threat posed to women by strangers.

5. These data also show similar differences between rural and urban violent crime rates (see Bachman, 1992).

6. Bankston and Allen (1980) point out that there are significant variations in the homicide rate, depending upon the nature of rural communities and residences.

7. Cain (1973) notes a similar phenomenon in England, where rural police officers are much more likely to live quite near or in the police station from which they work. The same is not true in urban centers.

8. For an analysis of rural sheriffs in Oregon, see Gibbons (1972). Gibbons concludes that rural sheriffs continue to police public order issues rather than pursue violent offenders.

9. Bartol also notes research showing that minorities and the poor, particularly poor women, do not fare well in rural courts (see Rural Justice Center, 1991, 1993; Sitomer, 1985). In the next chapter I will discuss how some of this research addresses the plight of battered women.

3

Woman Battering
and Criminal Justice

Introduction

We saw in Chapter 2 how rural areas are generally seen as being much
less susceptible to the blight of violent crime. Nevertheless, I pointed
out that the research literature on violent crime in rural areas pays
very little attention to the phenomenon of rural woman abuse, and
more specifically, to the physical and sexual victimization of women
at the hands of men they cohabit with. In this chapter, I show how the
extensive research literature on domestic violence in general has
ignored, or devoted little time to, the interpersonal victimization of
rural women. At the same time, the extensive studies conducted on
the criminal justice response to domestic violence have also failed to
address rural regions.

This chapter comes in two parts. In the first part I introduce the
phenomenon of woman abuse by exploring its historical and political
construction as a social problem. Remaining cognizant of the fact that
historians are reluctant to give a transhistorical definition of "domestic
violence" or "family violence," I explore the political struggle over
terminology and particularly the implications of using the term *domestic*

violence in preference to *woman abuse* or *woman battering*. Having laid out my own position in this debate, I outline the nature of woman battering and how the term will be used in this book. I then examine the research on the criminal justice response to domestic violence, focusing especially on law enforcement and judicial responses.

Woman Battering

The Historical and Political Construction of Domestic Violence

Elizabeth Pleck (1987) identifies the unique laws passed against domestic violence in the Puritan colonies in Massachusetts in 1641 as the first wave of reform against woman battering. The motives of the Puritan reformers in passing these laws were mixed. While Pleck acknowledges the humanitarianism and altruism of the reformers, she also points out that these laws were passed to address a form of "wicked behavior" that threatened the fabric of their divinely or-dained settlement (p. 5). Although the laws against excessive beating of wives and children remained on the books in Puritan colonies, they were rarely invoked against abusers. For example, Pleck's analysis of the beating of Elizabeth Ela by her husband in Haverhill in 1681, informs us that the authorities in Puritan colonies were reluctant to interfere on behalf of abused wives. In regard to violence within families, Pleck comments, "there were severe limits to the extent of Puritan communal vigilance" (p. 31). Likewise in other periods of history, Pleck points to the intersection of a number of social forces that lay behind campaigns against family violence. For instance, she notes the campaigns against family violence in the 1870s in the United States were also directed at controlling the ranks of working-class and migrant families (p. 5). In the early 1960s, campaigns against the "newly discovered" phenomenon of child abuse were led by pediatricians and radiologists who were interested not only in the plight of injured children, but also in extending the reach of medicine into the arena of social problems (Pleck, 1987, pp. 164-181).

Other authors have noted the enduring presence of domestic violence. Ann Taves's (1989) analysis of the life of Abigail Abbot Bailey reveals considerable levels of woman abuse in Bailey's family during the last quarter of the 18th century in New England. This abuse involved wife battering and the sexual abuse of the Baileys' 16-year-old daughter by the husband and father, Asa Bailey. Deborah Fink (1992) documents male violence against rural farm women in Nebraska between 1880 and 1940. She highlights the way in which physical isolation rendered farm women vulnerable to the rage of their husbands. Fink tells the story of a Boone County man whose father had beaten his mother. The man explained that

> women couldn't leave the farms because they had no transportation of their own. . . . Even if she had transportation, a woman would not ask anyone for help, because the prevailing attitude held that she had made her bed and must lie in it. People didn't talk much about marital problems, because such things were private. (p. 79)

Linda Gordon (1988), in concert with the above mentioned historical works, argues that family violence is a historical and political construct. Using information drawn from the case files of three different child protection agencies in Boston, she identifies wife battering, child abuse, child neglect, and sexual abuse as the main forms of family violence that have assumed the stature of social problems at different times in history. In the United States, the image of the battered wife became a prominent feature of the temperance discourse from the 1830s. By the 1870s, wife battering was widely frowned upon and illegal in most states. However, as Gordon (1988) observes, woman battering became much more of a social problem when the feminist movement was strong. During some periods "experts" addressed wife battering and sexual assault, while at other times they focused on child neglect, which they constructed as a female crime (p. 4). For example, Gordon highlights the ways in which during the Progressive Era wife battering was concealed as a form of family violence.

Like Pleck, Gordon points out that family violence was typically associated with impoverished immigrant families, and as such, this association fed into the hegemonic depiction of these families as pathological or out of step with mainstream white Protestant American mores. Most women in her study were poor immigrants. Their poverty and immigrant status seemed to be the key factors that determined their inclusion among the ranks of the socially "problematic." These distinguishing characteristics seemed more important than their ethnic identities, although Gordon does acknowledge the significance of ethnic variation and its relation to family violence. At the same time, Gordon cautions that she had no way of knowing the proportion of middle- and upper-class families that engaged in family violence. Given that many poor immigrant families did not engage in domestic violence, Gordon warns that it is dangerous to conclude that poverty, unemployment, and immigrant status were the causal roots of this violence.

While the poor, the unemployed, and various immigrant groups swelled the ranks of those who engaged in "officially recognized" family violence, the social workers who labeled families as being in need of state intervention were largely white, native born Protestants. However, the targeting of family violence was not an expression of a simple monolithic social control impulse. It is important to note that Gordon emphasizes the role that victims of domestic violence played in shaping the involvement of various agencies. This acknowledgment that battered women sought the protection of social workers and tried to influence social policy formulation, recognizes the active resistance of battered women to family violence and warns us about neatly separating social control responses from the agendas of those targeted for regulation.

The Struggle Over Terminology

The work of both Gordon (1988) and Pleck (1987) reminds us that the phenomenon of family violence is seen differently at different moments in history. At times child abuse is a prominent part of the family violence discourse, at other times wife abuse is of paramount importance. The framing of one or more aspects of family violence as a social problem depends upon the power of various groups to have their perceptions and definitions written into the public agenda. Researchers have emphasized different aspects of family violence and explained those phenomena in different ways. The debate over how to explain and contextualize family violence lies beyond the scope of this book. However, some of the emergent foci and competing explanations are noteworthy and helpful in our search for theoretical tools to explain the phenomenon of rural woman battering.

Some researchers focus on a constellation of abusive relationships within the family, including violence between siblings, parental violence toward young children and teenagers, the physical abuse and

neglect of the elderly, courtship violence, and violence between intimate partners (see, e.g., Gelles & Straus, 1988; Straus & Gelles,
1995). This research focus, known as the "family violence" perspective, argues that factors such as unemployment, poverty, cultural
norms that sanction violence, and familial structures lay at the root of
intrafamilial violence (see Gelles, 1974, 1979, 1985; Gelles & Straus,
1988; Steinmetz, 1977, 1977-1978; Straus, 1973, 1976, 1979, 1980a,
1980b, 1980c; Straus, Gelles, & Steinmetz, 1980). For these researchers the focus is firmly on family violence rather than male
violence within families. It should be noted that these researchers
argue that wives commit a significant amount of violence toward
husbands. Using survey instruments known as the Conflict Tactics
Scales (CTS) to conduct structured face-to-face or telephone interviews, Straus et al. (1980) found that in those couples where only one
partner reportedly committed acts of violence toward the other, the
proportion of wives and husbands committing violence was comparable. Among these couples, 12.8% of husbands and 11.7% of wives
committed acts of violence toward their spouses. Findings such as
these led Steinmetz (1977-1978) to posit the existence of battered
husband syndrome, which she deemed worthy of research attention.[1]

Later research by Straus and Gelles confirmed their 1975 survey
findings that, "in marked contrast to the behavior of women outside
the family, women are about as violent within the family as men"
(cited in Kelly, 1990, p. 122). They back up this controversial finding
with reference to two national surveys and 10 other supporting studies
that supposedly reveal that there is "little doubt about the high
frequency of wife-to-husband violence" (cited in Kelly, 1990, p. 123).
The authors then qualify this apparent symmetry in interspousal
violence by stating that the consequences of the violence are usually
more dire for women and that women often use violence out of
retaliation and self-defense (Gelles & Straus, 1988, p. 90).

Straus and Gelles (1990) found a 27% decrease in the rate of wife
beating between 1975 and 1985. According to these authors, this is a
highly significant decrease and translates roughly into 432,000 fewer
wives being beaten by husbands than if the 1975 rate continued to
operate in 1985. There was no real change in rates of wives' overall
violence or acts of severe violence against husbands over the same
period. In discussing the reasons for the possible decline in wife
beating over the 1975-1985 period, the authors point to the emergence of more equalitarian forms of marriage, economic changes that

placed less stress on "intact families," more alternatives for battered women, the availability of treatment programs for abusive men, and increased deterrence produced by changing public attitudes and increased law enforcement responses to domestic violence.

The apparent "sex symmetry" in interspousal homicides has led some authors to propose that spousal killing is a similar process for male and female perpetrators (see McNelly & Mann, 1990; McNelly & Robinson-Simpson, 1987; Steinmetz, 1977-1978; Straus & Gelles, 1990). Their argument stems from U.S. interspousal homicide data showing that for every 100 men who kill their wives, roughly 75 women kill their husbands.[2] However, there are two major problems with such a proposition. First, the pattern of sex symmetry is seen only in the United States and not in other countries and is therefore of questionable worth in terms of making generalizations (see Dobash, Dobash, Wilson, & Daly, 1992, p. 81). Second, and most important, the raw numbers tell us nothing about the motives behind the killing and the history of abuse prior to the incident. Dobash and Dobash (1992) observe there is a marked difference in the nature of male and female perpetrated domestic homicides. They comment,

> When the woman dies, it is usually the final and most extreme form of violence at the hands of her male partner. When the man dies, it is rarely the final act in a relationship in which she has repeatedly beaten him. (p. 6)

Feminist perspectives on violence within families challenge the accuracy of the family violence school argument that husbands and wives engage in similar amounts of violence. As Kurz (1993, p. 258) points out, the CTS, which provided the methodological underpinning of family violence research, fails to ask who initiated the violence, whether the violence was committed in self-defense, or who was injured by the violence. Other researchers argue that the scale is too broad to distinguish among very different kinds of violence.[3] When such distinctions are made, researchers find that it is men who control women through violence (see Breines & Gordon, 1983; Dobash & Dobash, 1979; Russell, 1990) and women who bear the brunt of serious injuries (Kurz, 1987; McLeer & Anwar, 1989; Stark, Flitcraft, & Frazier, 1979).

Feminist researchers are more apt to use the term *woman battering* because it better conveys the gendered asymmetry of violence between adult partners in intimate relationships. The position of feminists is supported by a number of studies that draw upon records from a variety of sources including the police, courts, physicians, hospitals, shelters, and National Crime Surveys (see, e.g., Byles, 1978; Chester & Streather, 1972; Dobash & Dobash, 1977/1978, 1979; Gaquin, 1977/1978; Levinger, 1966; Lystad, 1975; Martin, 1976; McLeer & Anwar, 1989; O'Brien, 1971; Stark et al., 1979; Vanfossen, 1979; Warshaw, 1989). According to Dawson and Langan (1994), women are much more likely to be the victims of intimate violence than men. On average, from 1987 to 1991, females experienced over 10 times as many incidents of violence by an intimate as did males. As an annual average over these years, women experienced more than 572,000 violent victimizations committed by an intimate, compared to approximately 49,000 incidents committed against men (Dawson & Langan, 1994, p. 2). The heavy overrepresentation of men among the ranks of perpetrators of family violence is consistent with their general overrepresentation among the ranks of violent offenders (see Dobash et al., 1992, p. 72).

Terms like *domestic violence* strongly imply that there is a gendered symmetry to interpersonal violence in families. Such notions of symmetry, be they express or implied, fly in the face of the studies referenced above. Kathleen Ferraro (1989a) notes the way in which legislative intervention against interpersonal violence against women has been accompanied by a shift in the language used to describe that violence (p. 157). Legislative language employs terms like *domestic violence, family violence,* or *spouse abuse,* which fail to disclose the fact that it is largely men who abuse women. The language of the law therefore poses as an objective and neutral code that ends up obscuring the systemic use of violence by men against women. This violence, for many feminists, is much more than just a crime problem. Unlike the family violence school, feminists theorize woman battering and abuse within the structure of patriarchy. I concur with Kathleen Ferraro (1993) who observes that, "It is vital that battering not be viewed only as a crime but also as a manifestation of structured gender inequality" (p. 175).

The framing of woman battering within the context of patriarchal relations in general is supported by the work of Michael Smith (1990). Smith found that "women who report their husbands' espousing a patriarchal ideology within the family, are more likely than those who do not report such expression, to recount being assaulted by those husbands" (p. 268).

My focus in this book is on intrafamilial male violence and emotional abuse directed at women. It is my belief that this form of abuse is the most significant form of adult interpersonal abuse in rural families in Kentucky. I do not focus on child abuse or abuse within homosexual families. This is not because these other forms of abuse are not important. Phenomena such as child abuse by mothers[4] and lesbian battering[5] remind us that abusive behavior is also engaged in by women. Nevertheless, it is my argument that interpersonal violence must be framed against wider social forces such as patriarchal relations.

The Nature of Woman Battering

I categorized my ethnographic findings on the victimization of rural women in terms of physical, sexual, and emotional abuse. This classification is largely consistent with that of Tong (1984), who distinguishes among four forms of woman battering. Physical battering includes assaultive behavior such as punching, kicking, choking, and burning. Sexual battering includes forced sexual intercourse with violence or the threat of violence. Psychological battering refers to consistent attacks on the self-esteem of women that often include intimidation and threats of violence. It is the unidirectional flow of this emotional abuse and the duration of the abuse that distinguishes it from occasional acts of emotional abuse engaged in by partners in most cohabiting relationships. Tong argues that consistent psychological battering can throw the recipient into a state of confusion because societal messages continually imply that the marital bond should produce the most intimate and caring relationship of one's life. Finally, Tong identifies what she calls the destruction of property and pets as another distinct form of battering in which the abuser destroys personal items and animals dear to the victim, and serves menacing notice that the victim may be next.[6]

Much has been written about the dynamics of the battering relationship. Lenore Walker (1984) describes battered women as being more likely than nonbattered women to believe in traditional sex role stereotypes. These beliefs in part account for their reluctance to leave violent men. To leave would mean that perhaps her children would be deprived of a father. In addition, battered women may have less confidence in their ability to make it on their own. The abuser is more likely than nonabusive men to have grown up in a home where he has experienced or witnessed abuse as a child. These experiences condition the abuser to believe that his violence is not problematic and that the victim is largely responsible for precipitating the violent episodes. The abuser may or may not convince the victim that she is partially or wholly responsible. According to Walker (1984), battered women suffer from a condition known as *battered woman syndrome* whereby they assume the persona of victim. They suffer from learned helplessness, a trait that makes them increasingly submissive and despondent. While the battered woman tries to evade abuse, the abuse continues. Her belief in the inevitability of abuse is strengthened by the fact that government agencies do little to help and support her, or even recognize the nature of her problem and the considerable personal resources she is drawing upon just to stay alive. Associated with the learned helplessness is depression, low self-esteem, and dependency.

Battered woman syndrome can be used as part of a self-defense strategy in the United States for battered women who have killed their abusive partners.[7] The use of battered woman syndrome to defend battered women charged with murdering their abusers is a thorny one for academics and advocates. For example, in the case of *People v. Humphrey* (56 Cal Rptr. 2d 142, 1996) the California Supreme Court expanded the scope of expert testimony on the syndrome. The defendant, Evelyn Humphrey, shot and killed Albert Hampton, her long-time abuser, after a period of abuse. The inferior courts in California found her guilty of manslaughter and sentenced her to 8 years in prison. As expert witness for the defense, criminologist Lee Bowker (1997) testified that Evelyn suffered from battered woman syndrome and that her case was "about as extreme a pattern as you could find" (p. 22). Bowker's testimony that Evelyn suffered from an extreme form of the syndrome was deemed by the California Supreme Court to be relevant to both the question of the "reasonableness" of the defendant's perception that she needed to use lethal violence, as well as to her "subjective belief" of the need to kill in self-defense. The state supreme court concluded that the inferior courts erred in not allowing the jury to weigh evidence of the syndrome in making up its mind about "reasonableness."

Used in this way, the use of battered woman syndrome secured Evelyn Humphrey's release. For some advocates, activists, and academics, however, the syndrome comes dangerously close to depicting some battered women as psychologically flawed. In the Humphrey case, Bowker emphasized the way in which battered women become very finely attuned to the escalation of violence by their abusers. This fact probably helped the supreme court to decide that such perceptiveness on the part of battered women is clearly relevant to the issue of "reasonableness." However, to the extent that the possession of battered woman syndrome depicts battered women as passive, nonresisting human agents, advocates and researchers alike argue that the syndrome stereotypes battered women as being unable to make choices. Such inability invites the accusation that these women lack resistive qualities and therefore partially acquiesce in their own victimization. If she is passive, then her passivity is the reason she does not leave,[8] rather than the dearth of social supports that battered women will often seize upon and use if they know of their existence and can readily access them.[9]

Dobash and Dobash (1992) challenge the psychiatric/counseling discourse on battering and identify it as part of the wider tendency in American culture to psychologize what are in reality social problems. Concepts such as battered woman syndrome and learned helplessness fail to acknowledge both the human agency of battered women and the constraints of patriarchal structures upon those human choices. Rather, the psychological discourse overemphasizes the passivity and dependency of battered women at the expense of acknowledging the acute obstacles they have to overcome and the tremendous resistance and coping skills they display. As Angela Browne (1987) puts it, battered woman syndrome "contributes in a subtle way to an image of maladjustment or pathology. Just the use of the term 'syndrome' connotes impairment to most people, including judges and jurors" (p. 177).

My ethnographic findings concur with the thoughts of Browne (1987), Dobash and Dobash (1992), and Jones (1994). In Chapter 1, I clearly highlighted the agency and resistance of battered women in rural areas. However, my interviews also revealed the acute sensitivity to escalating violence that Bowker testified to in his contribution to the defense of Evelyn Humphrey. The interpersonal violence experienced by battered women in rural Kentucky is, in my opinion, consistent with what Bowker (1997) refers to as "dominance enhancing behavior" (p. 18). Using a similar approach, Jalna Hanmer (1996) argues that male violence in general is "designed to control, dominate and express authority and power" (p. 8).

Rural Woman Battering

In Chapter 2, I noted how violence against women was one of the galvanizing forces at the recent World Conference on Women (Maran,

1996). While the already comprehensive literature on woman abuse continues to expand, it fails to address adequately the phenomenon of rural woman battering. As I noted in Chapter 2, the extant research literature shows rural areas are far less likely to witness violent crime than urban areas. The explanation given for lower levels of rural violent crime is that rural communities are smaller in size and population, more culturally homogenous, and have a stronger "collective moral conscience" that limits violent behavior. However, the often-used logic that urbanization and industrialization generate more violent crime does not appear to hold true for woman battering. I have mentioned the research of Ronet Bachman (1994), who finds that women in central cities, suburban counties, and rural areas are all equally likely to report being the victims of intimate violence (p. 7).[10] My research findings are consistent with those of Bachman (1994) and suggest the extent and forms of woman battering in rural families differ little from those in urban areas. Therefore I contend that rural woman battering does not follow traditional criminological axioms concerning the social generation of violence.

While the research literature has marginalized or ignored rural woman abuse, it has also failed to address the response of rural criminal justice agencies to woman abuse. It is in this direction that my analysis now turns.

The Criminal Justice Response to Woman Battering

In Chapter 2, I presented a number of research studies that show the "connectedness" between rural criminal justice agencies and the communities in which they attempt to enforce the law. In this section of Chapter 3, I explore the police and judicial responses to woman battering and highlight the failure of the extant research to address adequately women's perceptions of these responses.

Policing

There is widespread agreement about the historical failure of the police and the courts to confront domestic violence (see, e.g., Buzawa & Buzawa, 1990; Hanmer, Radford, & Stanko, 1989; Sherman, 1992; Tong, 1984).[11] My own research into the policing and judicial response to interspousal violence in Lane County, Oregon, between 1853 and 1960, shows the police almost never arrested spouse abusers and the judiciary almost never sentenced them to jail time (see Websdale, 1992).

Before 1984, police rarely made arrests at the scene of domestic disputes. This changed with the passage of pro-arrest and mandatory arrest laws. Pro-arrest laws require that police should make arrests under certain conditions. Pro-arrest laws expand the discretion of officers when deciding whether to arrest. For example, in Montana, arrest is the preferred response to domestic violence cases when there is an injury, the use or threatened use of a weapon, and the violation of a restraining order [Montana Code 46-6-311(2)]. Kentucky has a pro-arrest policy that recommends that police may arrest where the officer has probable cause to believe the suspect has intentionally or wantonly caused physical injury and presents a danger or a threat of danger to others if not arrested (Kentucky Revised Statute 403.715). Mandatory arrest laws force police to arrest under certain circumstances. The conditions under which mandatory arrests are made vary by state. For example, under Arizona Revised Statute 13-3601, police must arrest if they have probable cause to believe that an abuser has inflicted physical injury, or used or threatened to use a deadly weapon, unless police have reasonable grounds for believing that the victim is safe. Likewise, the increased availability of protective orders, which legally restrained violent partners from future abuse, furnished women with more options to confront the violent behavior of their partners (see Dobash & Dobash, 1992, pp. 168-169). Both the introduction of mandatory arrest laws and the increased availability of protective orders are part of a wider social movement to confront violence against women. However, as Sherman (1992) points out, these developments are also part of a broader criminal justice and political initiative supporting punishment over rehabilitation, victim's rights, and "law and order" campaigns (pp. 104-109).

The recent debate about the policing of domestic violence has been an important aspect of the much broader criminological discourse concerning deterrence in general. Roughly $4 million was spent by the National Institute of Justice (NIJ) investigating the deterrent effects of the mandatory arrest of domestic offenders (see Lerman, 1992, p. 218, note 6). In the first of these experiments, in Minneapolis, mandatory arrest of violent spouses was shown to be a more effective police response than either separating the parties or referring the parties to counseling. Compared with the other strategies, mandatory arrest was significantly correlated with a reduction in the revictimization of women (Sherman & Berk, 1984a). Subsequent experiments in the cities of Milwaukee, Colorado Springs, Miami, Charlotte, and Omaha failed to replicate the Minneapolis findings convincingly. Sherman (1992), in summarizing the outcomes of the experiments, cautioned that mandatory arrest may in fact exacerbate the abusive behavior of batterers who have less of a stake in "conformity." Among these groups Sherman lists unemployed men, unmarried men, and African American men.[12]

Objecting to the argument that mandatory arrest does not work, Stark (1994, p. 32) argues that none of the studies on mandatory arrest combined arrest with aggressive prosecution and incarceration. Abusers receive short jail terms, if any at all. Stark argues that in those jurisdictions that have combined arrest with prosecution and imprisonment (e.g., Lincoln, Nebraska; Quincy, Massachusetts; and San Diego, California), violence has been reduced. Stark argues that if mandatory arrest is combined with more consistent prosecution, conviction, incarceration, or treatment, or a combination of these, then such arrest strategies do reduce recidivism (see Stark, 1993a, p. 662). Dutton (1987) reports a Canadian experiment in which the arrest of batterers was combined with prosecution and treatment. He notes that batterers who received arrest, prosecution, and treatment were 10 times less likely to reoffend than if they received arrest alone.

Garner, Fagan, and Maxwell's (1995) and Fagan's (1996) analysis of the NIJ arrest experiments concludes that we still do not know whether arrest reduces recidivism. Not only were the results from the NIJ experiments mixed, but so many variables were used, so few prosecutions undertaken, and the experiments were limited to misdemeanor arrests only. In referring to arrest and prosecution experiments in Indiana, Fagan (1996) finds that "severe violence" is reduced if the threat of arrest or prosecution is present. He calls this presence "The Sword of Damocles" effect.

Feminist criminologists continue to cite evidence of the low level of police intervention and arrest of batterers (Stanko, 1989, p. 49). Stanko (1989) notes that an arrest made in a domestic altercation does not carry the same degree of prestige as other arrests (p. 51). Other feminist research draws attention to the fact that police have failed to arrest batterers even when the victims are in serious danger and where the victims request an arrest (Ferraro, 1989b, p. 61). For many feminist criminologists, the ongoing failure of police to intervene effectively to protect battered women is part of a wider pattern of disadvantages faced by women in a patriarchal society. Ann Jones (1994) makes the point that the presence of mandatory arrest laws does not mean that police officers will make arrests when the law allows them to. Rather, many officers will continue to use their discretion and "abet the batterer and deprive his victim of her safety, her freedom and her constitutional rights " (p. 142). Jones's comments are even more important when we contextualize them against the fact that only about one seventh of batterers come to the attention of police (Dutton, 1995, p. 241). This last observation is a stark reminder that police often see the tip of the woman battering iceberg.

The NIJ experiments on the effectiveness of mandatory arrest in deterring batterers from future violence have provided us with immense amounts of information about the policing of domestic violence. However, the work published from these studies has largely ignored the opinions of battered women. For example, Sherman (1992) reports on women's perceptions of policing and specifically whether the police spoke to the victim and suspect, whether the victim saw the police handcuff the suspect, if the victim felt safe after the police left, and if the suspect got out of jail within a few hours (p. 331, table A2.12; in regard to the Charlotte experiment see Hirschel & Hutchison, 1992, pp. 109-112). We also learn of women's views on whether the perpetrator subsequently left the scene, whether the argument continued, whether there were new arguments that day, whether the suspect or victim engaged in further violence, and if the victim bailed out the suspect (Sherman, 1992, p. 336, table A2.13). However, women's responses are basically simple yes/no replies to researchers' questions. At no point do women express how they feel about police performance or their victimization in general.[13]

A number of feminists criticized the NIJ experiments for their failure to consult battered women for their thoughts and feelings about police performance at domestics. The empiricist framework of the NIJ studies prioritizes quantitative data such as police calls and arrests. This hierarchy of credibility effectively decontextualizes women's victimization from the broader field of gender power relations (see Bowman, 1992, pp. 201-203; Zorza, 1992). According to Berk, Campbell, Klap, and Western (1992), in their Bayesian analysis of outcomes at all the NIJ sites, "the "cleanest" story is told from the treatment assigned (arrest, separation, counseling) and the official data. . . . Nevertheless there may be some interest in seeing how well our findings hold up in the weaker ('less clean') data" (p. 195). The implication here is that the opinions of battered women on police performance at domestics are somehow less than clean.

Feminism has raised the marginalization of women's voices in social science and history as a major political issue. Feminist researchers have encouraged us to theorize the personal experiences of women as political. Feminist studies of the policing of domestic violence have been much more willing to access women's experiences and perceptions of policing. For example, Ferraro's (1989a) study of the implementation of a presumptive arrest policy in Phoenix, Arizona, included 17 interviews with women who called the police. Interviewers asked women about their reactions to and their evaluations of police interventions (pp. 176-178 and p. 183, n. 5).

Part of Jill Radford's (1987) research in the London borough of Wandsworth involved interviewing 314 women about the policing of male violence. Radford reports that women interviewed were "very unimpressed by the response of the police" (p. 38). In particular, she comments,

> few women reported incidents to the police. Their main complaints were that the police were not interested, were slow to respond, did not follow up the initial report or tell them what had happened, or that they expressed attitudes that were racist and/or hostile to women. (p. 37)

A number of feminists see police failure to intervene and protect women in domestics as one way in which the patriarchal state has reproduced the domination of men (see Edwards, 1989; Hanmer, 1978; Hanmer & Saunders, 1984; Hanmer et al., 1989; Walby, 1990). Stanko (1989) notes,

> Police action cannot by itself stem the tide of violence against women. . . . Police protection within the context of male domination does not and cannot promise women autonomy. . . . More arrests of violent men—the only solution to battering available to the criminal justice system—will hopefully assist more women in acute danger. (pp. 67-68)

With some exceptions (Bell, 1986, 1989; Brown, 1984; Decker, 1979; Gagne, 1992; Websdale, 1995a; Websdale & Johnson, 1997a; Weisheit et al., 1994b, pp. 4-5), studies on the policing of woman battering have traditionally dwelt upon urban contexts and ignored rural areas. Indeed, both the NIJ experiments and the feminist studies of policing woman battering have focused almost exclusively on urban settings. There are at least three major concerns associated with the failure to examine the policing of rural woman battering. First, the voices of rural battered women remain subterranean, and a valuable source of feedback on police practice is lost. Second, we miss the opportunity to explore some of the idiosyncrasies of policing communities that are more likely to be socioculturally and physically isolated. Third, we run the risk of formulating rural law enforcement policies and procedures for intervening in domestics on the basis of information gathered primarily in urban settings.

Some of the earlier classic studies of crime in small towns do not mention domestic violence as either a minor or a serious form of disorder warranting police attention (see Dinitz, 1973; Esselstyn, 1953; Gibbons, 1972). Esselstyn (1953) makes passing reference to a number of offenses that the Star County, Illinois, sheriff's department would largely ignore. Although not expressly stated, these offenses would probably have included domestic violence. Domestic violence would probably have been included among those offenses that police could know little about or where a report "won't do any good," or may "threaten community harmony" (p. 182). Esselstyn reports there are some offenses where it is "regarded as unwise to resort to formal legal sanctions" (p. 182).

Decker's (1979) analysis of the rural county sheriff in Pine County, central Indiana, includes a brief discussion of the policing of domestics. Usually the sheriff does not send someone to investigate, and even if he does there is rarely an arrest made. Domestic affairs are reported as being "one of the most difficult and distasteful" tasks for the officers (p. 107). In his observational study, Decker reports that the sheriff's first instinct in a domestic case is to define it as a problem for another agency.

> Unless a law has clearly been violated he (the sheriff) is hesitant to investigate. To a large degree there is no advantage to be gained by sending a deputy to check on the situation. . . . Few wives press charges and pursue legal action against their spouses. (p. 108)

In an attempt to learn more about domestic violence, Schulman (1979) conducted a telephone survey of 1,793 Kentucky women who were married or living with a male partner. Notwithstanding the problems associated with learning intimate details of people's lives over the phone, Schulman's study reports a number of important findings about the differences among women's perceptions of the policing of domestics in urban, suburban, and small town/rural settings. Rural women were more likely than urban and suburban women to report multiple violent victimizations to police (Schulman, 1979, p. 39, table 12). They were also more likely to report the police took longer to attend the scene of the domestic dispute. In 25% of all the violent incidents reported to the police, the police took longer than an hour to attend, and in 22% of those reported incidents police did not respond at all (p. 40, table 13). Sixty-nine percent of women living in suburban areas reported that the police arrived at the scene of their domestic disputes within 5 minutes, compared to only 6% in rural areas and 4% in urban areas. Consistent with the findings on response time, Schulman observes that suburban women report much higher levels of satisfaction with the way police treated them than either urban or rural women. Fifty-four percent of urban women compared with 22% of rural women and 6% of suburban women reported being "very dissatisfied" with police treatment.[14]

Stephen Brown's (1984) survey of 41 police officers and 84 battered women used closed-ended test items to explore police responses to domestic violence in a small southern city with a population of 25,000. He found that officers rarely made arrests of batterers or referrals to social service agencies. Brown points out that battered women are severely hampered by an "entrepreneurial" system of law (p. 286). Under this system, victims of crime must themselves activate the law on their own behalf. The most common response of officers was to attempt to mediate the dispute by talking with the batterer. Although Brown's research was conducted in a small southern city, we learn nothing of the influence of small city life on police practices and little about women's subjective experiences of policing.

Daniel Bell's (1984a, 1984b, 1985, 1986, 1989) studies of a large number of domestic cases in Ohio include urban, suburban, and rural police jurisdictions. At all jurisdictional levels, police were unlikely to make an arrest at domestic disturbances. However, when they did make an arrest at a domestic, Ohio police were more likely to do so in urban areas. As with Brown's study, we learn some useful details about police responses. However, as with Brown, we learn little of the social influences on rural police response or women's perceptions of police performance at domestics.

Patricia Gagne's (1992) ethnographic work examines the lives of four women in a small, rural, central Appalachian community. In so doing, Gagne frames the abuse experienced by these women in terms of the broader social control of women by men and the failure of rural police to protect them. She comments,

> the social control of women is achieved in a variety of ways, of which violence is only one. In terms of men's behavior, the social control of women begins with the objectification and devaluation of women. For women, it begins innocuously with their deference to men. In the current research, deference resulted in residence in an area where employment opportunities and police protection for women were lacking. (p. 412)

Gagne's ethnography is an important piece of work because it links the rural sociocultural milieu, and specifically its stereotypically gendered fabric, to both the control of women and police passivity to domestic disturbances. Gagne (1992), in recognizing the idiosyncrasies of rural regions in exerting different forces on women's lives, points out that because "the women of Raven Ridge lived in a geographically isolated, economically depressed area . . . the means of social control used by men may not be generalizable to more urban or economically prosperous areas" (p. 413).

My own ethnographic research identifies those specific characteristics of rural regions that impact the policing of domestics (Websdale, 1995a). After interviewing 25 battered women in rural Eastern Kentucky and a number of police officers, social workers, judges, attorneys, and spouse abuse shelter workers, I found support for three basic propositions about the policing of woman battering.

The first is that the physical isolation of the rural milieu provides opportunities for batterers to engage in particular forms of abusive behavior. Similar control strategies would be either more visible or less effective in urban areas. This isolation also makes it difficult for battered women to leave or otherwise resist violent men. Rural households in Kentucky have significantly lower telephone subscription rates, and this may mean that some rural battered women could not call the police even if they wanted to. The physical isolation of some rural residences makes it more difficult for police to arrive quickly at the scene of a domestic dispute and may be one reason battered women in Schulman's study reported much longer response times for rural police.

The second is that rural family life, gender roles, and patriarchal ideology generate acute forms of sociocultural isolation that render rural women particularly vulnerable to battering and passive policing. Of particular importance here I document the patriarchal attitudes of rural police officers and the way in which these attitudes mitigate against a timely and effective response to domestic calls.

The third is that rural battered women experience acute difficulties in utilizing the limited but potentially supportive services of the state. These acute difficulties and limited state provisions tend to reproduce, in a complex and often contradictory fashion, the power relations of rural patriarchy. The greater homogeneity and cohesiveness of rural areas makes it generally more likely that battered women who do use state services will know the personnel providing those services.

The elected nature of sheriffs and the close ties between small town police departments in rural Kentucky and men in the community has produced what some respondents have called an "ol' boys network." Sheriffs in particular are reluctant to move against men who supported their election. At another level, the abject poverty faced by some rural communities, especially in Eastern Kentucky, has produced a subterranean economy that deals in illegal drugs, bootlegging, stolen property, gambling, and prostitution. In addition to my own research, a number of studies have highlighted the complicity of local police in these illegal (but often socially approved of) activities (Davis & Potter, 1991; Potter & Gaines, 1992). This complicity, I argue, makes it more difficult for local police to enforce the law against abusers who are involved in the subterranean economy, or at least know of its existence and police acquiescence in it.

Courts

Courts in the United States were reluctant to intervene in family disputes and often gave husbands free rein to punish their wives for their "wayward" behavior. Under English common law, the laws of chastisement gave husbands a legal right to beat their wives. This law was confirmed into American law in the case of *Bradley v. Mississippi*, 2 Miss. 156, 158, (1 Walker 1824), which allowed husbands to beat their wives with a rod or stick, provided the instrument was less than the diameter of the base of a man's thumb. From the 1860s, in the United States, some jurisdictions began to overturn or at least restrict men's legal ability to beat wives. In the case of *North Carolina v. Black* (60 N.C. 162, 163, 86 Am. Dec., 436, 1864), the court held that husbands could not inflict excessive or permanent injury on their wives and expect to remain immune from prosecution for assault. In 1871, a Massachusetts Court held that "a rod which may be drawn through the wedding ring is not now deemed necessary to teach the wife her duty and subjection to the husband" (*Commonwealth v. McAfee,* 108 Mass. 458, 11 Am. Rep 383, 1871; cited by Tong, 1984, p. 128).

In spite of the reformist nature of the Black and McAfee decisions, however, police and courts rarely confronted severe violence against wives, whether or not it resulted in excessive or permanent injury. Some states passed specific laws outlawing woman battering. For example, during the Progressive Era, the state of Oregon passed "whipping post laws" that allowed for the public flogging of batterers at the whipping post. However, Pleck (1987) could find no instances of Oregon batterers being whipped for their wife-beating behavior (p. 119). My own research in Oregon also uncovered no such examples of the actual enforcement of the whipping post laws (see Websdale, 1992).

In general, the court treatment of batterers is a much neglected area in criminology. The failure of the courts to prosecute is noted in a number of studies (Field & Field, 1973; Okun, 1986; Parnas, 1967; Police Foundation, 1976; Tong, 1984). Domestic assaults are usually misdemeanor offenses or first offense felonies. These types of cases are generally taken less seriously by the courts. As Stanko (1982) has pointed out, there is also a bias against prosecuting offenders "known" to victims. Langan and Innes (1986), using National Crime Survey data, note that one third of misdemeanor domestic violence cases would have been defined as rape, robbery, or aggravated assault, all felonies, if the perpetrator had been a stranger.[15]

Judges can issue temporary or permanent protection orders, sentence the batterer to a short jail term for misdemeanor assault, or, more rarely, a longer jail term for contempt of court, if he contravenes the terms of the protection order (see Finn, 1989).[16] Perpetrators may be sent to counseling groups as an alternative to serving jail time, although the rehabilitative effects of these groups seem limited (see Harrell, 1991; Tifft, 1993). There are a number of well-documented problems with protective orders in domestic cases (see Buzawa &

Buzawa, 1990, pp. 54-65). Abusers often do not understand the intent behind the order or the consequences of breaking the order. On other occasions, abusers sense it will be easy to evade the order and suffer no consequences. Sometimes, abusers reject the order and see it as an inappropriate intrusion on the part of the state into their "private" family affairs. This may especially be the case in rural communities where the family is more likely to be seen as a privatized unit beyond the legitimate reach of government.

These criminal justice "solutions" are directed at the "pathological" offender. He is either separated temporarily from the victim through court orders or incarceration, or attempts are made to modify his behavior (counseling) in order to reduce the likelihood of revictimization. Such solutions typify criminal justice solutions insofar as they are profoundly astructural. They provide quick temporary "fixes" for the problem of crime, the locus of which resides in the criminal tendencies of individuals rather than criminogenic social structural conditions. As Fagan (1996) argues, domestic violence is not the kind of social problem that is very amenable to criminal justice intervention.

Sherman (1992) reports tremendous variation in the way in which the courts dispose of domestic violence cases. In the Milwaukee experiment, the prosecutor decided to press no charges. Only 37 initial charges were filed out of the 802 arrests made in the Milwaukee experiment. Sherman found the lack of court-imposed punishment to be surprising given that a large number of battered women appeared willing to prosecute after an arrest had been made. As Sherman notes, it is a widespread misconception that victims of domestic violence do not cooperate with prosecution.[17] Out of the 802 arrests in Milwaukee, only one batterer was punished in a way that included incarceration (see Sherman, 1992, pp. 336-337). This lack of prosecution in Milwaukee stemmed from the fact the prosecutor's office was swamped with domestic cases. Sherman concludes that prosecutors could not handle the volume of new cases arising out of the new mandatory arrest practices. This was the same in Minneapolis, where there was also virtually no prosecution. Sherman and Berk (1984b, p. 7) report that only 3 out of 136 arrests in Minneapolis resulted in court sanctions. These findings for Milwaukee and Minneapolis stand in stark contrast to the other federally funded research in Omaha and Charlotte. Dunford, Huizinga, and Elliot (1990) note a court ordered sanction rate of 64% in Omaha (p. 193). These sanctions included jail, probation, and fines. Hirschel, Hutchinson, Dean, Kelley, and

Pesackis (1990) reported a 17% conviction rate in the Charlotte experiment (p. 148). However, in the Charlotte experiment, of those men convicted and sentenced, less than 1% served any jail time.

As my ethnography will show, rural battered women's use of the court is not only an attempt to secure actual protection. It can also be an act of symbolic resistance and a powerful negotiating tool in a strife-ridden relationship. It is hard to understand the intent of battered women in the court system without asking them about their motives. By asking battered women why they chose to prosecute and why they chose to drop charges, David Ford (1991) shows that battered women can use the threat of prosecution as a means of empowering themselves in their struggle against their abuser. The myth that battered women will not follow through with prosecution of their abusers assumes new meaning when viewed through the lens of Ford's research. Rather than seeing battered women who do not follow through with prosecution as irrational, Ford argues the dropping of charges by battered women is one more way those women can assert some control in their conflictual relationships. Ford (1991) observes, "In making a significant threat to prosecute by initiating steps to invoke the process, a battered woman is able to exercise power that was previously missing in her relationship" (p. 331).

Likewise, Barbara Hart (1993) highlights the complex relationship between battered women and the courts. Unlike victims of stranger-violence, battered women face the threat of retaliatory violence during the predispositional phase of their cases. Hart also points to the refusal on the part of some court personnel to see battered women as true victims. She notes, "battered women frequently report that criminal justice system personnel appear to consider them 'unworthy victims' who are clogging up the courts with unimportant family matters" (p. 626).

As I will demonstrate in Chapter 5, the behavior of judges in domestic cases can make a world of difference to victims. For example, Barbara Smith (1980) found that victims voiced greater satisfaction with the court system if judges appeared knowledgeable about domestic violence, made appropriate referrals to community support agencies, and suitably admonished batterers about the seriousness of their actions.

However, in addition to exploring the complex relationship between battered women and the courts, we must not lose sight of the fact that when compared to assaults by strangers, domestic assaults are dealt with more leniently by the courts. We must also not forget that male and female domestic "disputants" do not come to the court as freestanding adversaries in the way the court and the legal system usually define opposing parties. Ann Jones (1994) puts it nicely:

> In any conflict, the law casts the parties as adversaries, but conflict between parties who share a household and perhaps children is never that simple. A battered woman may want her husband arrested to deter him from beating her again, but if feeding the children depends upon his wages, she may not want him jailed or even prosecuted. In that case, the prosecutor is likely to say that she's wasting the court's time; and the judge may admonish her instead of her assaultive husband. . . . Is this man, who is at once her husband and her assailant, her adversary or not? The battered woman may have to answer yes and no—an answer which disqualifies her complaint. (pp. 24-25)

Laudable as all of this research on the courts and domestic violence is, nearly all of it has been conducted in urban areas. As I noted in Chapter 2, the limited research literature on rural courts emphasizes the "connectedness" of the court to the community (Fahnestock & Geiger, 1993). One way of reading this research is that rural courts might be more sensitive to the needs of victimized women who are members of the community. However, as Fahnestock (1992) indicates, this connectedness does not necessarily work for battered women. Due to limited opening of the rural courtrooms and court offices, the use of part-time prosecutors, and the lack of education of court employees including judges on the dynamics of domestic violence, many rural battered women are not well served. In addition, because battered women know court employees in rural regions they also report being ashamed to go to the court and open their marital difficulties to public scrutiny. My own research, like that of Fahnestock (1992), questions the assumption that because rural courts are more "in tune" with community needs, they will act to protect battered women more effectively than urban courts. My research pays close attention to the relationship between rural judges and the community and the way in which informal contacts between judges and batterers influence judicial decision making.

Conclusion

I have now discussed woman battering and how it is understood in the historical and social scientific research literature. In particular,

I emphasized that rural woman battering has attracted little research attention. I also highlighted the need for more research on rural law enforcement and judicial responses to woman battering. Much of the research on the policing/judicial handling of woman battering has not taken adequate account of the experiences/opinions of battered women themselves. The next two chapters move toward addressing the neglect of the rural policing (Chapter 4) and court handling (Chapter 5) of woman battering. Although using a variety of sources of information, these two chapters deliberately prioritize the experiences and opinions of rural battered women themselves.

Notes

1. For a discussion of the failure of battered husband syndrome to assume the status of a social problem see Lucal (1995).

2. The actual number of spousal killings from 1976 to 1985 are estimated at 18,417. Of these, 10,529 were wives and 7,888 were husbands. See Maxfield (1989, p. 677) and Mercy and Saltzman (1989). For a broader discussion of the issue of spousal killing see Wilson and Daly (1992). A recent report shows that for U.S. spousal murders, women represented 41% of killers (Dawson & Langan, 1994, p. 1).

3. For a thorough discussion of the theoretical and empirical limitations of the CTS, see Dobash et al. (1992), and Dobash and Dobash (1992, chap. 8).

4. According to the family violence school researchers, mothers are slightly more likely to use violence against children than fathers and to use more severe and abusive forms of violence (Straus, Gelles, & Steinmetz, 1980, p. 65). There are a number of reasons for this including the fact that mothers typically spend much more time with children. See Linda Gordon's account of Mrs. Kashy's abuse of her daughter and Gordon's description of Mrs. Kashy's attitude as "patriarchal" (in Gordon, 1990, p. 182). However, it is important to remember that child sexual abuse is typically perpetrated by males (see Russell, 1981).

5. For a discussion of the theoretical implications of lesbian battering see Mary Eaton (1994). See also Claire Renzetti's (1992) analysis of abuse in lesbian relationships in *Violent Betrayal*. Liz Kelly (1996b) cautions,

> Acknowledging that some lesbians use violence does not undermine the fact that the power they hold within a relationship is not, and cannot, be the same as that held by men in heterosexual relationships. It is an interpersonal use of "power over," not backed up by social systems outside the relationship (p. 39).

According to Kelly, there is no empirical basis at the moment for concluding that violence is as prevalent in lesbian relationships as it is in heterosexual relationships (p. 44).

6. There are many ways of classifying abuse. Lee Bowker (1997) regards battering as "dominance enhancing behavior" taking at least one of five forms: psychological/verbal/cultural; physical; sexual; economic deprivation; or social isolation.

7. For a recent discussion of the introduction of battered woman syndrome into the English legal system see Chan (1994). For a recent analysis of the contribution of social psychologists to the use of battered woman syndrome in U.S. courts in cases where battered women have killed their abusers, see Schuller (1994). Excellent coverage of specific case law on the use of battered woman syndrome in the courts can be found in the publication *Domestic Violence Report.* See *Domestic Violence Report,* December/ January 1997 (p. 22) for a discussion of the expansion of the admissibility of expert testimony on battered woman syndrome in self-defense claims in California.

8. For a good discussion of the issue of "Why doesn't she leave?" see Ann Jones (1994, chap. 7).

9. Battered women will, for example, follow through with criminal charges against abusers, and actively and vigorously take charge of their own lives, if they are provided with adequate supports. This includes their choosing to end the battering relationship rather than engaging in activities such as family counseling (see Fleming, 1979).

10. See also Bachman and Saltzman (1995).

11. In this section I retain the term *domestic violence* to maintain a sense of continuity with the extant research literature.

12. For further discussion see Hirschel and Hutchinson (1992), and Berk, Campbell, Klap, and Western (1992). For a detailed and perceptive critique of the NIJ experiments, see Garner, Fagan, and Maxwell (1995) and Fagan (1996).

13. My comments here are directed at the absence of women's perceptions of policing and criminal justice in published books and articles. I recognize that the researchers who conducted the Charlotte experiment, for example, asked extensive background questions of women. However, women's responses did not filter through into the published article on this study. In fairness to Hirschel and Hutchison (1992), their long form final report contains more information from women.

14. For a discussion of the sampling errors in this research see Schulman (1979, pp. 62-64).

15. There are a number of other factors that come into play to work against the prosecution of woman batterers (see Buzawa & Buzawa, 1990, pp. 54-65).

16. In Kentucky, victims attend domestic violence court to obtain an Emergency Protective Order (EPO; a temporary 14-day protective order prohibiting the alleged abuser from having contact with her, living at their family residence, etc.) or a full Domestic Violence Order (DVO; valid for 3 years). These orders are designed to protect women from abuse. In other states, protection orders are known by a different name. For example, in Hawaii they are called "restraining" orders, and in Florida "injunctions."

17. Ann Jones (1994, p. 143) highlights a 1977 study in California showing that with the help of Victim Assistance programs, only 10% of battered women in Los Angeles and 8% in Santa Barbara refused to cooperate with prosecutors. For further details see "Immediate Arrest in Domestic Violence Situations: Mandate or Alternative," 14 *Capitol University Law Review* 243 (1985), cited by Jones (1994, p. 261, n. 36).

4

Policing Rural Woman Battering

The Compromised Enforcement of Law

Introduction

One of the principal characteristics of rural patriarchy is the combined geographical and sociocultural isolation of women. I have already discussed the relationship between the structure of rural patriarchy and women's victimization. In this chapter, I explore some of the ways in which rural woman battering is policed. It is not my suggestion that the policing of rural battering neatly reproduces rural patriarchy. Rather, the policing of rural woman battering is complex, contradictory, and multifaceted. Different agencies respond to violence against women in different ways, producing a mosaic of social control initiatives that tensely coexist alongside other responses of the patriarchal state. Specifically, I will address the patriarchal attitudes of some rural police and the relationship between rural police and batterers. I also scrutinize some of the intricacies of patronage politics and policing; the impact on policing of low rural tax bases; the allocation of police services in remote rural regions where physical conditions may make it more difficult for police to respond to domestics and where lower telephone subscription rates sometimes mean that rural women cannot call for police support. The fact that abusers are often known to rural police officers (for a variety of reasons) sometimes compromises police responses at rural domestics.[1] This "rural compromise" in policing occurs in a number of ways. I discuss the way in which some sheriff's departments are in the habit of telephoning "known abusers" to tell them to collect court orders limiting that abuser's access to his partner. A small number of abusers are also police informants and this, my ethnographic evidence suggests, sometimes compromises the police when it comes to enforcing domestic violence laws against those men. It is less likely that police will enforce domestic violence laws against their informants, especially if informants are providing information on drug manufacture, sale, and distribution. The police themselves are sometimes corruptly involved in illegal activities, especially drug running. If their involvement is known to abusers, it may also limit the ability of corrupt officers to enforce domestic violence laws against abusers. However, as the evidence will demonstrate, the greatest component of the rural compromise is the fact that local rural police (sheriffs and small town departments) often know the abuser socially, often share his worldview, social connections, and even have relatives in common. I refer to this rural matrix of connections among men as the "ol' boys network." This phrase is used commonly in Kentucky in a number of settings but I've never heard it used more frequently than by the women who provide direct service to women who have been battered. The ol' boys network sometimes militates against the enforcement of domestic violence laws and the extension of unconditional police support to rural battered women.

It is not my argument that all rural police agencies and their officers deal with domestics in the same way. The policing of rural domestic violence is not a monolithic phenomenon. Of the 50 women I interviewed, only 40 had had dealings with the police over their battering. Of those 40, 10 (25%) were pleased with how the police handled the situation. Twenty-six (65%) were dissatisfied with the police handling of their cases, listing a range of reasons, many of which I will highlight. The remaining 4 women reported that they were neither pleased nor displeased and are best described as having an indifferent opinion about police response. These statistics convey a general sense that roughly two thirds of battered women I interviewed identified a variety of problems with the response of rural police to their domestic plight. This level of dissatisfaction points to the existence of a serious social problem. It is the task of this ethnography to explore the character of that problem.

The Components of Compromised Policing

Patriarchal Attitudes

By *patriarchal attitudes* I refer to that cluster of collective values, beliefs, and ideas that deem rural women to be subordinate to rural men. It is not my argument that these patriarchal beliefs are absent in urban communities. Rather, I speculate that the forms these beliefs take may be more extreme and less tempered with an exposure to issues of women's rights. Patriarchal attitudes are best seen as a continuum of ideological sentiments that prescribe the social locus of women, often tying them closely to their biology as reproductive receptacles and nurturers. At times, and with a majority of abusers, these attitudes are tinged with misogynism. Among a significant number of local rural police officers this constellation of patriarchal attitudes includes certain ways of understanding the social circumstances of rural battered women in astructural ways. In particular, we find some officers blaming women for their own plight and failing to understand the immense amount of courage, resistance, and artistry exhibited by those so brutally victimized in their own homes. I include among these attitudes a failure to treat domestics seriously, especially when there may be a threat of lethal violence.

These patriarchal attitudes must be understood against the wider societal position of women in general and also against the history and sociocultural milieu of rural life in Kentucky. We find examples of "old Eastern Kentucky standards" in Harry Caudill's (1963) classic *Night Comes to the Cumberlands.* At one point Caudill notes,

> But it was in the faces and hearts of the women that the land's tragedy, folly and failure were most deeply etched. In their world the man was a tyrant who ruled his house with medieval unconcern for his wife's feelings or opinions. She rarely sat down to eat a meal with him, it being her duty to "wait on" him. When a stranger was present she stayed discreetly out of sight. . . . Her girlhood was spent in graceless toil and crowned by an early marriage. (p. 80)

For sheriffs and small town police to enforce the letter and spirit of Kentucky's relatively new Domestic Violence and Abuse Act (1984, amended 1992) in many cases requires them to confront local patriarchal norms.[2] In a variety of situations and for a variety of reasons, confronting these norms and enforcing the new laws against the weight of rural patriarchal custom proves problematic for many officers.

Rural patriarchal attitudes among local police sometimes mean they are less willing to intervene in domestics and less inclined to arrest husbands, who they feel should be in a dominant position in the family. Ronnie, an officer with the Lovelace municipal police, put it as follows:

> *Ronnie:* I feel that at times we are sticking our nose where it doesn't belong.

Ronnie also felt it was time to balance the scales of justice when it came to domestic violence. With all the recent press coverage of domestic violence and the plight of rural battered women in Kentucky, Ronnie was concerned that batterers' perspectives were not being recognized.

> *Ronnie:* And we need to catch both sides of the story. Not just one. It seems like the female is always the one believed. And a lot of times that's wrong. Female pulled a gun on the male, the male goes to jail. Wait a minute. That's not justice.

This quote is interesting because at no point does Ronnie consider why the female would pull a gun on her abuser. Neither does he note that most of the offensive violence comes from men.

Patriarchal explanations are often pitched in terms of biology. We find this in the words of municipal officer Sawyer. These sentiments are common among local police in rural communities.

> *Websdale:* Why do you think there are so many men doing this to women? As opposed to the other way around?
>
> *Sawyer:* There've been a few situations where I guess women, just very few, have actually assaulted men. I think that just has to do 'cause of their size.

Even if size is the reason why women are less likely to use violence against their male intimates, then surely this provides the reason why women sometimes pull guns on men. Again, this logic did not enter into either Ronnie or Sawyer's discussion of the one-way nature of male violence.

Battered women report that a significant number of rural police fail to take woman battering seriously. Sally lives in the small town of Sale in Eastern Kentucky, which I visited on a number of occasions. Just as the pain of years of battering is inscribed on the bodies and souls of many women in this town, so too the physical landscape bears the deep scars of bygone days of coal mining. In this sense, the cut-and-run coal mining capitalist and the cut-and-stay patriarch have a lot in common. During my time in this ravaged little community, you could slice the tension of class and gender struggles with a razor. According to Sally and several other women I talked with, local police failed miserably to take woman battering seriously. In discussing her own abusive relationship, Sally castigated local police.

> *Websdale:* So the police took him down to the station and let him go?
>
> *Sally:* He beat me home you know. We lived about 11 miles out of town (Saleville).
>
> *Websdale:* How did you feel about that?
>
> *Sally:* Awful. . . . Well in Saleville it's very poor, I can tell you that right now. It's bad today. My daughter has been abused, she's been slapped and her husband got a gun out right in the city limits and shot it. City police came. Didn't do a thing. . . . You might as well not call 'em. It's like the sheriff told me. He said, "I can take 'em upstairs and book 'em and they can beat me back down."

We see this failure to take woman battering seriously in the case of Patricia Taylor, who, as I noted in Chapter 1, was brutally murdered in the small community of Pine Knot in McCreary County by her partner James Naegele. In the Taylor case, her neighbor suspected Taylor was being beaten and called the local sheriff's department. The neighbor has a mild speech impediment and the sheriff's department told her that if she made any more prank phone calls they would come and arrest her. Sheriff McArthur Swain's office told reporters that officers had responded to domestic calls at the Taylor-Naegele residence before, but that Patricia Taylor had not wanted to press charges. It is difficult to discern the reason for the failure of the sheriff's department to respond to the neighbor's call for help on Taylor's behalf. Given the history of domestic disturbances at the residence, it is highly likely that the failure to attend was just one more example of rural police failing to take woman battering seriously.[3]

Mary Hamilton was murdered by Ronnie Hamblin, the husband of Hamilton's granddaughter. According to Melissa Hamblin, Mary's granddaughter, the murder could have been averted if the Whitley county sheriff, H. D. Moses, had taken the domestic turmoil seriously. Earlier that week Melissa tried unsuccessfully to have her husband arrested, claiming he had beaten her and fired a gun at her. Melissa commented: "I talked directly to him and he did not want to come out and get him. . . . That's his job, to protect and serve. That's what he's getting paid for" (*Louisville Courier-Journal,* March 28, 1994).

While battered women reported fewer problems with the state police taking woman battering seriously, there have been a number of accusations that the state police have not enforced the law as they should have. In Chapter 1, I also introduced the murder of karate instructor Ella Hunter by her husband Phillip Hunter, which occurred on January 31, 1993. At the time of the murder, she had in her bag a copy of the protective order that had been issued limiting her husband's access to her. Relatives and co-workers claimed that Phillip Hunter had violated the terms of the protective order on a number of occasions and that the state police knew of these violations but did not arrest him. Captain Robert Forsythe of the Pikeville State Police admitted he had responded to a call about the couple on October 7, 1992. At the time of his response, the protective order had been entered into the statewide crime computer. However, he neglected to check whether the court order was in place before responding to the call. Between the time the order was issued (October 2, 1992) and the time it was finally entered into the crime computer (3:19 pm on October 7, 1992), the state police received six calls concerning the Hunters. Under Kentucky law, police are required to arrest abusers who break the terms of protective orders. After Ella Hunter's slaying, the state police in Pikeville instituted a new policy requiring officers to check whether protection orders are in place if they are responding to domestic disturbances.

June, who lived in a remote region of rural Eastern Kentucky, was wrestling with a number of problems in her life when we talked. She was organically impaired by her alcoholism. We got along well and I met her a number of times at the shelter. On one particularly poignant occasion she shared her feelings about the way local police treated her with contempt.

> *June:* They always acted like smart alecks. Laughed at me all the time.
> *Websdale:* Did that hurt your feelings?
> *June:* Very much. Very much.

I have acknowledged the decline of capitalist coal mining alongside the enduring structure of rural patriarchy. However, we must not exclude from our consideration the role of race. For some of the small number of African American women who live in rural communities in Kentucky, the policing of their intimate victimization also bears the hallmark of racist as well as sexist policing strategies. It is clear from my conversations with these women that rural black women are doubly isolated. Not only do they experience the typical geographical and sociocultural isolation endemic to rural communities, they also are marginalized as members of a small minority. Of the five black women I interviewed in rural Kentucky, two were adamant that race was a significant reason why their domestic plight was not taken seriously by police. Brenda attests to the role of race in her failure to receive police protection in one of the few small western Kentucky towns with a relatively high African American population. Her words resonate with the research evidence (see Chambliss, 1994; Chesney-Lind, 1997; Prejean, 1993; Stark, 1993b) and case law (e.g., *McKleskey v. Kemp,* 481 U.S. 279, 1986) that attest to the racist nature of the criminal justice system. In the following excerpt, Brenda lives these issues.

> *Brenda:* He locked the door behind me. . . . I could not leave the house. He started beating my head against the wall. . . . I whispered to my daughter to go and call the police. They took forever to come. . . . When the police did come out there, they didn't do anything to him. They didn't arrest him or nothing.

Websdale: They didn't do anything to him?

Brenda: No. I think because he was white and I was black. That's why I feel they didn't do anything to him. . . . They seen me all beat up and . . . they heard me screaming.

We cannot assume that patriarchal structures are the same in Caucasian and African American communities. However, the few interviews I conducted with African American women caution that we must look beyond the machinations of gender bias in order to grasp fully the cultural nuances of the policing of African American domestics.

Regina found herself in a chilling situation with her violent husband. The local (municipal) police department in the small rural town of Everest is located within a few minutes driving time from her residence. The night Regina was severely beaten by her abusive husband, he left the house vowing to "finish her off" when he got home. Afraid for her life, Regina called the Everest police department just after 7:30 p.m. when her husband left. She told them about the beating and her husband's threat.

Regina: They didn't even come to the house to get me until 10. That's two hours. The police officers were a joke.

She called the police station while she was waiting and talked with the dispatcher:

Regina: I didn't know where he was and I didn't know what time he was comin' home. And I didn't want to be there when he got home, especially if he walked in the door and saw I had a bag packed. That would have really ticked him off.

Many cases reveal ways in which some police take the batterer's side, share the batterer's understandings of the situation, or have similar interests in asserting a man's right to control his wife. It is possible that when police fail to take these situations seriously, we are also witnessing misogyny.

A good illustration of what I mean by common interests among men emerged in a conversation with Chuck, a Lovelace patrol officer. He felt that under certain conditions a "good man" might assault a woman.

> *Chuck:* It's a frustrating situation. . . . There's times that . . . I have to . . . arrest a gentleman . . . and actually the woman really deserved it . . . she does stuff that would actually cause a good man to slap a woman.
> *Websdale:* Give me some ideas.
> *Chuck:* Like a woman's cheatin' on her husband. And he catches her at it.

Some police officers at least imply that some battered women deserve to be victimized because they do not properly fulfill their roles as wives and mothers. Ralene, a spouse abuse shelter director in Central Kentucky, talked of how police sometimes judge battered women on the appearance of "their" households.

> *Ralene:* Police officers sometimes comment that, "I went into the house and the house was filthy and the kids were dirty. Last night's dishes were in the sink." Therefore the woman was not a good wife, mother, housekeeper, and deserved every-thing she got. Or she was drunk. He was drunk, that's okay. A woman that drinks is worse than a man that drinks. Women are not supposed to be that way.

Rural police officers vary considerably in their attitudes toward domestic calls. Many feel frustrated because in most cases the victim will not file a criminal complaint against her abuser. Few officers expressed either an awareness or a concern for the social and economic difficulties faced by battered women that, among other things, work against her filing criminal charges. According to some police, if battered women remained with their batterers, it was because they had chosen to. Notions that people are self-sufficient and survive and thrive because of their own choices and energy are important in rural regions. The lingering effects of Jeffersonian self-sufficiency, even in the wake of large-scale agribusiness, still underscore aspects of the rural collective conscience. The rural prescription as applied to women is that they, too, albeit in different ways, can pull themselves up by their own bootstraps. This may include battered women being able to "choose to" extricate themselves from violent relationships.

Sergeant Cross, who works in a small municipal police depart-ment, likened the "illogic" of battered women returning to their abusers to a rational-thinking individual who, after experiencing the pain of putting a finger in a candle flame would then, fully cognizant of the pain, return the finger to the flame. This of course is a plain statement of the "battered women as masochists" explanation.

> *Cross:* It would be like sayin' that I could learn to stick my hand in a candle flame. . . . I'm sure after a while they want it. . . . They say "he's threatenin' to shoot me." I say, "you need to go file for divorce." They go "yeah, but I love him." Horseshit. In two months it's gonna be the same thing again. I'll guarantee it. Get back to the same thing of puttin' your hand in the candle flame.

It is not just local rural police who diminish the significance of domestic calls. As we rode together, state trooper Davis saw many victims of domestic violence as being manipulative and rather undeserving of police support. His outlook betrayed more than a hint of misogyny.

> *Davis:* A lot of them were fabricated . . . that man has taken all that he can take . . . that's the way he lashes out . . . and boom. Call the State Police. I want his ass out of here. And I just don't really see that's right . . . It's bullshit is what it is.
> *Websdale:* As a rough guess, what would you say the percentage of bullshit ones is to legit ones?
> *Davis:* Probably 70-30. . . . All you see on TV and in the newspapers are the legitimate cases. The ones where the wife has been severely beaten and the police haven't responded. They don't tell you about the 99% of the calls that don't amount to shit.

Suzanne, who lived in a small rural town, had clearly been beaten and yet received little support from local police. In the end, police told her to take her child to her mother's and allowed the abuser to remain in the apartment where the assault had occurred. This typified rural cases where the abuser was allowed to stay in the home and was not arrested for assault even when there appeared to have been probable cause to have made an arrest.

> *Suzanne:* I was pregnant with my second child and that was the first time I ever called the police on him. I was about eight months pregnant. He threw a set of keys and hit me in the

eye. Cut my eye. So I went next door and called the police. And I told 'em that I wanted him arrested. He had hurt me. And they talked me out of the arrest. They told me, "well, you don't want to do that. That's your husband."

In Suzanne's case it is noteworthy that she tells us the police dissuaded her from pushing for an arrest because the abuser was her husband.

My interviews with police officers and battered women revealed a range of patriarchal attitudes among local police that translated into various styles of handling domestics. The handling of domestics by the Ipcress Municipal Police Department, located in a small town surrounded by economically depressed and "dry" counties, illustrates well the complexity of police responses.

One cold night in the spring of 1992, after conducting an interview at the spouse abuse shelter served by the Ipcress Department (among other police agencies), I talked with Laurie, the night shift supervisor. Laurie was on edge because an abuser had issued a death threat on Carol, whom I had just interviewed. Carol had been transported to the shelter from the one at which she was originally housed because of her husband's threats to kill her. Laurie and I talked in the main office, me keeping half an eye on the security screen. In general, the Ipcress Department was perceived by the women I interviewed to have a good record on domestics. This meant they attended quickly and enforced the law, while being polite to victims of violence. Chief Stanza of the Ipcress Department was adamant that his department took violence against women seriously. When I interviewed him, he told me as much. At one point he commented:

> *Stanza:* If an officer attends a domestic and there is probable cause to make an arrest and the officer doesn't arrest . . . I want to know why he doesn't.

Laurie basically confirmed that Chief Stanza was supportive of battered women and when he was on duty his officers attended the shelter quickly if there was any problem. However, her impression of Stanza's Lieutenant Rum, who took over when Stanza was on vacation or not on duty, was most unfavorable. Laurie's assessment of Lieutenant Rum was consistent with my own after I had conducted an interview with him.

Rum told me he did not think the perpetrator of domestic violence should do jail time for his first offense.

> *Rum:* Actually if they do it a second time I think they deserve some time in jail. And maybe the first time go with some sort of diversion agreement with if it happens again you have to serve this time.

That night as Laurie and I sat chatting about whether or not Carol's abuser would find the shelter,[4] I asked her if she had called the Ipcress police. She told me she had but that Chief Stanza was on vacation and that Lieutenant Rum was in charge. Laurie said Rum would not take the threat against Carol seriously, adding that Stanza would have. No patrol car (to my knowledge) attended the shelter that night or kept an eye on things in the surrounding area. Given that many people in the area knew where the shelter was, and that Carol genuinely believed her abuser would kill her if he could, the threat seemed dangerous enough to me.

As it turned out, the abuser did not find the shelter. Laurie gave up working at the shelter and Carol moved on. A year later I heard from another source that Chief Stanza had been removed as Police Chief by the mayor and the municipal council. One of my key informants in the area told me that while on the surface Stanza was supportive of the shelter and battered women, he had been taking advantage of his contacts at the shelter. Apparently he had been visiting ex-shelter residents (about half a dozen, according to my source) and propositioning them for sexual favors. It is not clear whether this was the reason Stanza was removed as chief. The situation at the Ipcress Department cautioned me about jumping to conclusions about the public and private posturing of small town chiefs. It also reminded me that patriarchal attitudes can manifest themselves in both overt and covert ways. Small town departments can be really effective in domestic disturbances, but we cannot assume that patriarchal attitudes are not present in the form of a thinly disguised paternalism.

The Ol' Boys Network

The personal biography of many of the rural police that I interviewed was steeped in the traditions of their rural locale or community. If they had not lived there all their lives, these officers had spent many years growing into the community. This degree of enmeshment was one of the reasons they were hired as local police in the first place. This was not the case with state troopers. Although many troopers know the region they patrol, they often do not have the same kind of intimate knowledge of local goings-on. Many interviewees, from judges and police to social workers to battered women themselves, identified an "ol' boys network" of local police officers and some abusers. This network of friendship, commonality of interests, occasional involvement of police and local men in illegal activities, and outright collusion between the police and these men to oppress women, all make it more difficult in rural areas for women to rely upon the protection of local police.

Susan reported that nearly the whole community knew that her husband beat her brutally on a regular basis. However, the local police officer in the small town where they lived in Western Kentucky did not offer her any protection. She told me the local constable was her husband's brother and refused to arrest her husband. Susan also noted it was common knowledge that the constable beat his own wife and that confronting domestic violence was not part of his "calling" as a law enforcement officer.

> *Susan:* Beating your wife is a normal everyday thing. The constable [her husband's brother] didn't come and arrest him.

Doris, a case manager at a shelter in Central Kentucky, told me that the shelter had worked hard with local law enforcement to increase their awareness of woman battering. In the county in which they were located, this seemed to have paid rich dividends. The shelter served eight counties, however, and in the more remote rural counties of their service district, local police seemed very ineffective to her.

> *Doris:* I had a young woman in the other day say that she couldn't get anything done because her husband was a sheriff's nephew. And they never at any time arrested him even though she even gave them information on his drug dealing. They didn't even bother. What could she do? It's the good ol' boy syndrome.

I interviewed Astrid in an urban shelter although she came from a small rural community. The county sheriff was her abuser Joseph's third cousin. In talking with Joseph's previous wife, Astrid learned the sheriff let Joseph get away with all kinds of violence, particularly against women, without doing anything more than fining him.

> *Astrid:* The sheriff is his [third] cousin. His ex-wife said that Joseph seems to get away with a lot. . . . Every time he gets arrested for terroristic threatening or something, they smack his hand and take his money, that's all they do.

State troopers, while generally more detached from the communities they police than local sheriffs and municipal police, can also be a part of the ol' boys network. Janis recalls one incident where state trooper Patterson attended her residence after she had been confined to her house for 3 days by her abusive husband Donovan, during which time Donovan beat Janis and raped her on multiple occasions.

> *Websdale:* How did you feel about Patterson's response?
> *Janis:* I felt like . . . anything that I told him was gonna be repeated back to my abuser. Patterson was good buddies with the brother of my abuser.

Janis also felt great discomfort at Patterson's approach to interviewing her after her 3-day ordeal with Donovan.

> *Janis:* We started talkin' about the rape and sodomy. Especially when it come to the sodomy he got very, like glarin' at me and he's like talkin' to me about things that didn't even concern it. . . . I got the sense that he was comin' on to me in a way. And here I'd been abused for three days and everything else. And I felt like this officer was gettin' turned on by talkin' about what happened to me. He told me I could press charges. He said they would never go nowhere.

Bernice, a young woman with two young children when I met her in the Lovelace shelter, recounted a long history of violent victimization. She finally broke free with the help of shelter employees and social services workers. The local police were of little assistance.

> *Websdale:* Did you ever think about calling the Clinton County Sheriff's Department?

Bernice: It wouldn't have done no good. They wouldn't have done anything.

Websdale: How do you know that?

Bernice: Both of 'em like David. They would do anything in the world for him. Anything to keep him out of trouble.

Cynthia, a rural battered woman, was rather typical of women who did not call the police.

Cynthia: I was too scared to call because the officers knew my husband, I knew they wouldn't do anything.

Bertha described how the connections between her abuser and local police affected police handling of her situation.

Bertha: There were two or three officers that went to school with him and they treated me like dirt.

Websdale: So they knew him socially?

Bertha: Yeah, before they was even policemen. One of them . . . he looked at Kenny and he says, "Kenny, give me one good reason to put that bitch in jail and I will." And he's never liked me. And he's always been softy, softy to Kenny.

"Knowing the man" also results in some local police not serving Emergency Protective Orders (EPOs) on abusers. These orders are issued by judges at ex-parte hearings and prohibit the alleged abuser from coming within a certain distance of the complainant and restrain him from engaging in future acts of violence. This order remains in place for up to 14 days, when the judge conducts a full Domestic Violence Hearing at which time he or she can issue a Domestic Violence Order (DVO), which imposes similar, often more detailed restrictions on the abuser for up to 3 years.[5]

Most of the women I interviewed who had taken out EPOs against their abusers reported that local police served them in a tardy manner, thereby delaying the extension of legal (but not de facto) protection to them. Excerpts from dissatisfied women include the following:

Marjorie: The police officer would not fill out the EPO. He excused himself because he was a friend of my husband. He got another officer to fill out the EPO.

Emma: Police were friends of my husband's. They did not like women. One officer told my husband how to beat the law.

One might think that knowing the man would make it easier for the officer to locate the abuser and serve the EPO. However, time after time women reported that it took many days to serve protective orders because local police could not find the abuser. My findings here are consistent with one report that showed that in fiscal year 1993-1994 in Kentucky, 28% of EPOs were never served.[6]

In rural communities, "knowing the abuser" is not the only interpersonal connection that plays out during the policing of domestics. In a much smaller number of cases, local police knew the victim and were not connected with the abuser. Keanne describes how her relationship with the sheriff got her fast, effective support during her domestic.

Keanne: The sheriff was very fast. When they told him who it was, he was like, there ASAP. See I've known Sheriff Scott since I was this high (Keanne points to her waist). I grew up with his daughter. And my parents and him, you know, we all socialize together.

Patronage Politics and the Rural Compromise

Kentucky sheriffs are elected to 4-year terms. In Kentucky, a newly elected sheriff brings in his or her own deputies, who do not necessarily have to have policing experience. In many of the poorer rural counties where I traveled and interviewed, sheriffs' deputies had other jobs to supplement their income. Deputy Roberts put it as follows:

Websdale: What made you come into law enforcement work?
Roberts: I needed the bread, for one thing. It gets rough on the farm.
Websdale: How did you get hired?
Roberts: I know the sheriff.

Attorney Carr commented that sometimes the nature of the sheriff's response to woman battering depended on the numbers of potential voters the victim or the batterer could influence.

> *Carr:* I think . . . it goes back to the political systems in these small counties. . . . They look at who has the biggest family and they kind of judge it on that. If the man is from out of town, I think she might get more help if she's got a big family in that county.

District Judge Santee, who felt he did a reasonable job of disposing of domestic cases, commented on how the familial ties between sheriffs and abusers meant that sheriffs in some counties would not serve protective orders on abusers they are related to.

> *Judge Santee:* I've had a number of women come into my county from neighboring counties because they are kin to the sheriff and the sheriff won't serve the protective order.

State Supreme Court Justice Stumbo expressed a similar view.

> *Justice Stumbo:* You get an abuser who is a member of a politically powerful family, you're just not going to be able to do anything with him. These are all elected positions [sheriffs, district and circuit court judges] and it's a matter of "What have you done for me lately?" in order to get reelected. You put somebody in jail, why there goes that whole voting block.

Virginia alludes to the way in which a number of women keep quiet about their interpersonal victimization because of the lack of willingness of local sheriffs to investigate.

> *Websdale:* Was the sheriff elected and do you think that has something to do with the fact that domestic violence wasn't policed tightly or at all?
>
> *Virginia:* Yeah I do. There's a lot of domestic violence in that county that the women don't even open their mouth about because they know there's nothing going to be done. They're like me. They can't seem to get away with their children and if they go without them they've lost them and have to fight for them.

The Low Tax Base and Compromised Policing

Because the tax base is often low in rural counties, particularly in Eastern Kentucky, many of the people I interviewed told me there was insufficient money to provide even the rudiments of a local police service. This meant a number of sheriff's departments could not provide the services vital to the well-being of battered women. District Judge Jackson accentuated the difficulty faced by underfunded sheriff's departments:

> *Judge Jackson:* Sheriff Patton in Hayes County knows everyone in that county and even though he may have some opinions about domestic violence that you may not agree with or I may not agree with, he is a good man. He has handled domestic violence the best way he could handle it. And he had no one to help him. He gets one deputy and himself. They don't even have a secretary. They don't have the radio capability to call in state police if they need a backup. It's an extremely dangerous situation.

On the surface, the lack of funds for policing appears to be a plausible reason as to why battered women might not receive adequate service from rural sheriffs. For example, if sheriffs did not have the funds to send their deputies to training school to equip them better to handle domestic calls, we might expect battered women to report an inferior response from untrained officers. Deputy Roberts, who worked a remote region of Eastern Kentucky, had received little training at all. He expressed a desire to receive more training in order to handle domestics better.

> *Websdale:* Do you feel like it would be better if you were trained?
> *Roberts:* Yeah, I would say so. There's a lot of things that I wouldn't know what to do.
> *Websdale:* And the reason you're not trained is the county doesn't have the money to train you?
> *Roberts:* Yeah.

It is unreasonable to expect police officers, especially if they are officers to supplement their income, to be up-to-date on all the latest developments in their many lines of law enforcement work without providing them with adequate training. It is clear from my interviews and my riding with rural police that there is much more they could do at domestics. Not one officer I talked with mentioned taking photographs at domestic scenes. When I rode with officers they did not carry cameras to photograph injuries or video recorders to record what happened at domestic scenes. Officer accounts of domestic disturbances did not appear to be the kind of detailed accounts that a prosecutor might desire in order to prosecute effectively on criminal charges. For example, the officers I talked and rode with did not appear to solicit statements from a range of either witnesses or victims, including children. They did not seem alive to the virtues of recording the body language and demeanor of witnesses. Neither did many officers discuss the significance of hidden injuries as a way of eluding their probable cause requirement for arrest. An awareness of the significance of doing things like taking photographs is a trainable skill. Unless the officer is taught to connect the taking of photographs with the potential prosecution of abusers (perhaps without the help of the victim), we should not expect photographs to be taken. These are issues of which urban departments and their officers, with much more access to training, still do not take adequate heed.

However, better training of local police is at best only part of the answer to improving law enforcement response to domestics. It is clear that the better funded sheriff's departments tend to respond more professionally to domestic calls. Those that have a written policy, lower response times, better communications, and liaison networks with other agencies, especially the state police, tend to intervene more effectively and appear more likely to arrest in a manner consistent with the spirit and letter of the law. However, I found tremendous variation in the response of so-called poorer sheriff's departments.

In Bush County, for example, there is a university and a regional hospital. The unemployment rate is relatively low for the region. The Bush County sheriff's department is relatively well funded. Nevertheless, the spouse abuse shelter that takes women from Bush County never contacts the sheriff because he often refuses to get involved in domestic cases. My personal experience partially confirmed this view after the Bush County sheriff stood me up on three separate occasions for an interview. Neighboring Mondale County has a very low tax base. Since the decline of the coal industry, unemployment levels are very high there. The main town in this geographically large county bears many of the visual scars of economic depression. Mondale

County's Sheriff Hem had little law enforcement experience and worked as a teacher and a social worker before being elected as sheriff. His predecessor is serving time in federal prison for drug running. However, a number of battered women and several spouse abuse shelter employees could not speak highly enough of Hem's performance at domestics.

My point here is obvious. The response of local sheriff's departments to domestics is in part a product of the resources they have to work with. But performance at domestics transcends resources and goes well beyond training. Sheriff Hem prioritized domestic calls in a manner that the Bush County sheriff, whose staff had far better resources and training in domestic violence, would not do. Put differently, an adequate tax base and the training of rural police in the field of domestic violence is not a necessary or sufficient prerequisite to ensuring a sincere, sensitive, and professional response that is supportive of battered women.

Remote Rural Locations: Delayed Protection

Police in rural areas face unique difficulties of covering vast distances in short periods of time to arrive at emergency situations. With domestic calls, this may mean the difference between finding a dead victim or a situation that has cooled down.[7]

Again we find tremendous variation in response by agency. In areas where the sheriff is more withdrawn and less committed to policing domestics (e.g., Bush County), the state police are much more likely to play an active role in the policing of domestics. However, the allocation of state police units in Kentucky is far from even. In some Eastern Kentucky counties, for example, one patrol unit can work three large counties in one shift. State trooper Davis talked of the difficulties associated with responding to domestic calls in rural regions.

> *Davis:* You're on one end of Bush County and there's no road like
> this [wide, well surfaced] . . . and you're called to the opposite
> end of Clinton County. A domestic in progress. As hard as
> you can run, lights and siren, you're looking at best at 40
> minutes. That's hard runnin', that's 100 plus most of the way.[8]

Blanche lived in the small town of Chains in Mondale County. Over the course of 7 violent years she called the municipal police to her house 25 to 30 times to deal with domestic violence. She reports one of the most common complaints of battered women in rural areas, namely that police took a long time to arrive. Her residence was 20 to 25 minutes from the police department in Chains, but it usually took police a lot longer to arrive.

> *Blanche:* They take their good ol's time getting there.
> *Websdale:* Like how long? Give me some sense.
> *Blanche:* Like for instance this time it took them a good hour and a half to two hours to get to me. He could have killed me. . . . For instance, the time he broke my ribs the cops was already called but they hadn't arrived yet.

Judge Ball from Hoover County, a coal mining county in Eastern Kentucky, told me,

> *Judge Ball:* the mountainous terrain makes it very difficult in some cases for local police to attend domestics quickly.

Although the situation has changed significantly over the past 10 years, Judge Ball points out that many local police see women choosing to remain in battering relationships. This perspective on the part of local police, coupled with their long response times, sometimes causes problems in the policing of domestics. Judge Ball, as if citing the extant research findings, told me that rates of domestic violence are "extremely high in Hoover County compared with the very low levels of other forms of violence."

No Phone

Police learn most of their information about crime and disorder from the public. Without this feedback it is unlikely the police are going to stumble upon domestic disorder in the regular course of patrol work. One of the most common ways of getting the attention of police emergency services is to use the telephone. Rural women are at a distinct disadvantage here. First, as noted, telephone subscription rates are significantly lower in rural communities. Second, some abusers disable phones or take phone receivers with them when they leave the house. Given the often limited availability of other forms of communication in rural areas, the compromised access to telephones disconnects women from yet another potential source of contact, solace, support, intervention, and perhaps in some instances, survival.

The use of technological aids such as telephones to help battered women is an increasingly promising development in some urban centers. For example, officers I have ridden with at the Metro-Dade Domestic Violence Unit have told me of their cellular phone program in which battered women have access to cellular phones that only dial the nearest police department. These phones are donated to battered women for use if they feel threatened. Other urban developments serve to inform police of immediate threats to battered women. For example, the use of a variety of technological aids, from silent hostage alarms to miniature VCRs that survey the exterior of women's houses, tip off the police that women are in acute and immediate danger. While these innovations might work well and bring police quickly to the scene of a potentially lethal incident in urban areas, they will not serve to reduce the response time of rural officers who, with all the knowledge in the world of the immediate threat of lethal violence, cannot negotiate rural terrain easily.

Rural Police Serving EPOs by Telephone

EPOs are served on abusers by local police. These documents stipulate that the alleged abuser must not come within a certain distance of the woman he is alleged to have victimized and that he is restrained from committing further acts of violence. There is a pro-found irony at the heart of the serving of these EPOs. On the one hand, local sheriffs are often proud that they know their constitutients, their constitutients' whereabouts, their contacts, and their lifestyles. This local knowledge is part of the intimacy of rural policing and rural social life in general. However, when we come to scrutinize the serving of EPOs more closely, we find these local connections can suddenly evaporate and these men are not as readily accessible as they once were.

Some sheriffs in Kentucky have found it expedient to telephone abusers and ask them to come to the sheriff's department to be served with their EPO. The procedure depends upon sheriffs and their deputies knowing a large number of the men that they police. For some sheriffs, the telephone method of serving papers works well and offenders appreciate the informality and implied trust. Apparently, in only a few cases do abusers abscond after being called. However, the possibility of suspected abusers disappearing after being called by the sheriff seems to be real. This possibility could expose victims to more violence. Doubtless the telephone approach saves the sheriff's time. If the abuser refuses to come to the sheriff's office, the sheriff can then develop a plan of action. If the abuser agrees to come in, however, then the sheriff can be fairly certain the abuser will be cooperative. The attendance of the abuser after a phone request for attendance may hail a certain solidarity between sheriff and abuser as to the rules of the game. A batterer might think that his offense is less serious because the sheriff telephoned him rather than sought him out to serve the summons. With "serious" crimes like burglary, theft, robbery, and drug dealing, the police usually do not telephone suspects and ask them to drop by the office. The failure to serve papers may also signal the sheriff's reluctance to serve papers on friends and acquaintances.

Sherry Currens, Executive Director of the KDVA, recalled one incident of the lax serving of an EPO. She comments: "The sheriff, who knew the man he was supposed to serve with an order, called the man and told him to pick it up. . . . Predictably, the man never picked up the order and the woman was left unprotected" (*Lexington Herald-Leader,* February 5, 1995).

Informants

Police officers use informants in all kinds of settings to provide information that will lead to the apprehension, conviction, or both, of criminals. For the past decade or so the United States has been in the grip of a "war on drugs" that has led to a massive increase in incarceration rates. Some have argued that this war provides the justification for the proliferation of criminal justice "services" and the massive expansion of the prison system (see Chambliss, 1994, 1995; Christie, 1993). The U.S. Supreme Court has gone out of its way to support the war on drugs by effectively eroding Constitutional rights such as the Fourth Amendment, and police seem intent on targeting the relatively powerless when they make arrests for drug possession (see Chambliss, 1994).[9]

This moral panic about the evils of illicit drug manufacture, sale, distribution, and use indirectly impacts the policing of domestic violence. Police in Kentucky, as elsewhere, will cut deals with low-level drug sellers or users in an attempt to catch the bigger growers, dealers, and distributors. They will also use informants to lead them to growers and drug runners in return for various favors, including immunity from prosecution. One key informant, a journalist who writes for a small town Kentucky newspaper, related a story of a low-level drug runner carrying several garbage bags of marijuana in his vehicle when he was stopped by a police officer for a suspected DUI. When the police officer asked the man if he could search his vehicle the man consented and the officer discovered the marijuana. As the case unfolded, the man gave the police the names of the growers in return for immunity from prosecution. The growers were subsequently apprehended and convicted. The identity of the informant was kept as confidential as possible, although the journalist told me that the informant's home had recently burned down under mysterious circumstances.

There is no need to dwell on the extent of marijuana growing in the economically impoverished state of Kentucky. Suffice it to say that drug manufacture, sale, and distribution is a huge subterranean industry that is constantly changing its mode of operation in response to the attempts by police at eradication. Police use of informants is part of this eradication program. A number of battered women and shelter directors pointed out that it is more difficult to get certain police agencies to serve protective orders against batterers if those batterers are police informants. Teresa, a spouse abuse shelter director put it candidly:

Teresa: EPOs may not be served if the abuser is a police informant.

In those cases in which woman batterers are also police informants, the need to gather information on drug operations sometimes takes precedence over the need to enforce domestic violence laws and protect battered women. In fact, we might say, a little melodramatically perhaps for some, that the "war against drugs" is more important than the "war against women."

Although deals with police informants are also common in urban areas, it is much less likely that those officers will be called to the scene of the informant's home if there is a domestic dispute. It is the sociocultural cohesion of the rural milieu that makes batterers who are also police informants more likely to get away with domestic assault.

Providing hard empirical evidence on these kinds of compromises is almost impossible. However, it is less difficult to document the appearance of a compromise around police informants. This kind of documentation moves us into the realm of public perception and rumor. Ethnographers must deal with rumor because in many ways, and especially in rural areas, rumor and gossip are a central component of social life. Bearing these observations in mind I will now discuss one case that has served as a lightning rod for numerous concerns about the "rural compromise" when it comes to the policing of rural woman battering.

In Chapter 1, I introduced the case of Johnny Jacobs, who was indicted for murder by a grand jury in March 1991 after killing his wife by shooting her in the face in January 1991. While awaiting trial before the grand jury, Jacobs spoke with two FBI agents about his ex-wife's parents, Claude and Donna Hall, and their son, Claude Hall, Jr. The Halls had been under investigation by the FBI for some time. In September 1990, police found roughly 4,500 marijuana plants in a field near the Halls' home. The field was allegedly surrounded by booby traps with explosive devices. On February 6, 1991, Jacobs gave police permission to search a mobile home in Wayne County where he had lived. There officers found prescription bottles with Claude Hall Sr.'s, name on them. Instead of finding prescription medication inside the bottles, they found marijuana seeds. I have already documented how the case proceeded and the Halls received very lengthy prison terms for their involvement in marijuana growing.[10]

Stories run rife about this case, and various claims-makers argue a number of different positions. There is probably no way we will ever know what happened in this case. However, several things are clear. Johnny Jacobs, who killed his wife in January 1991, who led the FBI to the Halls in February 1991, and who was indicted for murder by a grand jury in March 1991, was finally convicted of manslaughter on October 16, 1995. Johnny Jacobs was sentenced to 10 years in prison for his crime. However, much to the disgust of his ex-wife's family, he remains free on appeal bond and is living in Knott County at the time of writing. Some people in the area spouse abuse shelter system (where Claudia was never a resident) feel that certain guarantees were made to Jacobs early in the process that resulted in him being treated very leniently by the judicial system in return for informing the police about the marijuana growing operation. When I asked an informant at the Kentucky Bar Association whether some kind of deal was struck in this case, the informant commented, "Anything is possible." In another conversation with a judge who also presided over Knott County during the time it took to dispose of the Jacobs case, I asked whether the federal agencies that went after the Halls for marijuana growing could have cut some kind of deal with the state judicial system to go easy on Jacobs. The judge commented, "Deals are cut all the time, but I have no comment on this particular case."

Whatever the "truth," my point is that a suspicion of impropriety has been established around the use of Jacobs as an informant. That impropriety, for some, resulted in the failure to convict a wife murderer in a timely and just manner. As I noted in Chapter 1, this impropriety was amplified by the swift and highly punitive conviction of the Halls for marijuana growing.

Police Corruption and
Compromised Law Enforcement

An important contemporary issue in police corruption is the connivance of officers in illegal drug operations and other subterranean activities such as bootlegging, auto theft, gambling, prostitution, and money laundering. The details of this corruption are important for our study of domestic violence because they once again suggest ways in which local rural police may be compromised around the enforcement of domestic violence laws. Rather like the Prohibition days, when a commodity that large numbers of the population use is criminalized and the penalties for its use escalated to the point of the ridiculous, then the process of deviantization produces a backlash. Under these conditions of restricted supply and high demand, the price of illegal drugs and other commodities/services rises and the delivery to consumers becomes much more of an art form. Part of the art of providing this service involves ensuring that some law enforcement officers do not interrupt the subterranean supply. In Kentucky, where roughly two thirds of the counties do not even permit the sale of alcohol and where poverty and unemployment rates are often so high, there has developed a widespread culture of resistance to the punitive criminal justice thrust to eliminate the illicit drug experience.

This culture of resistance, born out of a pastiche of creativity, negotiation, daring, and hopelessness, is not limited to Kentucky. The manufacture, distribution, sale, and use of illegal drugs is highly publicized in urban centers, where it is described in terms of "urban blight" and the "disease of addiction." In urban areas, though, corrupt officers have much less contact with the community, especially with regard to domestic cases. Consequently, the degree of compromise at domestics produced by rural abusers knowing that police officers are actively or passively involved in corrupt activities is probably likely much greater than in urban centers. As Potter and Gaines (1992) observe, rural areas have an abundance of "drug dealers, bootleggers, prostitutes, gamblers, loan sharks, auto thieves, fences and the like" (p. 37). Drawing attention to the conviction of dozens of sheriffs in Kentucky, Tennessee, and Georgia for involvement in drug trafficking, they conclude that "corruption is as critical a determinant of rural law enforcement and politics as it is to social control in our big cities" (p. 37).

The pursuit of corruption related to drug running in Kentucky began in a big way in 1986 in economically depressed Morgan County. A total of 16 people were indicted, several of whom were prominent, elected officials. Among those indicted was the sheriff of Morgan County and the county judge, both of whom had protected drug dealers and connived in the distribution of cocaine.[11] In the spring of 1992, during my many interviewing/observation trips, I stopped in West Liberty, the county seat of Morgan County, where the sheriff's department is based. Stopping at a local restaurant for a toasted cheese sandwich, I engaged the proprietor in a long conversation that eventually drifted to the topic of the sheriff, who had been indicted. The proprietor told me that he/she thought the incarcerated sheriff was a well-respected pillar of the community and would vote him in again in a heartbeat if he were to ever come up for reelection. The proprietor's reason was that the ex-sheriff understood the people of Morgan County and was always there to help them.

Beginning in August 1989, FBI agents posed as cocaine traffickers from Chicago. They sought protected airplane drop-off sites in Eastern Kentucky and guaranteed safe escort of their cocaine out of the counties in which the drops were made. According to the indictment, Lee County Sheriff Johnny Mann was the first to agree to protect the shipment. Mann accepted payment of $39,000 for his part in the operation. Sheriff Mann's role was to protect both cocaine and marijuana shipments from both police detection and interference. It was Mann who introduced the agents to Wolfe County Sheriff Lester Drake, who ended up taking $17,000 for his role in guaranteeing safe passage of the drug shipments, and Owsley County Sheriff Billy McIntosh, who earned $12,000. On March 9, 1990, Mann introduced the agents to Beattyville Police Chief Omer Noe, who received $5,000 for his efforts. On June 14, 1990, Lester Drake introduced the agents to one of his "trusted" deputies, Wilson Stone, who shared $4,000 with Drake. Finally, on June 19, Mann introduced one of the agents to Breathitt County Sheriff Dean Spencer, who made $8,000 for his services.[12] At the trial, tape evidence emerged in which both Mann and Drake talk about going easy on some lawbreakers and about taking money to protect local bootleggers and marijuana growers. Sheriff Billy McIntosh is heard saying that he had given up helping the state police raid marijuana patches because it made him too many enemies.[13]

There are multiple ironies in all of these cases. Sheriff Mann, from Lee County, was known for conducting raids against marijuana growers in his county. He even took Lee County Judge Executive Bud Reese along with him to vouch for the fact that he had destroyed the plants that he found on the raids. Reese himself was the ex-Police Chief of Beattyville, the little town from which the FBI also caught Police Chief Noe. Chief Omer Noe taught a drug prevention program at the Lee County middle school![14] In other words, we see a front-stage antidrug rhetoric and a back-stage connivance in illegality.

It is too simple to explain the behavior of these corrupt officials by using the language of moral indignation and attributing their behavior to individual character flaws. To regard these convicted officers as greedy self-serving hypocrites is also to miss the latticework of structural and historical forces that furnish certain members of the community with what Richard Cloward (1959) once called an "illegitimate opportunity structure."

In their study of vice and corruption in rural settings in Kentucky, Potter and Gaines (1992) identified 28 organized crime networks in five Eastern Kentucky counties. They note, as do many others, that the "marijuana industry is the cornerstone of Eastern Kentucky's agricultural economy. Local law enforcement officers have estimated that as many as 40 percent of the residents in the areas under study are employed in the marijuana industry" (p. 40). Further analysis by Potter and Gaines shows that 25 of the 28 networks relied on corrupt relationships with public officials and police (p. 42); 11 relied on official acquiescence or a deliberate choice on the part of officials not to intervene against the illicit operations (p. 43); 16 of the networks were managed and coordinated by people who were related to each other; 5 of the criminal networks had relatives who occupied influential positions in county government or law enforcement; and finally, only 4 of the networks used outright bribery of public officials to protect their illegal operations.

Police acquiescence or connivance, or both, in drug dealing in Kentucky is common. Likewise, as we have seen from Potter and Gaines, a large percentage of the population also seizes upon these illegitimate opportunities. The drug industry is endemic to rural Kentucky, probably as it is endemic to many other rural regions of the country. It is especially prevalent in Eastern Kentucky where counties live in the grip of such grinding poverty. As Robert Merton (1938) once put it, people adapt to adverse structural conditions and "innovate" or find new ways of making a living and moving toward realizing the American Dream.

Given the deeply embedded cultural acceptance of the marijuana industry, it is not surprising that sheriffs who consistently move against these operations endanger their chances of being reelected.[15] In parts of Eastern Kentucky where the annual per capita income is between $7,000 and $9,000, marijuana growing is highly lucrative. As Potter and Gaines (1992) indicate, a well-tended marijuana plot of 60 square feet can yield up to $60,000 worth of high-grade marijuana (p. 40).[16]

Seven of the 50 battered women I interviewed talked cautiously about these rural subterranean economies. A number of other battered women alluded to such networks, but were reluctant (understandably) to discuss any details. Of the utmost importance here is that large numbers of men in the community, some of whom are batterers, access these subterranean commodities and services (drugs, illegal weapons, prostitution, gambling, chop shops [auto body shops using parts from stolen vehicles]) and probably know of the acquiescence or, much less often, the outright corrupt involvement, of law enforcement personnel in these ventures. When these police officers attend domestic disturbances in which batterers know of the officers' acquiescence, connivance, or other kind of involvement in subterranean illegalities, then those officers will be less likely to enforce the law and protect women.

Ariel lived in a secluded part of Nixon County. She was the only battered woman with a bachelor's degree that I interviewed. Ariel made numerous references to the corrupt activities of local criminal justice officials. She appeared well informed and her allegations of impropriety were consistent with the comments of other key informants and interviewees. She talked of her and her abuser engaging in illegal activities with the sheriff, a judge, other attorneys, and the county attorney in Nixon County.

> *Websdale:* Do you have any sense that there's any other form of
> . . . illegal activity with the sheriff's department?
> *Ariel:* . . . Yeah.
> *Websdale:* Now, what do you base that on?
> *Ariel:* Because I've been there. You know, when they're there. I've
> been in a poker room before where you know when
> everybody's there. The judge and the attorneys, the county
> attorneys, etc.

One law enforcement ritual I heard of from a number of interviewees was the "front-stage" public display of burning the proceeds of a major marijuana find. The burning feeds whatever public momentum there is for the war on drugs, yet in some cases the local police strip the marijuana buds and burn only the leaves and stalks. One well-connected journalist, who writes a crime column for a local newspaper in rural Kentucky, told me of having suspicions of the local sheriff, who would make a public display of aerial searches for marijuana patches. However, when the reporter began to explore those areas searched, it was only to find that the sheriff consistently failed to search those areas where local word has it that he connives with growers.

Ingrid, whose husband was a marijuana grower, was unequivocal when I asked her about local police knowledge of marijuana growing operations.

> *Websdale:* Did you ever get the sense that law enforcement
> officials in the area knew about people growing marijuana?
> *Ingrid:* Oh, there's no doubt in my mind. I also know that the
> sheriff we had before this one, stripped the buds from the
> plants before burning the rest of the plants. There was a
> picture of the burned plants in the papers. . . . I do know of
> well-off people in Roosevelt County that were arrested years
> ago. They grow marijuana. The next thing you knew all the
> policemen in town had brand new cars. Nobody got put in
> jail, nobody served any time. It was dropped. Yeah, you just

accept that kind of thing. They're the ones that own businesses. If they get put away, the businesses will shut down and what's left?

Ingrid clearly did not want to go on record as saying that she knew "big growers." However, she was so well informed, and her information was so consistent with other data I had collected in the rural region she was talking about, I felt she had her finger on the pulse of this subterranean economy and culture.

> *Ingrid:* I know that if I reported certain people that I know grow marijuana, nothing would happen to 'em. Because there's people that they buy, that the big buyers have under control. There's just no sense in even admitting that I know, risking my life for anything like that.

My ethnographic data suggest that if law enforcement personnel are involved in activities like the marijuana industry and bootlegging, they will be compromised around the enforcement of domestic violence laws. First, to enforce the domestic violence laws against a batterer who is either a consumer or supplier of illegal goods or services (liquor, gambling, prostitution, drugs, illegal weapons, and stolen property), might expose the acquiescent and/or corrupt officer to the wrath of the batterer, who might blow the whistle on the officer. Second, enforcing the law against someone involved in the popular activity of supplying illegal goods and services might greatly diminish a sheriff's chances of reelection. As Potter and Gaines (1992) put it in the context of subterranean economies, "the active enforcement of the laws creates some serious political dangers . . . a few hundred votes can easily swing an election. . . . The extended family of the arrestee may control a hundred votes or so itself" (p. 52).

Larissa and Pauline talked guardedly about what a number of other informants described as very high levels of corruption in Reagan County in Western Kentucky. Unemployment rates run very high and the coal mining boom days are long gone. An illegitimate opportunity structure flourishes, in which, apparently, a large number of local officials partake.

> *Websdale:* Do you have any sense of the degree of illegal activity in Reagan County?

Larissa: I think there's a lot of it going on. I live right next door to drug sellers. Ah, that's all my neighbors have been.

Websdale: What do they sell?

Larissa: Pot mostly, I don't know. I don't ask 'em (laughing). I don't even speak to 'em. The Vegas City police department's known for being very corrupt. There's been murders that all involved drugs and cover-ups. Big time cover-up. I think it was ten years ago there was a, a, very serious, ah, episode of a young girl being murdered and everybody knew who it was. It is still being talked about.

Pauline: The murderer retired or resigned a year ago from the Vegas City police department when the FBI came in and re-opened the investigation. This girl was pulled out of her apartment with her roommate in the room right next to her and savagely murdered.

Larissa: They found her in the trunk of her car.

Pauline: What everybody says is that she had been pregnant. The officer's name is Johnny Turner and it was his child. She also knew a lot about illegal drug activity and Turner was involved.

Larissa: She, she just threatened to name names. And the interesting thing about it was everybody knew who did it. And to this day he's a free man.

Janis said she felt that all the things she reported to state police would get back to her abuser. She alluded to the existence of a "mini-Mafia" but declined to elaborate.

Janis: He [state trooper] was good buddies with the brother of my abuser. And that's the same way with the Sheriff's Department. That's the main reason why they didn't respond. They asked these people [abuser, his brother and their friends] before they even ran for sheriff, if they should. The people that I was with are almost mini-Mafia. That's as far as I want to go on that. I don't want to dig myself a hole here.

From this excerpt it is clear that the state police are sometimes involved in the rural compromise. They, too, know abusers in the community and can pass on information contrary to the best interests of battered women. However, the overwhelming majority of women who complained about police corruption and its impact on the policing of domestics, referred to the sheriff and small town police.

State trooper Goople, when pressed as we rode together in his patrol car, conceded that sheriff's departments may not pursue batterers because of the close and potentially corrupt ties among batterers, their extended families, and sheriff's department personnel.

> *Websdale:* I've heard sheriff's departments haven't responded to domestics because . . . they've been involved in other [illegal] activities with the husbands.
> *Goople:* Well, I think there's probably some accuracy to it.

Conclusion

Our common sense might tell us that the more the police are in tune with community sentiments, the more likely they are to be of service to the public and be sensitive to public demands. Weisheit, Falcone, and Wells (1994a) observe that the state police who operate in rural areas are much more detached from the local cultural milieu. Consequently, their relationship with the community is much less intimate (p. 564). These researchers argue that local rural police are much more accountable to the community because of their ties with the community. While this may indeed be the case for a number of offenses that take place in public space, it is clearly not the case for offenses within the family. Women, and others I interviewed, are emphatic in their view that local police are less responsive to the needs of battered women than are state police. This is one of the central ironies in the policing of rural woman battering. Paradoxically, the more detached the police are from the community, the more likely they are to enforce domestic violence laws. Rural women mentioned that state police are more likely to make arrests, remove men from the home as opposed to removing women from the home, and inform battered women of their rights under the law.[17] In general, the state police are also more likely to take battered women seriously and not collude, or appear to collude, with batterers.

My ethnographic findings therefore offer a different take on the viability of rural police departments as the "ideal type example of community policing" (Weisheit et al., 1994a, p. 566). To date, community policing programs have been noticeably quiet about the problem of violence against women in families (see Websdale, 1995b). If the notion of community policing is really about the police being more accountable to the public, then my research suggests that that accountability must be extended to battered women. For battered women, the more detached state police do a much better job of protecting women's interests.

On the surface, the Kentucky state police are the best trained to deal with domestics. They display a greater awareness of the liability issues, a firmer grasp of how to deal with EPOs and DVOs, and are more alive to the dangers of false arrest. This awareness probably derives in part from their training and the fact that they see their jobs more as careers than do sheriffs and their deputies. Another reason rural battered women are more confident the state police will assist them is that the state police are more detached from local politics. Their continued employment as state troopers does not depend upon the votes of extended families.

The more supportive response of the state police at domestics is recognized by both spouse abuse shelter workers and battered women alike. However, state troopers, especially those who have closer ties with the community, can, as we have seen, still be compromised around enforcing domestic violence laws. They can still have patriarchal attitudes and can be dismissive of battered women. However, they tend to be much less a part of the rural patriarchal loop or "ol' boys network," about which many battered women have complained bitterly. They are also more committed to the dictates of rational-bureaucratic legal codes. These codes have often worked against women. In Kentucky as elsewhere, however, this has changed. Some historians and criminologists have come to recognize the law as much more of contested terrain (see Smart, 1989; Thompson, 1975), rather than an instrument wielded by the powerful in a monolithic manner against the relatively powerless. The state police, caught in a contradictory location in this contested terrain, cannot merely reproduce customary social control initiatives that have, and still do, perpetuate rural patriarchy. The state police have less room to maneuver than elected sheriffs who must negotiate an entirely different set of customary political balances.

We ought not carry battered women's seemingly bifurcated perception of local and state police performance too far. The ethnographic evidence certainly does not support the crass interpretation that all or even most sheriff's departments or small town police are consistently compromised when it comes to protecting battered women. Neither should we see the state police as a panacea. Finally, it is crucial to reemphasize the geo-cultural context of which the policing of rural woman battering is but a part. The sociocultural isolation of women and the control tactics of abusers coexist with long-established traditions of rural patriarchy. It is this isolation and the historical sinews of rural patriarchy that undermine the potential power of local police to confront woman battering.

Notes

1. For a quantitative appreciation of the differences between women's perceptions of police performance in rural and urban Kentucky see Websdale and Johnson (1997a).

2. Under Kentucky law, police "shall" make a warrantless arrest for misdemeanor assault if there is visible sign of injury caused by the abuser and if the abuser poses a future threat to the safety of others.

3. For more details of this case see the *McCreary County Record,* July 11, 1995. At time of writing, the administrator of Taylor's estate is planning to sue the McCreary County Sheriff's Department in federal court.

4. Not a particularly difficult thing to do given that at least half of the local school children knew the location of the shelter.

5. At the time I conducted the research the period for which DVOs were granted was just 1 year. It was extended to 3 years in 1996.

6. See "Nearly a Quarter of Domestic Violence Orders Never Served" in the *Ashland Independent,* September 10, 1994. Also see Captain Neil Brittain, Commander of the LaGrange State Police Post, in the *Lexington Herald-Leader,* "Kentucky's Failure to Protect Victims Concerns Abuse Panel," September 10, 1994, p. B4. Brittain notes that 27.8% of the 22,221 protective orders issued in Kentucky in fiscal year 1993 were not served. The reasons for this poor service record could stem from a failure to report served orders to the state computerized system, or the direct failure of law enforcement officers to serve the orders. Marsha Weinstein, then Executive Director of the Jefferson County Office for Women, commented, "I'm afraid we've got safe and unsafe counties." Her comments are consistent with my own ethnographic observations.

7. Evelyn Zellerer (personal conversations with the author) reports that in parts of rural Alaska, police can reach some communities only by airplane. The implications for arriving in a timely manner to a domestic dispute are obvious here. In my own ongoing research in Florida, detectives with the Metro-Dade Domestic Violence Unit have talked with me at length about the problems with reaching domestics in the remote rural communities in the Florida Keys. Response time is one problem. The vulnerability of the officer is another.

8. Having ridden an 8-hour shift with Davis, at one point during which he turned his car around, in a manner reminiscent of the car chase scenes in *The French Connection* or Steve McQueen's *Bullett,* and pursued a motorist for some strange reason, I can personally attest to the "hard runnin'."

9. There is a lot of case law attesting to the erosion of civil liberties and the increased power of police to search and seize. For example, *Illinois v. Gates*, 462 U.S 213, 1983; *California v. Greenwood*, 486 U.S 35, 1988; *Florida v. Bostick*, 498 U.S 1021, 1991; *California v. Acevedo*, 500 U.S 565, 1991; *Arizona v. Evans*, 1995.

10. According to the Halls' attorney, Ned Pillersdorf, the Halls still deny being involved in the operation.

11. See *Licking Valley Courier*, January, 1, 1989, "Former Sheriff Begins Jail Term."

12. See *Lexington Herald-Leader*, August 17, 1990. When the convictions were handed down, Spencer was the only one of the six police officers the jury did not find guilty.

13. See *Lexington Herald-Leader*, July 21, 1991.

14. See *Lexington Herald-Leader*, August 17, 1990.

15. In regard to bootlegging in dry counties, Davis and Potter (1991) similarly note that if a sheriff moved against bootleggers, he would have a "very difficult time" getting reelected (p. 156).

16. We must not be misled into assuming that these illicit subterranean drug economies are all-male operations that therefore involve some corrupt or "disinterested" rural police networking with rural men alone. In reality, women are actively engaged in rural drug running and other illicit operations. Davis and Potter's (1991) analysis of 21 bootlegging operations found that women had pivotal management roles in 11 of them. In fact, women represented 27% of the total of 92 participants in the 21 operations (p. 150).

17. In our quantitative analysis of 510 battered women's perceptions of police performance at domestics in urban and rural areas (less than 10,000 population), women reported the state police to be significantly more effective than local police (sheriff and municipal) when it came to performing these tasks. See Websdale and Johnson (1997a).

5

Courting Revictimization

The Courts and
Rural Woman Battering

Introduction

I have already alluded to the allegedly more intimate relationship between the courts and the citizenry in rural communities (see Fahnestock & Geiger, 1993). We simply do not know whether this intimacy translates into real protection for rural battered women. As I noted in Chapter 3, battered women and their abusers do not enter courtrooms as freestanding adversaries. We must not lose sight of this important point, which is as relevant to rural regions as it is to urban centers. In order not to lose sight of the structural constraints imposed upon women by the dictates of the domestic violence code, I begin this chapter with a brief overview of the role of the courts and domestic violence law in Kentucky. My ethnography identifies rural battered women at the intersection of a complex array of social forces. On the one hand, they clearly negotiate their relationships with the legal system in general and the courts in particular. Their active strategizing around how to use the courts is a testament to their courage and resistance. On another level, it is also clear that women are subject to structural forces they have little control over. These forces do not stem only from the masculinist strictures of domestic violence law that tend to ignore the power relations that women are subject to. They also derive from the multiple layers of cultural prescriptions and social expectation that bear direct relation to the rural sociocultural milieu itself. In order to explore these seemingly disparate threads of women's experience that speak simultaneously to women's agency and their subordination to broader social structural currents, I break my presentation of ethnographic findings into two parts. In the first section I discuss how women negotiate the courts and the rural judiciary. Second, I address those structural themes that tend to frustrate agency and undermine women's resistance. In particular, I discuss women's overall perceptions of judicial performance, the rudeness of judges, the sentencing of feuding couples to church, the failure of judges to appreciate the complex difficulties faced by battered women, and the social connections between abusers and judges.

Rural Courts and Woman Battering in Kentucky

Catherine MacKinnon has done much to debunk the objectivist posturing of a system of liberal law that depicts parties in disputes as "adversaries." For MacKinnon (1987), "the state is male in the feminist sense. The law sees and treats women the way men see and treat women" (p. 140). In similar fashion, "the state, in part through law, institutionalizes male power" (p. 141). One of the dangers with this kind of interpretation is that it sees male power as omnipotent. As Carol Smart (1989) indicates, such omnipotence leaves little room to theorize the resistance of women. Smart argues, "Yet law remains a site of struggle. While it is the case that law does not hold the key to unlock patriarchy, it provides the forum for articulating alternative visions and accounts" (p. 88).

Domestic violence law continues to work against the interests of women. Men and women, as domestic "disputants," do not come to the courtroom as freestanding and unfettered adversaries in the sense that liberal law suggests. Historically, husbands have enjoyed certain rights over wives' bodies that they did not enjoy over other women. The historical research I discussed in Chapter 3 showed how husbands were allowed to beat their "wayward" wives. Up until recently, husbands could not be found guilty of raping their wives because the law upheld husbands' rights of unfettered sexual access as part of the marriage contract. This began to change in the late 1970s, and during the 1980s most states introduced marital rape laws. Kentucky's marital rape law was passed relatively late, in 1990, and has a number of restrictions making it difficult to prosecute marital rape (see Russell, 1990, p. 379).

In general, the law fails to take sufficient account of the public/private divide in social life. Men and women in families cannot enter courtrooms as independent adversaries because they come from familial situations where men have considerable power over women. This failure to recognize the disadvantaged position of wives vis-à-vis their violent husbands is compounded by the fact that the courts have always upheld the marital bond wherever possible. In Kentucky, for example, judges are mandated to dispose of cases in ways that "strengthen and maintain the biological family unit" (Kentucky Revised Statute [KRS] 600.010 [2] [a]). The formal mandate to uphold the marital bond has lessened, evidenced, for example, by the fact that courts are much more willing to grant divorces than they were just a century ago. Nevertheless, the sanctity of marriage continues to affect the way judges think about disputes between husbands and wives.

While criticizing the law as androcentric, I follow Smart in acknowledging that the rational-bureaucratic legal code can work for women. In fact, the introduction of such a code was resisted in the state of Kentucky, a state that clung to the vestiges of a more traditional legal system based upon local magistrates and judges operating within the framework of rural fiefdoms. In 1975, a constitutional amendment was passed reforming the judicial system. From that point on, judges had to be attorneys and could no longer run for office as affiliates of particular political parties. As Chief Justice Robert Stephens pointed out in 1990, judicial candidates "may not endorse other candidates whether judicial or otherwise; they may not make pledges or promises of how they will conduct their official duties . . . ; they may not personally solicit funds" (Stephens, 1990, p. 3, cited in Miller, 1994, p. 156).

This progressive constitutional amendment had been debated since 1923 and supported by a number of groups, including urban civic and political leaders, the League of Women Voters, the Kentucky Bar Association, the Kentucky Circuit Judges Association, and the urban press.[1] Because they would lose their judicial fiefdoms, many rural magistrates, county judges, justices of the peace, and other judicial officers opposed the amendment. The progressive amendment is best seen as part of the shift that Max Weber once described, from more localized and traditional legal norms to the rational-bureaucratic code of law. The Kentucky amendment was narrowly passed with 54.6% of the electorate voting it in. However, it is highly significant for our purposes that the amendment was defeated in fully 86 rural counties.[2] This failure to pass the amendment in rural areas is indicative of the resistance to the introduction of rational-legal codes over law based on what Weber (1948) calls traditionalist authority (p. 296). Significantly for our purposes, the most important characteristic of traditionalist authority is what Weber calls "patriarchalism." He defines patriarchalism as "the authority of the father, the husband, the senior of the house, the sib elder over the members of the household and sib; the rule of the master and patron over bondsmen, serfs, freed men" (p. 296). Rational legal authority, on the other hand, does not rest upon

> piety toward the possible incumbents of office fiefs and office prebends who are legitimized in their own right through privilege and conferment. Rather, submission under legal authority is based upon an impersonal bond to the generally defined and functional "duty of office." (p. 299)

Although my portrayal of rural patriarchy looks much more closely at the power relations of gender, there are a number of parallels between Weber's analysis of legal developments and the disjuncture between urban and rural politicos in Kentucky over the transformation of the judiciary. The reluctance of rural communities in Kentucky to embrace a more rational-bureaucratic legal code has particular relevance for the enforcement of domestic violence laws that have made incursions into family life possible. These incursions have been especially controversial in more traditional rural communities.

Rural judges try individual cases of domestic violence in district courts in Kentucky. The district court is the center of local jurisprudence and disposes of what the law deems to be mostly minor offenses. Battered women have a number of routes available to them under Kentucky's Domestic Violence and Abuse Act (1984, amended 1992).[3] If women pursue criminal charges against their abusers, then the charge is usually a misdemeanor assault charge and is heard in district court. If they pursue civil remedies, these usually take the form of seeking protective orders from the court in order to keep their abusers from harming them further.[4] On the rare occasions when women pursue felony charges against their abusers (e.g., marital rape, kidnapping), the case is heard in circuit court. The fact that most cases of domestic violence are heard in the district court system in Kentucky (as in other states) signifies that violence against women within families rarely ends up being treated as "serious" crime. As I have already noted, national surveys show that if a batterer's violence were directed at strangers it would be much more likely to qualify as a felony offense (Langan & Innes, 1986). The importance of the trivializing of violence against women in the courts cannot be understated. The courts' failure to take domestic violence seriously tells us that the rational code is not that "rational" after all when it comes to violence against women.

I asked Kentucky District Judge Alder what would happen to an abuser who beat up his wife. Alder replied the abuser would serve maybe one night in jail.

> *Websdale:* This guy assaults his wife . . . police arrest him. How long does he spend in jail for that assault?
> *Judge Alder:* It depends. Chances are if it's a first time, he'll spend that night and he probably will get a probated sentence. The reason that he will probably get a probated sentence is because [of] the way our process works on the criminal charge. Of course the domestic violence case is not criminal in nature.

When pressed about just how much the judiciary can do for battered women in rural communities, Judge Alder, who presides over a well-to-do, racially homogeneous county in Western Kentucky, acknowledges they can do little.

> *Judge Alder:* I don't think that the victims have any confidence in the court system. I know they don't. They don't have any belief that I can help them.
> *Websdale:* Can you? Do you honestly think that given the way the system is structured, the time that men will do, that you can really help them?
> *Judge Alder:* Honestly?
> *Websdale:* Yeah.
> *Judge Alder:* No.

Negotiating the Rural Courts

If one thing stands out from my conversations with rural battered women about their relationship with the court system, it is their initial hesitancy and concern about entering it in the first place. It is at this initial stage of deciding whether to proceed against their violent partners that women engage in some of their bravest acts of resistance to the rural patriarchal order. It is hard for those of us not in those situations to appreciate the magnitude of the socio-legal obstacles faced by rural battered women. The decision to go to court in a rural county where you, your abuser's family, or both are perhaps well known, is to lay out a lot of personal details. In rural communities more so than urban ones, these details are often deemed best left behind closed doors. We saw in disturbing detail in Chapter 1 how women's decisions to resort to the court can provoke homicidal rage from some abusers.

We must add to these difficulties the fact that rural women may be especially estranged from rural courthouses. Rural women are often not in tune with the cultural capital spoken in courtrooms, where attorneys and judges use obscure legal jargon. Summoning the courage to go to court, reveal intimate details of your life, and at the same time risk your life and perhaps the lives of your children, requires enormous courage. Having made this decision, many battered women I interviewed drew upon the support of court advocates based in the rural shelters to help them through the arduous process of going to domestic violence court. As Hanna, a shelter director put it to me:

> *Hanna:* The good court advocate will learn what battered women want and what their heartfelt strategies are, and use these strategies as the basis for her advocacy work in the courtroom.

It is clear from my interviews with rural judges and battered women that these two groups come from different social classes. In relatively cohesive rural communities these differences in social class background are perhaps more acutely experienced and publicly acknowledged than they are in urban centers. Judges have a very high social standing in the community and have high incomes compared with the families of the battered women I talked with. In addition, all but 17 of the 125 district judges in Kentucky are men. These class and gender differences between rural battered women and judges amplifies the alienation battered women feel.

While I stress the significance of rural women's resistance to their own interpersonal victimization, we must not romanticize women's behavior when they enter the domestic courtroom drama. For the most part, rural battered women's cases are mediated through the support of the legal advocate. It is unrealistic to expect that battered women's resistance takes the form of them engaging judges over legal technicalities or other more esoteric aspects of the law. Rural women state their case in court and sometimes argue their points. But rural women, for the most part, do not engage in outright expressions of rage in open court, in part because their advocates have prepared them in the more calculated art of "ideal" courtroom behavior. However, rural judges differ in their willingness to allow court advocates to support battered women. In a number of rural areas where domestic violence is taken less seriously by the police, we also find judges intervening to reduce the support extended to battered women by shelter-based court advocates. Advocates report that some judges will not allow them to proceed to the bench with the battered woman seeking relief.[5] The exclusion of advocates from deliberations at the bench leaves battered women in a very precarious position at a critical juncture in their process of trying to break their ties with their abusers. This exclusion has become such an obstacle to successful advocacy, especially in certain rural counties, that House Bill 315 was passed in 1996 to guarantee the rights of victim advocates in court. Among other things, House Bill 315 allows victim advocates to accompany the victim in court proceedings, confer with the victim in a reasonable manner, and address the court as directed by the court.

In using the courts, Elizabeth actively weighed the pros and cons of having her abuser locked up. She had heard that Judge Jackson was severe with abusers and this knowledge caused her some consternation and added to her already mixed emotions.

Websdale: Have you had many dealings with Judge Jackson?
Elizabeth: Well, once. And he's firm. And I've been afraid to have anything done against Marvin [her abuser] because I know he will serve time. I want him to serve time but to me I don't want to put someone in jail. To me that's cruel because they never get to see the outside world that much and I know what I went through when Marvin was in jail for six months. It was hard on me. And I'm lookin' at that again. What kind of

financial situation would I be in? I'd rather him be out working and getting child support from him, than him being in jail and not working.

Sonia learned from her experiences in domestic violence court that her abuser did not want to do jail time or have his name published in the local press as an abuser. She told the judge exactly what she wanted out of the legal proceedings and the judge granted her wishes. Note how Sonia learns new techniques of reducing her abuser's violence through her active observation of his courtroom demeanor.

Sonia: Oh yes. He would be afraid to miss. You know, to get in trouble with the law or anything like that. He, he'd be scared to death of that. And the hitting part has eased up because he's afraid if, if I really feel like he's really gonna start in and really get bad, I tell him, "you can go on and hit me but you'd better kill me because I will have you arrested and your name will be in the newspaper." So in the last year, the physical part of it has really declined a lot.

Websdale: And you think it's because of the strategy of saying, "it's going to be in the paper."

Sonia: Uh huh.

Websdale: Did you get that strategy from seeing the way he behaved in court?

Sonia: Uh huh.

Lenore found the judge very supportive and wise to her husband's abusive behavior. She planned her court strategy down to the finest detail, including where she wanted her abuser to be able to have supervised visits with her child. Lenore got all she requested with relative ease.

Lenore: Judge Cash at the last EPO hearing said, "What would you like for child visitation?" I said, "I would like supervised visitation." He said, "Okay." I'm like, "Huh, that was easy." And he said, "Where would you like it?" I said, "I'd like it at his grandma's house." He said, "Okay" and I said, "I already asked her and she said it would be fine."

When battered women decide to take their victimization to the courts, they serve notice to their abusers that things must change. For the abuser, this move means they may have to face new and very public consequences for their violent behavior. This public pronouncement on the part of battered women through the forum of the open domestic violence court is particularly telling in rural areas where people know each other and where domestic violence orders are published in the local press. It is not surprising, given the shift in the dynamics of the violent rural relationship, that the abuser will be greatly angered. He will be angered not just because he faces potentially new consequences for his action, but also because she has gone public and because he has lost some control. Evidence from urban areas shows just how dangerous it can be for women to go public and enter the arena of the courts. Ann Jones (1994) documents a number of press accounts of the slaying of women, children, and court employees by enraged men whose partners were seeking remedies such as a divorce, protection order, child custody, or child support (pp. 29-30). Courtrooms can be so highly charged during some of these proceedings that women rightly fear and call for protection. For example, on January 19, 1993, a group of Dallas judges walked off the job, protesting a lack a courtroom security after Van Hai Huynh murdered his wife, injured a bystander, and then committed suicide.

Many women who resorted to the rural courts reported how this action enraged their abusers. Stephanie, under threat of death, was one such woman who weighed the pros and cons of proceeding to court. Even with heightened courtroom security, note how she reports feeling the safest she's ever felt and also her most vulnerable.

Stephanie: I filed for divorce. They sent him papers and things blew up. He told my attorney he was gonna kill me. And I had to go to court yesterday. So he called me the night before I went to court and told me that if I showed up in court he'd shoot me on the courthouse steps. Well I was afraid and I called the city police here, and asked them if they would at least go with me. I didn't know if I would make it into the courtroom or not. Surprisingly enough, I got a wonderful response. I couldn't believe it. They came to my house and both of them took me over here. They got between me and got me up to the stairs, took me inside, set me over with the attorneys, not with the rest of the people, so I could watch the doors so I could let them know when he came in. And, I never felt so secure in my life but at the same time, I felt helpless because I'm waiting for this man to come through the door and blow me away. This is a terrible thing to have to live with. And it lasted almost three hours. He never showed. So when we got up with the judge, the judge very calmly said, "I know we have a problem. Everyone has looked for him and he's not here. If I fall to the floor, I suggest you do the same. Now let's carry on with business." And he just said it very calmly like it was just a matter of fact. So they were waiting for him to come in and he didn't.

These simultaneous feelings of safety and vulnerability lie at the heart of many rural battered women's experiences in court. Such contradictions, combined with the central contradiction that battered women and their abusers are in conflict and yet share their lives, makes it impossible for women to enter the courtroom as the pure adversaries of the men who beat them.

In this section I have tried to emphasize the active process of women's involvement in the judicial disposition of domestic cases. As noted, the pivotal act of resistance to the rural patriarchal order comes when battered women decide, with or without the support of court advocates, to proceed to obtain protection from the court. These brave decisions, taken amid a rural sociocultural climate that recommends against the airing of family problems, are not always welcomed by rural judges. In the next section we will see how women's resistance to rural patriarchy through the court is met by a number of well-entrenched obstacles.

Revictimization From the Bench

Attorney Parks, who represents battered women who have killed their violent partners, emphatically agreed with my suggestion that a significant number of battered women felt revictimized by judges.

Websdale: A significant number of the rural battered women I have interviewed reported feeling as if they had been revictimized by the judges who disposed of their cases.

Parks: The women I represent and numerous others I have talked with report the same thing. I agree with your findings 150 percent.

Women's Perceptions of Rural Judges

Women I interviewed generally reported a more positive feeling about the way rural judges worked with them, compared with the way they were dealt with by rural police. Of the 50 women I interviewed, 31 had various experiences with judges. Of these, 16 (52%) were pleased with the judge's handling of their case and reported the judge to be any combination of polite, helpful, sympathetic, and fair.

Both Keanne and Clara felt the district judges in their small rural communities worked well on their behalf.

Keanne: The judge just got really perturbed with Chris and he said, "You say it didn't happen, she says it did, so since you can't get your stories straight stay away from her, no physical contact, nothing whatsoever. If you are seen around her, talk to her, six months in jail." I won. I was happy because the judge had looked at me and he said, "Good luck."

Clara: The judge was really good. The child support was set at $15 a week. That was the minimum because John wasn't working. And John said "I'm not gonna pay any child support." The judge said, "You can pick up pop bottles for $15 a week. Either you do that or you go to jail."

Two women were "indifferent" to their judge's performance. Thirteen women (42%) were dissatisfied with the ways judges treated them.[6] Those with negative impressions cited their perception that the judge was biased, rude, dismissive or even all three. In some of these cases women described what is most accurately called judicial harassment.

We cannot accept these percentages at face value. The sample size is small and based on battered women who, for the most part, negotiated the courts with the support of shelter-based court advocates. Perhaps more important than the sample size, however, is the fact that the numbers tell us little of the evaluative criteria used by women to assess the performance of judges. One thing we must bear in mind, particularly with rural battered women, is their degree of physical and sociocultural isolation. This isolation, as we saw in Chapter 1, may be a product of the controlling behavior of abusers and their desire to live in geographically isolated regions. The isolation may also reflect the violent regulation of women's movements even if the couple live in a small town or near other families. Rural women's isolation means they may not be exposed to the behavior of men other than their abuser. Such isolation may reflect a deliberate control maneuver by their abuser. Whatever the underlying reason, battered women will likely use their abuser's violent behavior as a measure of men's behavior in general. Using their abuser as a touchstone in this way may lead rural battered women to inflate their assessment of the performance of rural judges, who are mostly male.

Inflating the performance of rural judges may also stem from the general deference afforded to judges in small communities by large numbers of citizens and not just battered women. To obtain a protective order from someone of much higher social standing may automatically evoke a sense of awe and appreciation, even if the judge is merely doing his or her job. These comments are intended to provide a context for understanding rural women's appreciation of the judiciary. They are not intended to undermine the sterling contribution made by a number of rural judges to the safety and well-being of battered women. That roughly equal numbers of battered women report being pleased with judges as report being dissatisfied with them, warns us about drawing sweeping conclusions that the entire Kentucky rural district judiciary is systematically opposed to the interests of battered women.

Just as the structure of rural patriarchy does not mean that all men dominate all women, it does not take the entire rural judiciary to act in overt and concerted ways to undermine the safety of battered women. If anything, the ethnographic evidence suggests that the judicial response to rural battering and battered women, like that of the police, is complex and uneven. We must add to this the fact that the structure of rural patriarchy is also perpetuated by the role of the courts and the nature of domestic violence law, as well as the individual behavior of judges.

Judicial Rudeness

Celia found her district judge to be inattentive and rude.

Celia: He didn't listen. He was just rude. He'd sit there and say, "Straighten up."

Vanda, who for various reasons wanted the protective order removed against her abuser, found the judge to be unsympathetic.

> *Vanda:* When I went in front of him and asked him to cancel the domestic violence ruling he asked me why I'd signed it in the first place. And I broke down and started crying because I felt like I couldn't make anybody understand. I lied for my husband. I told the judge that I had lied. He told me to go to social services and to go and speak to my lawyer immediately. There was an undercurrent of disgust and anger in his voice. He was almost sarcastic in the way he went about it.

Caught in the cross fire between her need for safety and her need for economic security, Vanda felt that lying to keep her husband from going to jail was the best strategy available to her at that time. When she later admitted her deception to the judge, she thought he might at least understand her motives. From Vanda's vantage point it seems the judge could not get past the fact that she had lied. For the judge, Vanda and her abuser were supposed to be rationally acting adversaries. Lying to prevent her husband from being jailed, ultimately in order to protect herself economically, was something that warranted compassion and understanding on the part of a judge, not contempt.

Anita complained that Judge Ellison dismissed many of her comments and ideas about how to dispose of her domestic case.

> *Websdale:* How was Judge Ellison's demeanor toward you?
> *Anita:* He shut me up. He told me, "Miss Jones, I don't want to hear this."

Judicial dismissiveness was reported by nearly all of the women who reported dissatisfaction with judges. It is not my contention these judges are dismissive only with battered women. Indeed, the same kind of authoritarian judicial behavior directed at others in court may not be seen by those others as dismissive. In other words, what is perceived as dismissive by battered women may be perceived differently by others who come before the bench. In a three-way conversation between myself, a spouse abuse shelter director, and a district judge, it emerged that what may be perfectly standard operating procedure for a judge, may be perceived as rudeness by a battered woman.

> *Pam:* Judge Jimmy Buck is very aggressive with people. Sometimes I feel like he's over aggressive with the victim. He's like a doctor who needs to go back to medical school and go through Bedside Manner 101.
>
> *Judge Alder:* Jimmy is that way to everybody, though.
>
> *Pam:* But a victim has been through too much already and doesn't need it from somebody who's supposed to be there to protect her. He makes her feel like she is the abusive party. He has yelled at them.
>
> *Judge Alder:* I'm glad you bring that up because that's something that as a judge I have to watch, myself. I cannot fathom a woman taking that abuse. And when they do and they go back and back and back again, I get frustrated. And sometimes I want to take 'em and shake 'em and say, "What are you doing? Let us help you."

Edith, who had been brutalized and shot at on a number of occasions by her abusive husband told me she was treated with contempt by Judge Smith.

> *Websdale:* So the judge thought you were lying?
>
> *Edith:* Yeah. He didn't let me talk. Whenever I started to answer somethin' he'd just say "shut up."

The rural judge who rudely dismisses battered women from the pulpit of the courtroom bench precisely reproduces the very ceremonies of degradation those women report experiencing in their homes. From the architecture of domination in which the judge stares down at those in court, to the near ritualized dismissal of some battered women, the rural judge can present the mirror image of the batterer.

Sentencing Conflictual Families to Church

Images of women's place are also intimately tied up with religious culture. The stronger influence of fundamentalist religion in rural areas bolsters this ideology of separate spheres of social action for men and women. A number of researchers have identified the church and fundamentalist religion in rural regions as the disseminators of a powerful form of patriarchal ideology (Kuczynski, 1981; Navin, Stockum, & Campbell-Ruggaard, 1993; Whipple, 1987). Jack Weller (1966) once wrote that, "The church in Appalachia is, beyond doubt, the most reactionary force in the mountains" (p. 126).

A number of judges have recommended that the parties to a domestic dispute attend church as one way of "improving" their relationship. Judges I talked with also told me that battered women would sometimes refer to the fact that their abusers were attending church with them as a sign that his battering behavior was a thing of the past. A number of advocates saw sentencing couples to church as just one more way that patriarchal ideology is reproduced. Instead of a woman being subject to the male head of household, she and her abuser attend church where the authority is no longer the judge but the pastor, or more distally, a male God. Pam, a spouse abuse shelter director in Western Kentucky, told me of a judge who sentenced perpetrators and victims of domestic violence to church so that they could learn the virtues of the Christian family. She contended this family form was based upon the ascendancy of husbands over wives.

Pam: We have a judge in Adams County who orders couples to go to church together. He continues to do this.

Pam and a number of other shelter directors expressed concerns that Christian religious ideology would recommend that women remain in violent marriages and try to fix them. Because religion is a crucial aspect of cultural life in rural Kentucky, the support battered women derive from their religions, their pastors, or both, is a matter of considerable importance.

Several women shared that they felt their pastors expected them to fix broken marriages. Both Tonya and Laverne describe the way in which fundamentalist religious values reinforced rural patriarchy and identified wayward women as the source of strife in marriage.

Laverne: In our congregation you're supposed to treat your wife with respect, but wives are supposed to take a submissive role. After you're beaten you're supposed to go back and make amends.

Websdale: So if you went to, say, your preacher, local preacher in Reagan County and said "my husband's assaulted me," what would the response of the preacher be?

Laverne: Oh, gosh (laughing). I went a lot. And, ah, I was told to stick it out, stick it out. Um, it was just a marital problem. It was me being obstinate and not being submissive.

As with all these issues, there are those who work with victims of domestic violence who see things a little differently. There are three rural shelters in Kentucky funded primarily by religious organizations (the Christian Appalachian Project) whose orientation is pro-Christian and who would dispute Pam's view. There are a good number of judges who would also dispute Pam's view. Circuit Judge Fonda makes referrals to pastors.

Judge Fonda: In this part of the country, I have a significant number of what I call Pentecostal beaters. Their perception is that they have got to get control of the heathens in their family. When you understand that and realize that these men to a large extent are concerned about eternal issues, then you've got a whole different ball game in the court.

Websdale: Tell me about it. That's interesting.

Judge Fonda: I think those of us who sit in the courtroom have to have some type of, of New Testament scriptural base to understand where they're coming from. If I have families who are involved in church, particularly if I know the pastors and know something about their counseling credentials, I will use pastors over more traditional therapists because the pastors have authority in the lives of those families.

Websdale: You've obviously heard stories, as I have and lots of people have, that women have gone to pastors in situations where they'd been battered and pastors have said to them, "endure."

Judge Fonda: Part of your great calling as a wife, yeah. I know my pastors and that won't happen.

There is no doubt that referring battered women to either a psychotherapist or a pastor can result in women being told that somehow they, rather than their abusive partners, are the source of the "relationship problems." For Circuit Judge Fonda, however, the realities of religious commitment in rural cultures must be taken into account and worked around, rather than simply be mechanically dismissed as a way in which rural patriarchy is reproduced.[7]

The Judicial Failure to Appreciate the
Difficulties Faced by Battered Women

There have been a number of rural cases in which judges have failed to recognize or adequately respond to the danger posed to battered women by their abusers. In the murder of Cammie Pigman in Hindman, Knott County, her abuser and killer, Isaac Pigman, had repeatedly threatened her over a long period of time. She was shot in the head three times by Isaac, who was apparently enraged at her finally divorcing him (see *Louisville Courier-Journal,* February 7, 1992, and February 8, 1992). Prior to the killing there had been numerous warning signs that Isaac was capable of using lethal violence. On November 22, 1991, Cammie swore out a warrant for his arrest for fourth degree assault and terroristic threatening. In an affidavit she alleged that he had kicked her and knocked her down and threatened to blow her brains out. The criminal charges were dropped at Cammie's request on November 26, 1991, the day after she had filed to divorce him. However, District Judge Kay Doyle issued a domestic violence order, valid until June 1, 1992, requiring that Isaac be restrained from committing further acts of violence and abuse. That order was still in effect the day Cammie was killed. On January 20, 1992, Cammie complained that Isaac had broken the protective order by threatening her over the phone. Kentucky state police arrested Isaac for contempt of court and he appeared in court on January 21, 1992. Acting on a motion from Knott County attorney Deborah McCarthy, Judge Kay Doyle ordered Isaac Pigman into a drug and alcohol treatment program at Humana Hospital, Lake Cumberland, for what she described as an open-ended period of time. Therapist Robin Moler filed an affidavit at the January 21 hearing recommending that Isaac receive drug and alcohol treatment. In that affidavit she rather ominously noted that Isaac Pigman was "suffering from major depression. . . . Due to the circumstances, I feel Mr. Pigman is capable of suicidal and homicidal actions" (noted in *Lexington Herald-Leader,* February 9, 1992, p. B4).[8] Isaac was sent to the program but was released after only 5 days and returned to Hindman, Knott County. The *Lexington Herald-Leader,* in concert with advocates for battered women, asked,

> The question is why Isaac Pigman wasn't behind bars before this tragedy occurred. . . . District Judge Kay Doyle ignored warnings that Pigman posed a serious threat to his wife. . . . Kentucky's judges have the power to protect women from violent men. Once again, a court has failed to use these powers fully. And once again, a frightened woman has suffered tragically as a result. (Editorial, November 11, 1992, p. A8)

Doris, an advocate for battered women who works in the Knott County region, told me that local advocates and battered women had a very low opinion of Judge Doyle.[9]

> *Doris:* Doyle did little for victims of domestic violence and nearly always decided cases in favor of perpetrators. Kay Doyle has a bad name locally for domestic cases.

Judges who tend to stereotype battered women and fail to appreciate the complexity of their situation also contribute to the perpetuation of rural patriarchy and, in particular, women's revictimization. Judge Steven told me that there are far too many domestic cases heard in his court. He dismisses between 10% and 15% of requests for EPOs because he says they are frivolous. In one case, he denied an EPO because a woman claimed her ex-husband threatened to kill her dog. As I have documented in Chapter 1, threats to women's pets constitute a particularly cruel and menacing form of abuse. This type of abuse, indirect as it is, meets the legal criteria required for the issuance of an EPO in Kentucky. Kentucky Revised Statute 403.720 requires only that the fear of imminent injury is produced by the abuser's actions. In all, according to Judge Steven, the disposition of domestics in Kentucky is "a big mess and it is driving judges crazy." Judge Steven knows of one rural judge who "says he won't even mess with domestic cases and just throws the paperwork away."

There are times when Judge Steven sends the battered woman to counseling because "she cannot be thinking right if she returns to the idiot." He contends that:

Judge Steven: Forty to fifty percent of the women who come in with black eyes end up saying they don't want to press charges. Most of these cases should be handled in a social services setting.

Judge Steven sees battered women who return to these abusers as "stupid."

Judge Steven: If they're so damn stupid to go back to this guy perhaps they deserve a beating.

District Judge Walter Maguire's well-publicized views on the family and domestic violence are replete with stereotypes about battered women and fail to point out the difficult and potentially lethal danger many of these women are exposed to. According to Maguire,

> our current domestic violence statutes, while well intentioned and moderately effective, have become and are becoming more and more trivialized by the current procedural scheme which encourages every "couple" or covered relationship to run to the courthouse every time a disagreement arises, harsh words are uttered or some real, or perceived "threat" is made. . . . The vast majority of "emergency protection" cases are not true "emergencies," and other agencies, principally social welfare agencies, are better equipped, staffed and trained to do "referrals."[10]

For Maguire, domestic disturbances emanate from pathological families set up to extract welfare payments from the state. He comments,

> I hold firmly to the view that it is all but impossible to strengthen and maintain "a family unit" whose principal connection to "family" seems to be . . . the primary purpose of acquiring or retaining certain government benefits, and in which violence is the principal and ongoing theme and dominant personality. . . . You cannot instill or restore sensitivity and stability where ignorance, abuse, addiction and/or mental or emotional illness is a dominant ingredient surrounding the conception and "parenting" of children.[11]

In a final broadside against advocates for battered women and others involved in the social movement against domestic violence in Kentucky, Judge Maguire argues that rather than developing regimes of public intervention to "protect about everyone from everything," we should instead acknowledge that "perhaps the best way to deal with complex social dynamics problems is to empower individuals to take individual responsibility and make sound decisions."

These arguments about empowering individual men and women to transcend their own behavioral limitations deny the patriarchal authority of batterers over their partners. As we saw in Chapter 1, there are numerous reasons why individual women cannot simply "choose" to leave violent men. For judges to ignore these reasons, or to argue that many of these cases are trivial or not emergencies, is to ignore the powerlessness and danger that many battered women feel in their homes in rural communities.

Attorney Simpson points to the way in which judges have a double standard in deciding certain child custody cases. In rural communities, in particular, if women do not come up to the standards of traditional femininity or the ideal of motherhood, then some judges have granted custody of children to fathers even although the father has battered his wife.[12] He comments,

> *Simpson:* I had a case and my partner has had more, in which there has been horrendous abuse and the man gets custody of the children because the woman wasn't a perfect little mother. A lot of judges seem to have the attitude that just because he abuses her doesn't mean he's necessarily a bad influence on the children.

Just as it is standard conservative rhetoric to blame the poor for the their own plight, so too in patriarchal circles it is commonplace to hear victims of woman battering being blamed for their victimization. Typical statements include, "Why didn't she just leave?" or "Why did she break the terms of the protective order and 'invite' him back into her life?" or "She must be stupid to stay with him." These kinds of statements focus on the victim and explain her fate in terms of her own behavior. This style of thinking, loosely labeled "victim blaming," constitutes a form of patriarchal ideology because it deflects attention away from the core problem, namely, systemic male violence against women. As Jan Pahl (1985) once pointed out, even to talk of the social problem of "woman battering" is to ignore where the real problem lies; that is, with "male violence."

The tendency for some rural judges to engage in victim blaming can lead to their admonishing and ridiculing women. In one case,

Linda Bolin had been hospitalized after being beaten with a baseball bat by her abuser Jeff Adkins. Bolin had filed charges against Adkins because he allegedly violated an EPO she had taken out against him.[13] During the hearing, Adkins proposed marriage to Bolin and she accepted. Presiding Judge Maguire admonished Ms. Bolin: "Ms. Bolin you're in serious need of help. I suggest very strongly that you . . . get yourself into counseling" (*Pulaski Week,* May 25-31, 1995, p. 1). Later in the proceedings, Maguire apparently commented (shaking his head),

> It's crazy. . . . Here he allegedly assaulted her, was deprived of his liberty for doing so, then comes to court and proposes. And the victim crumbles and says "yes" and that she's only afraid of him "when he's drinking." (*Pulaski Week,* May 25-31, 1995, p. 2)

The local newspaper carried an article by Dr. Don Whitehead, who offered some medical/psychiatric insights into the Bolin case. He comments:

> Very often the victim goes back to live with the abuser. Why? One way of understanding spouse abuse is to consider it an addiction—an addiction to a person. . . . Abuse victims return time and time again even though they know the relationship is dangerous. They are addicted. (*Pulaski Week,* July 13-19, 1995).

These commentaries on the Bolin case constitute a classic example of victim blaming. The discourse on the Bolin case is yet another play on the theme of "battered women as masochists." Both Judge Maguire and our medical expert who fed off of the case focused on the pathology of the victim, rather than on the much broader issue of systemic interpersonal male violence against women. As it happens, Bolin did not marry Adkins. She thanked Maguire publicly for recommending the counseling. My question with this case is, "Where is the discussion of Adkins's violence toward Bolin and interpersonal male violence toward women in general?"

Victim blaming was also a theme that emerged during the tragic homicide-suicide in Earlington, Western Kentucky, in which Leonard Morrow murdered his wife and two young children before taking his own life. On November 28, 1993, under the guise of taking his estranged wife Latonya and his children Christmas shopping, Leonard shot Latonya in the neck multiple times, his daughter Mynisha twice in the face, and his son, Leonard, Jr., once in the face. On October 1, 1993, Latonya Morrow had obtained an EPO restraining Leonard from contacting her or coming within 500 feet of her or members of her household. A full Domestic Violence Order was granted by Judge Soder on October 12, 1993. Leonard violated that order on October 23, 1993, by entering her home, shooting up the house, breaking all the windows, and smashing the furniture. As a result of his destructive behavior, Latonya Morrow filed a criminal complaint against her husband. The Madisonville police arrested Leonard Morrow on October 29, 1993. He came before Judge Soder on November 19, 1993, for violating the protective order. Judge Soder fined him $20 with $47.50 in court costs. A tape of the proceedings reveals Judge Soder saying to Leonard Morrow, "You're free to leave—good luck. . . . and no more violations of the domestic violence order" (*Louisville Courier-Journal,* December 1, 1993, p. A7).

Nine days after this hearing, the Morrow family members had all been shot dead. The social postmortem of the killings and their antecedents galvanized the small community. Within 24 hours of the killings, the Hopkins County Joint Child Fatality Task Force convened to determine the reasons for the death of the children.[14] The report makes the following points:

- that Latonya Morrow signed a statement with the Hopkins District Court on October 1, 1993, saying she would not drop the Domestic Violence Petition
- that Latonya, contrary to the terms of the existing EPO, drove her husband and the rest of the family to the October 12, 1993, hearing for the issuance of the full Domestic Violence Order. At this hearing, Latonya asked for the protective order to be dismissed because she and her husband were going to work their differences out. Due to her request, the prior condition preventing Mr. Morrow from coming within 500 feet of his family was lifted. Mr. Morrow was only restrained from acts of domestic violence and abuse.
- that at the November 19, 1993 hearing stemming from Leonard Morrow's breach of the protective order by destroying Latonya's residence, Latonya told representatives of the Hopkins County Attorney's office that she did not want to see her husband jailed or punished. It was for this reason that Judge Soder only fined Leonard a total of $67.50 and released him.
- that Latonya "inadvertently aided her husband in violating the Restraining Order by driving him to the courthouse" (*Hopkins County Joint Child Fatality Task Force Report,* p. 9) on October 12 and November 19, 1993

- that the judge and prosecutor were not aware that Leonard Morrow had used a gun to shoot up Latonya's home on October 23, 1993. Neither were they aware of the death threats Leonard Morrow made against his family to his co-workers. Also the judge had not been informed of Leonard Morrow's severe depression.

The report concludes by saying that "it does not appear that the system failed Mrs. Morrow," but rather that "Mrs. Morrow failed to allow the system to protect her." There was a storm of protest about this case. Advocates for battered women, Latonya Morrow's family, and the press in Louisville and Lexington attacked the Task Force and Judge Soder for failing to protect Latonya Morrow and her children. Helen Kinton, then president of the KDVA and director of the nearby Sanctuary Shelter in Hopkinsville, commented, "It's the responsibility of the system to protect its most vulnerable citizens. Nobody has taken into account Mrs. Morrow's fear" (*Louisville Courier-Journal*, December 7, 1993). According to Kinton, fear could have prompted Latonya Morrow to ask that charges against her husband be dropped (*Louisville Courier-Journal*, December 7, 1993). Hopkins County Coroner John Walters, the task force chairman, saw it differently, saying that Latonya Morrow "was not making any effort to avoid her husband" (*Louisville Courier-Journal*, December 7, 1993).

Other advocates pointed to the lack of information that the court had at its disposal about the Morrow case. For example, Hopkins County Deputy Sheriff Craig Patterson told the press that he knew that Morrow had used a gun to shoot up the house on October 23, 1993. However, this information apparently did not filter through to the judge or the prosecutor. Notwithstanding the failure of the judge and prosecutor to learn of Leonard Morrow's use of a gun on October 23, 1993, there was earlier evidence in court records that Leonard had used a gun against his wife in an earlier incident of domestic violence. Latonya Morrow stated in a September 30, 1993, court petition that her husband had threatened her with a gun at the same time that he assaulted her. Advocates argued that Judge Soder should have taken this earlier use of the gun into account and jailed Leonard Morrow after the October 23 disturbance. Margaret MacDougal, president of the Board of Directors of the nearby Hopkinsville spouse abuse shelter, argued that domestic violence was not taken seriously in Hopkins County. In an editorial titled "Unchecked Violence," the *Louisville Courier-Journal* agreed with advocates that Latonya Morrow should have received much better protection:

When Morrow pleaded guilty, it should have resulted in his getting locked up for as long as possible. . . . His gun should have been confiscated. For reasons that aren't yet clear, the prosecutorial system broke down. However, when a sick man repeatedly signals for help, and his wife sounds all the law enforcement system's alarm bells, and virtually nothing happens, that's called something else: unconscionable. (*Louisville Courier-Journal,* December 1, 1993)

Another way in which rural judges and criminal justice personnel fail to acknowledge the complexity of battered women's predicaments is seen when they argue that battered women misuse protective orders. Rural judges frequently express a concern that battered women contravene the spirit of protective orders when they invite abusers back into their lives and their homes while the orders are still active. In some of these cases, judges jail abusers for contempt of court. It is in the arena of protective orders that the perspectives of women themselves are especially important. For battered women, the court is a potential resource to restore some tranquillity (however temporary) into their troubled relationship. In many cases the significance of the protective order is both real and symbolic. Those women at risk of lethal violence know full well that the protective order will not stop their abuser from killing them. Criminal justice personnel are also cognizant of this fact. However, for a large number of rural women it seems that the shaming produced by the issuance of the order gives them a little more control than they had previously. This shaming process is likely to be more prevalent in rural communities than in large urban areas. From rural battered women's perspectives, the EPO and DVO are not just to stop him from hurting her again, but rather to tilt the power balance in the relationship in her direction. Consequently, when the shift in the power balance is effected, she is not too concerned about whether or not the spirit of the protective order has been flouted. Pam, a spouse abuse shelter director, put it as follows:

Pam: She can't violate the protective order. She's the one who went and got it. Many times, though, as women we want believe that men change. And many times the threat of them going to jail and people finding out that they're an abusive person, is enough to make life really wonderful for a year maybe. It is a little power that she's never had before. Women just want the abuse to stop and they want to have some peace

for a little while. And if that little piece of paper's gonna
ensure that they're gonna have it, then they're gonna use it.

Knowing the Abuser

I have already discussed the many ways in which patriarchal
structures are reproduced. In my analysis of the policing of rural
woman battering I noted the significance of the shared understandings
among men about the place of women. I do not suggest that there is
a conspiracy among men to keep women in their place. Rural patriarchy is far too deeply embedded and complex for such a simple
mechanism to be the motive force behind its history. Rather, we must
scrutinize the commonality of interests and experiences among men,
and especially groups of men, and the way these translate into certain
patterns of decision making. In particular, we must ask, "Who is
listened to?" "Who is believed?" "Who is able to speak?" and "Who
has the contacts with people in positions of power to get his or her
interests taken care of?"

Of the 125 district judges in Kentucky, 108 are men. This is only
to be expected given that women have been slow to enter the legal
profession in Kentucky, and that it takes time to become a judge.
However, we must move beyond representational issues and look
carefully at how men stand at the intersection of a mosaic of social
connections that tend to include other men rather than women. This
social "connectedness" of judges sometimes translates into a failure to
act in ways that benefit rural women.

Mavis reflected on the way in which the social links between her
abuser and the district judge ensured her abuser preferential treatment. Mavis also reports on how the cards were stacked against her
in this case because there was a man on the jury who had previously
beaten her.

> *Mavis:* As it turns out, my husband's father worked for the judge,
> and so the judge's son and my husband kind a grew up
> together on the same little farm. And, even though he'd done
> all these horrible things and could someday possibly rape one
> of their own children or run over 'em, in a car or something,
> drinking or something, they put more significance and more
> loyalty to him over me who had been hurt and never done

anything in my life. They showed him preference. And that's what it came down to.

The entire criminal proceeding was an ordeal for Mavis. She notes:

> *Mavis:* They wouldn't let me know when the arraignment was. There was one guy there, a sheriff, he finally did call me the day before. So I went into court to testify. And I'm having to testify with my abuser and his friends and his buddies and everybody there. I go in there and there's a man in there, who grew up with my husband, who hit me a long time ago. This man was on the grand jury. He hit me his self. And so I called the Commonwealth Attorney and I told him about the situation. Then I asked him if the guy on the grand jury couldn't be replaced by somebody else. And he said, "No, this is the way it is, this is the way it's going to stand." I was scared to death.

According to Blanche, the judge favored her abuser and his new girlfriend. She noted that because the judge knew the abuser's family, his demeanor was markedly different toward him in court. She comments:

> *Blanche:* He has let so many men go. . . . Me and my daughter was trash. And Kevin broke my ribs and I ended up in the hospital. Judge Feder . . . he'd always look over toward that woman and Kevin and smile. And he'd look over at me and my lawyer and give us looks like he was biting holes through us.

Sometimes it is not just a case of the judge being connected with the abuser and apparently favoring him. Blanche's case was also adversely affected by some of the courthouse workers who also knew Kevin. Again this kind of intimacy is much more likely in rural communities. Blanche observes:

> *Blanche:* All of them girls working at the courthouse went to school with him.
> *Websdale:* So you're seen very much as an outsider?
> *Blanche:* Yeah, they would always look down on me. Felt like to me they were thinking I was trash or something.

Like sheriffs, district judges are elected officials who are likely to know a number of the people who come before them in court. It is clear from a number of sources that the decisions of some judges in domestic cases are influenced by their degree of familiarity with the extended families of domestic disputants and their potential value as voters. This form of bias is probably less marked than it is with sheriffs because sheriffs and their deputies are more likely than judges to occupy social positions similar to those of batterers who are brought before the courts.

David, an attorney who had worked numerous battering cases put it as follows:

> *David:* And a lot of times you get judges and county attorneys who know one side or the other and they aren't real interested in enforcing domestic laws. Don't ask me to name any names cause I'm not going to.

Women's perceptions of judicial bias suggest there have been a significant number of cases of judges deciding cases in favor of perpetrators because of the connections between the judge and the perpetrator's family. Some women I talked with also felt there was what might be considered more outright corrupt ties between judges and abusers that worked against women's interests in court.

It is much more difficult to identify judicial connivance or acquiescence in certain illegalities than it is in the case of policing. It is possible that judges have fewer opportunities to engage in such illegalities, or less of a need because their salaries are much higher than those of local police officers. Having said this, there have been a number of Kentucky judges suspended or removed from office for misconduct.[15]

Tonya and Laverne, who reside in a depressed mining community in Reagan County, talked of Circuit Court Judge Carrol, who they allege is at the center of a number of illegal dealings in the county and with whom Laverne had a number of difficulties with her domestic case.

> *Tonya:* Judge Carrol has been a judge for years and years, he sits up there and fixes drunk driving tickets for the illegal place that sells the whiskey and stuff [Reagan County is dry].
>
> *Websdale:* He hangs out there?

Tonya: Yeah, yeah, that's his biggest hangout, so he knows.

Laverne: He's an alcoholic. He was arrested in Browtown and had to stay in jail there. It was in the paper. And the very next day he got out and was right there on the bench again.

Spouse abuse shelter director Hanna confirmed Tonya and Laverne's perceptions about Judge Carrol. Laverne had a tremendous child custody battle with her abuser, and the judge sided with her abuser. Hanna commented:

Hanna: And Judge Carroll is the big drug kingpin for everything that comes through Reagan County, including cocaine and marijuana shipments. It is well known that if you attend his court in the afternoons he is often drunk on the bench.

As I noted above, the mere fact that judges engage in corrupt behavior does not mean that they will exhibit bias in their disposition of domestic cases. Word gets around about corruption in small communities, however, and we should not rule out the possibility that the few judges who have tainted reputations are also viewed with suspicion by battered women simply because it is networks of men in those communities who are at the center of corrupt activities in general.

Tamara alleged that the handling of her child custody battle in circuit court was riddled with corruption.

Tamara: I mean, my daughter, my 11-year-old lives with her daddy because he had eight thousand dollars to bribe Judge Nostra in Livingston County. At the time I had no money and they just made sure I wasn't there in court. I had no idea when the court date was. They didn't try to get me for an unfit mother, they tried to get me for "financially unstable" which I was. But I wasn't a bad mother. And he got what he wanted because I wasn't there. I had no attorney and they knew that. It was just very carefully planned.

Websdale: So you think maybe somebody was paid?

Tamara: Oh, yeah. I'm sure of that. He told me he spent eight thousand dollars on that attorney and we never even had to fight in court. It shouldn't have cost him more than five hundred. There was no fight. And his attorney and the judge were foxhole buddies in the war. If his attorney wanted something, Judge Nostra was pretty much easy. You know, they were just too close.

The closeness between some rural judges and certain influential men in the community may make it more difficult for those judges to dispose of domestic cases in which those men are abusers, or in which their kin or close friends are abusers. The fact that judges must get the vote out to get reelected means they are indebted to those men in the community who help them do that. However, the evidence of strong links between judicial corruption and the compromised disposition of domestics is hard to come by and seems to be of much less importance than corruption and its compromising effects on the policing of domestics.

Conclusion

The law and the rural judiciary do not neatly reproduce rural patriarchy. Women do have a say through the courts, and many report favorable outcomes. The fact the law prescribes that woman battering is a misdemeanor offense tells us that this manifestation of violence is not taken as seriously as comparable, or even less heinous, offenses committed by strangers. In Kentucky, the late passage of the marital rape law, together with the restrictions attached to that law, reflect the miserable condition of women in that state. As in other states, Kentucky law continues to recommend that the judicial disposition of domestic cases bear in mind the need to maintain the family as a biological unit.

Domestic law does not necessarily paint battered women into a corner. However, the law and the courts offer women only a limited number of options. I showed how the decision to proceed against violent men through the courts is a major act of resistance by battered women. It is also clear that, having made this decision, women work the courts for their own benefits. In a sense I have tried to show how patriarchal patterns or structures are both lived out and indeed transformed by individual women. We ought not lose sight of the potency of women's resistance in the drama of the rural courts. Against the backdrop of people who know them and their families, rural women face the allegedly rational-bureaucratic legal code at a time when their lives are often in the utmost danger from their abusers.

Contrary to the limited literature on the relatively harmonious flow of cases through rural courts, my ethnographic labors suggest a more complex pattern of disposition of rural domestics. I reject the notion that because rural judges "know" many domestic "disputants" that they are therefore more sensitive to the outcome of cases and particularly to victims' rights. Almost as many of the battered women I interviewed were "dissatisfied" with the judicial disposition of their domestic cases as were "satisfied." The level of dissatisfaction may be even higher if rural battered women, who often experience extreme sociocultural and physical isolation, are comparing the performance of mostly male judges with the behavior of their abusers.

The reasons for battered women's dissatisfaction with rural judges and the courts are complex. I identified cases in which judges acted in ways battered women perceived to be authoritarian and disdainful. In these instances the robed patriarch, perhaps unwittingly, revictimizes women in a manner similar to that of the women's patriarchs at home. I also highlighted the pros and cons of "sentencing" battered women and their abusers to church; this sentencing is likely to be more common in rural communities, given the relative strength of the church in those communities compared with urban communities. Although judges, advocates, and battered women have various perspectives on this rural judicial practice, we must once again recognize the possibility of submitting women to yet another male authority, who, like the robed patriarch and her live-in abuser, has considerable power over her.

One of the most important ways judges contribute to the perpetuation of rural patriarchy is through their failure to appreciate the difficulties faced by battered women. I showed how some judges and courts resort to victim blaming. The Morrow homicide-suicide case in Hopkins County serves as a textbook example of victim blaming. Likewise, I attempted to demonstrate how the personal connections between judges and abusers can influence the disposition of rural domestics. Finally, some judges know abusers, abusers' friends, or both socially, and I explored how such interconnections can work against the interests of battered women.

Notes

1. For a broad discussion of the Kentucky judicial system see Miller (1994, chap. 8).

2. There are 120 counties in Kentucky.

3. According to Kentucky Revised Statute (KRS) 403.720, "Domestic violence and abuse" refers to "physical injury, serious physical injury, assault or the infliction of fear of imminent physical injury, serious physical injury, or assault between family members."

4. As noted earlier, in Kentucky battered women can secure an Emergency Protective Order (EPO) in an ex parte hearing. This order is valid for up to 14 days. To secure a full Domestic Violence Order (DVO), which is valid for up to 3 years and can be renewed, she must return to court for a full hearing. Since these protective orders are issued in civil court, the court makes its decision based on a preponderance of the evidence. States differ in the protections offered and the way in which they are offered. For example, in the rural state of West Virginia, which borders Kentucky, civil protection orders are issued by a magistrate court and are valid for only 90 days. Ex parte temporary orders are valid for only 5 days.

5. Under the 1992 amendments to the Domestic Violence and Abuse Act of 1984, domestic violence court was opened up to the public. However, although this gave advocates the right to attend court with battered women, it did not give them the right to advocate for the woman at the bench. This right was left to the discretion of individual judges.

6. This 42% dissatisfaction rate compares with 65% of interviewees (26 out of 40) who were dissatisfied with the way police treated them. As noted in Chapter 4, only 25% of women reported that the police did a good job at their domestic dispute.

7. For a discussion of the role of religious institutions in responding to domestic violence see Katherine Hancock Ragsdale (1995). For a broader discussion of the relationship between certain forms of religion and family violence see The U.S. National Conference of Catholic Bishops Committee on Women in Society (1992). For a general analysis of the way in which Christian beliefs encourage family violence, see Greven (1991). It is my position that the relationship between Christian religious ideas and violence against women is complex. At times, these values foster family violence. In other cases, it was clear from my interviews that religion was a powerful antidote to male violence.

8. Moler's point was consistent with other research showing that many men hospitalized for depression have fantasies about killing family members (see Hart, 1988, pp. 242-243).

9. This view was echoed by sources at the KDVA who also had a number of negative dealings with Judge Doyle. The KDVA conducted a full investigation of the Cammie Pigman murder, interviewing family members and other involved parties. These findings remain confidential.

10. Excerpt from letter written by Judge Maguire to Assistant Professor James Clark, University of Kentucky, School of Social Work, September 6, 1995. I am indebted to Judge Maguire for providing me with a copy of this letter.

11. Excerpt from letter written by Judge Maguire to Assistant Professor James Clark, University of Kentucky, School of Social Work, September 6, 1995.

12. Research shows that batterers who seek custody of their children have a better than even chance of winning it (see Mahoney, 1991, pp. 44-45). Bowker, Arbitell, and McFerron (1988) found that 59% of fathers who secured custody of their children had physically abused their wives (p. 162).

13. Bolin and Adkins had been in court a number of times about domestic violence.

14. Just as child abuse emerged as a major social problem before woman battering, we find that child fatality review teams far outnumber domestic violence fatality review teams. In those few communities where domestic fatality review teams have emerged, these teams have often been modeled after the structure and experiences of child fatality

review teams. As part of our ongoing research into domestic violence, Dr. Byron Johnson and I recently completed a nationwide poll of domestic violence coalitions and state agencies and found that only five states had official domestic fatality review teams and six states had unofficial (i.e., informal) ones. There is no real research or practitioner literature to speak of on domestic violence fatality review teams. For a starting point, see Linda A. McGuire, December 1994, "Domestic Fatality Review Teams," draft paper prepared for the National Resource Center on Domestic Violence (contact at 6400 Flank Drive, Suite 1300, Harrisburg, PA 17112-2778). The above details were reported in the Conference Highlights of the "Courts and Communities: Confronting Violence in the Family Conference," March 25-28, 1993. I am grateful to Merry Hofford, Director, Family Violence Project of the National Council of Juvenile and Family Court Judges, Reno, Nevada, for providing this information.

15. The 1975 judicial amendment created the Judicial Retirement and Removal Commission in order to better discipline judges. Although the content of its decisions are not public record, the Commission is a marked advance on the more traditional "all-or-nothing" practice of impeaching judges. The Commission is not a paper tiger. In December 1992, it suspended (with pay) Letcher County Circuit Judge Larry Collins. Collins had been charged with extorting $7,000 and some marijuana in return for protecting a drug dealer. Collins eventually served time in the penitentiary and lost his license to practice law.

More recently, District Judge Charles Huffman III, from Pike County, pleaded guilty in federal court to trading judicial favors among his friends and contacts for drugs. He was suspended from the bench on August 23, 1995, and is due to serve a year in the federal penitentiary. I am grateful to the Kentucky Bar Association and certain anonymous informants who provided detailed information on this case, most of which does not appear in this publication.

Just because judges engage in corrupt activities does not necessarily mean their effectiveness in protecting battered women is somehow impaired. There is no evidence to suggest that in either of these cases the illegal activities of the judges interfered with their ability to deal effectively with domestic cases. Sources in Pike County praised District Judge Huffman as an innovator in the disposition of domestic cases and as a judge who took violence against women seriously.

It is not my intent to go into great detail about judicial corruption in rural Kentucky. First, would be difficult to do because the files of the Judicial Retirement and Removal Commission are not part of the public record. The Commission is able to comment only on cases that have been decided by the Kentucky Supreme Court. There are only three other states that have such guarded access to the records of judicial conduct. This restrictive access is the subject of scrutiny by the Kentucky Supreme Court at this writing and it is hoped that it will change. The American Judicature Society compiles details of complaints and actions against judges on a state-by-state basis and publishes these in the *Judicial Conduct Reporter*. However, this is a statistical compilation and does not provide details on individual cases. In addition, the National Center for State Courts in Virginia does not keep information on judicial misconduct. This generally restrictive access to the misbehavior of individual judges makes it difficult to reach any firm conclusions about the nature and extent of the problem, or how it might impact the disposition of domestic cases in Kentucky. Second, local knowledge/suspicion/rumor, especially important in rural communities, of judicial malfeasance may be enough to tell some battered women they will not be dealt with fairly in district court. Such knowledge will be especially important if a woman's abuser is somehow linked to the corrupt activities.

6

Regulating Rural Women
The Patriarchal State

Introduction: The State and Social Conflict

Prior to the rise of "civilizations" (circa 10,000 years ago), societies survived largely through hunting and gathering. In these societies property was communally owned and there was no formal state apparatus. Disputes were settled through informal processes such as negotiation, self-help, avoidance, third-party mediation, and toleration (see Black, 1989, pp. 74-77; Michalowski, 1985, chap. 4). Most sociologists and anthropologists acknowledge that "law" appeared with the emergence of social inequality, an inequality that stemmed from the appropriation of surplus product by the few. In his classic work, "The Origin of the Family, Private Property and the State," Engels (1970) saw the rise of the Athenian state and the attendant development of a public police as a means of 90,000 free Athenian citizens keeping 365,000 slaves from asserting their interests (p. 546). In England, the shift from tribal communal ownership to "civilization" was accompanied by a change from rule-by-custom to rule-by-law (see Michalowski, 1985, chap. 4). As Michalowski indicates, the shift was also accompanied by growing social inequality. This connection between the rise of state societies and the consolidation of the social advantage of various ascendant minorities pervades many sociological interpretations of the state. The numerous Marxist interpretations of the state[1] derive in various ways from Marx's original (polemical) statement in the Communist Manifesto that, "The executive of the modern state is but a committee for managing the common affairs of the whole bourgeoisie" (Marx & Engels, 1970, p. 37).

Any systematic analysis of interpersonal violence against women must take account of the complex role of the patriarchal state. It is for this reason that I explore, through my ethnographic findings and other pertinent materials, the role of the state in Kentucky in managing gender relations. It is generally agreed that the modern state took its form from the patriarchal family (see Aries, 1962; Dobash & Dobash, 1979; Hall, 1984; Stone, 1977).[2] Embodied in this form was the separation of the public and private spheres of social life. Under this separation the home became a "man's castle" and was ideologically constructed as a refuge from the evils of industrialization. In spite of the widely acknowledged modeling of the modern state on the patriarchal family, most sociological theories of the state ignore the role of gender and the way in which the state reproduces patriarchal relations. Many sociologists accept Max Weber's (1948) definition of the state as

> a human community that (successfully) claims the monopoly of the legitimate use of physical force within a given territory . . . the right to use physical force is ascribed to other institutions or to individuals only to the extent to which the state permits it. The state is considered the sole source of the "right" to use violence. (p. 78)

Contrary to Weber, a number of feminists have argued the state has granted to male heads of households the "right" to use violence to keep their wives in line. Walby (1990) observes,

> The problem with the traditional Weberian definition in relation to gender is the notion that the state has a monopoly over legitimate coercion, when in practice individual men are able to utilize considerable amounts of violence against women with impunity. (p. 150)

Other feminists are reluctant to go as far as Walby in criticizing the Weberian definition of the state. For example, Frances Heidensohn (1992) points out we should recognize the "state may grant implicit licenses to some people (mostly males) which give them a degree of authority and legitimacy in the use of coercive power" (p. 12).

I employ the term *state* to refer to those organizations and agencies, both inside and outside of formal governmental structures, that regulate and manage the social, economic, and political conflicts of the citizenry. Although traditional theories of the state have tended to concentrate upon the agencies of central government, I include not only central government, legislatures, and their attendant bureaucracies, but also the criminal justice/legal system, welfare services, education, and health service delivery. The state does not simply impose "itself" on the citizenry in a monolithic manner. Rather, the ever-changing interface between the state and civil society is a contested one. State policies are molded out of the white heat of political conflict. This white heat derives from numerous intersecting struggles among social classes, gender groups, races, and ethnic groups.

There is a growing body of literature that addresses the way in which the modern state reproduces patriarchal relations.[3] Feminists such as Ehrenreich and Fox Piven (1983) and Fox Piven (1990) have argued the patriarchal state does not neatly and unproblematically reproduce the power relations of gender. Rather, the patriarchal state acts in contradictory ways in managing gender relations, and women themselves play an active role in influencing and formulating state policies as both activists (see Gagne, 1996) and consumers of state services (see Fox Piven, 1990, p. 250 and n. 3; Gordon, 1988). Fox Piven, citing survey data, states the mass of American women appear to have "a belief in the strong and interventionist state" (p. 250). She goes on to add, "I think the main opportunities for women to exercise power today inhere precisely in their 'dependent' relationships with the state" (pp. 250-251).

I have already discussed the ways in which the law enforcement and judicial handling of domestic cases reinforce rural patriarchy. In this chapter, I focus on the acute difficulties rural battered women experience in utilizing the limited but potentially supportive services of the interventionist patriarchal state. These acute difficulties and limited state provisions perpetuate, in a complex and often contradictory manner, the power relations of rural patriarchy.

Rural Woman Battering and the Patriarchal State

The nature of state intervention in rural communities bears directly upon the well-being of women who live in violent relationships with men. There is tremendous variation among rural regions in Kentucky. In general, rural Eastern Kentucky counties have much lower tax bases and are less able to provide a range of services to citizens. However, by their very nature, rural communities do share certain characteristics that make them less accessible, amenable, or both, to state intervention. I specifically address those aspects of the state service delivery that directly impact rural battered women.

Transportation

The low tax base in rural areas, the great distances to be covered, and the relatively small number of people puts the provision of public transportation out of the reach of rural governments. According to Seroka (1986), what rural voters want most from local government are adequate roads, sewers, garbage disposal, education, public health, ambulance services, police, libraries, fire protection, welfare, and the minimum of administrative staff to oversee their provision. The desire to have a minimum of administrative staff is consistent with a more generalized suspicion of government of all kinds and reflects the historical legacy of self-sufficiency that harks back to days when agriculture was the mainstay of the rural economy.

Taxi services are also difficult to access, even assuming battered women could afford to pay for such private transport or that women would feel safe riding taxis. Taken alongside the fact that in many violent relationships men will control, limit, or scrutinize women's use of "family" vehicles, the lack of public transportation is a particularly acute impediment for rural women. Many women conveyed their frustration about their inability to move themselves and their children out of their violent rural homes. Rural battered women's general physical immobility is a metaphor for their sociocultural isolation. In cases of extreme geographical isolation, the inability to escape may be an important contributor to women's vulnerability to lethal violence or to their strategizing about using lethal violence themselves as a form of self-defense.

Health Care

As Bushy (1993) points out, the health status of rural women is a much neglected topic (p. 187). While the medical research literature now recognizes woman battering as a major medical/public health problem,[4] it has yet to explore the health care needs of rural battered women. This is unfortunate because rural women face unique difficulties in accessing health care. In spite of the fact that a significant number of emergency room visits by women stem from battering (see Stark et al., 1979), the lack of confidentiality of health care delivery to rural battered women has not been addressed as a major issue. Many women I talked with said they did not feel confident they could obtain confidential medical care. Given the fact that people know each other's business more in smaller communities, women expressed great reluctance to entrust health care providers with the (sometimes shameful) fact that they were being battered. Sharing such information and knowing that it could get back to their abusers is a sufficient enough deterrent to accessing health care for a number of interviewees.

These concerns about lack of privacy are far outweighed by the paucity of medical/health services in rural communities.[5] Health services are particularly scarce in rural Kentucky, and people often have to travel long distances to see a physician. The Hill-Burton Act mandated that people must be treated at emergency rooms and that lack of medical insurance should no longer be a reason for not treating someone. For many battered women who did not have medical insurance, emergency rooms became the sites for the receipt of primary medical care. However, rural battered women often still feel vulnerable at hospital emergency rooms because of the lack of privacy.[6] As Stark and Flitcraft (1996) point out, the hospital emergency room has increasingly become the sole source of medical assistance for the "the poor, minorities, and large segments of the white working class" (p. 7). Given the acute poverty of most of the rural women I interviewed, reliance upon emergency room services in the aftermath of assault is often the only health care option available. It is clear from my interviews with police officers that they, too, see the emergency room as the automatic recourse for many rural women whom the officer perceives need medical assistance. The lack of confidentiality that battered women report at emergency rooms is therefore a critical issue in rural communities.

Many shelter workers in Kentucky also complain about the unwillingness of physicians to intervene or report cases of spousal abuse (as they are required to do by law). Likewise, many rural physicians appear to be unfamiliar with the dynamics of domestic violence. This unfamiliarity reflects a lack of training, but may also be linked to the rural patriarchal imperative that domestic violence belongs within families, rather than out in the open. Research based on urban centers shows that physicians are able to identify something like only 1 battered female patient in 25 (see Jones, 1994, p. 146). Whether or not rural physicians would fare better in their ability to discern battering remains to be seen. In my interview with Miranda, she described her very negative interaction with her local physician. She visited the physician to obtain birth control pills because she did not want to become pregnant again. Miranda was forced to have sex with her husband on numerous occasions. She told her physician she did not want to have more children and that her husband could "go all night long." Rather than asking whether Miranda was comfortable with having sex "all night long," or having sex at all with her partner, the physician laughingly asks what her abuser drinks. He then remarks that such a concoction might benefit him and enable him to perform longer in his own sex life.

> *Miranda:* The doctor laughed at me when I went back on birth control pills. I told him, I said "I don't want to bring another child into the world because my husband drinks all the time." And I said "he can go all night long." And the doctor thought that was real funny.
>
> *Websdale:* What do you mean?
>
> *Miranda:* He said, "What does he drink?" You know he said "maybe it could make me go all night long. Make love all night long." I would be so sore and raw that I could not walk sometimes. And so the doctor, when I said you know, "I can't do anything with him. He won't use protection or anything." And I begged for pills. And he said really. "What does he drink?" And I said "He drinks Kessler oil. Kessler whiskey." It's that sickening sweet smell. I hate that smell.

The inadequate delivery of rural health care services is particularly acute with regard to women's reproductive health. Given what some women describe as an attempt by abusers to keep them "barefoot and pregnant," the provision of safe abortion services is of great importance to some battered women. In spite of a general lack of information about the availability of abortion services in Kentucky, a significant number of rural battered women I talked with or heard of, considered having abortions at some point in their lives. Of those rural women, very few actually followed through and terminated unwanted pregnancies. The reasons for this appear to be complex and seem to vary somewhat by region of the state. The single biggest reason is the fact that abortion services are essentially only available in major urban areas such as Louisville, Lexington, and neighboring cities such as Cincinnati and Nashville. For rural women, the prospect of getting to these centers is often daunting.[7]

In my conversations with key informants, it is clear that religious values play a key role in the formulation of views about abortion services. It is difficult to say how these views play out across rural and urban regions of the state. Most informants agree that in regions where churches are more independent of mainstream denominations, and where conditions exist under which congregation members are freer to make their own pacts with their God, women's decisions to have an abortion are more likely to be respected. I found these kinds of churches more often in Eastern Kentucky. Ironically, given the general dearth of resources in Eastern Kentucky, we may find a cultural/religious climate that is more tolerant of rural battered women seeking abortions. Dolores, who grew up in Eastern Kentucky and had been involved in the early shelter movement there, had a number of contacts in the field of health services. She commented:

> *Dolores:* That element of the independence, and wanting to be off to yourself and left alone, that's still there. I think it's real interesting when you start looking at issues like abortion. If you talk to Eastern Kentuckians about that, even some fundamentalists, many will say, "It's a sin." But they'll also say, "It's nobody's damn business whether you have one or not. That's between you and your God." That is not something the government should regulate and the pro-lifers should get out of their faces because it's an individual choice. They'll say, "I don't believe in it. I think it's a sin. But it's not my place to tell you that."

In Western Kentucky, for example, a number of informants said that churches tend to be more mainstream than those in Eastern Kentucky and leave less to the individual in terms of them making "pacts with God." As Hanna put it:

Hanna: Western Kentucky churches tend to be more "big-brotherish" and play a bigger role in social life. They penetrate general cultural life much more. This is true for Protestant as well as Catholic churches. In Eastern Kentucky, there are more "charismatic" churches.

Rural battered women's access to abortion services is therefore influenced by a number of factors. Of major importance is the general dearth of health services, including access to abortion. This lack of access is bolstered by a patriarchal ideology, particularly acute perhaps in rural areas, that says that women should be barefoot and pregnant. However, we can see from the general discussion that this absence of rural reproductive rights is also fractured by regional cultural nuances and particularly the importance of different shades of religious affiliation.

Social Services

A key issue in the lives of rural women is the choice that they may have between leaving violent men and working the welfare land mines of the patriarchal state. For rural women this can be a crucially important dilemma because of their relative lack of educational qualifications, job opportunities, transportation options, and child care provisions. In rural communities, if women do decide to leave violent men, they have a choice between finding wage work to feed their children or relying on the shrinking provision of state aid.[8] Given the dearth of well-paid jobs in rural communities and the expansion of minimum wage service sector jobs, many women who leave violent relationships opt for state aid so they can parent their children.

Rural battered women report that seeking state assistance often involves interacting with people they know at social services departments. These social services personnel either do not understand battered women's plight or have little sympathy for welfare recipients in general.[9] It could be that the receipt of state aid in some rural areas is more problematic because of the presence of stronger antigovernment sentiments and widespread beliefs that rural folks "make it on their own." In addition, social services in rural communities tend to be underfunded and more difficult to access than in urban centers (see Bogal-Allbritten & Daughaday, 1990; Olsen, 1988; Reid & Whitehead, 1982; Yoder, 1980).

As Abramovitz (1994) and others have pointed out, the past 15 years have witnessed an intensification of right-wing ideology that essentially blames the poor for their own plight (see, e.g., Murray, 1984). Some rural women report that not only do some social service providers stigmatize them because they are poor, but also that those same providers implicitly accuse women of being accomplices to their own intimate victimization by lacking the willpower to leave. Of the rural battered women I interviewed, eight had negative experiences with social services departments or individual social workers and five reported positive experiences.[10]

Stephanie, a battered woman from a small community in central Kentucky, talked about the provision of social services. Her lengthy comments mirror those of many rural women I talked with about the provision of state aid. Note how Stephanie weaves a complex account of the ceremonies of degradation that she endures at the hands of the state, and the limited options she has.

> *Stephanie:* And you apply for aid from social services. And when you come out you get pennies. So what do you do? If you go get a job what happens? Then you lose what little pennies you have and you still don't have nothing. So it's really scary. You might only get beat twice a week but you have a roof over your head. Or you practically have to live in the slums. And you're trying to fight and make sure your kids don't stay on drugs but they're wallowing in that crap because you can't afford to get them out of it. So it's really frustrating, you know, that's why I stayed with him as long as I did. Even though he only worked part time, the money he made was good.
>
> You're trapped when you go out and try to get help and they demean you and make you feel like that you're a low life. Lots of people don't want to be in there. Don't want to be on welfare. They want to get off. I know I can make it in this world and I'm going to. One way or another I'll make it and my children will make it. If I didn't have my children, I don't know where I would be. Maybe out prostituting. I don't know. You do what you have to do. It's survival, that's all it is. Bottom line. And I survived for years living with that man, so I can survive now. But I just wish we had more support, I really do.

Social worker Stern exhibited more than a hint of victim blaming in her attitude toward battered women. We talked at length about this issue in the tiny and profoundly depressed town of Simpson in Eastern Kentucky.[11]

> *Stern:* I have a case that I worked with in this county for years and years. And the spouse abuse shelter sees this particular woman and they're gonna help her. They're gonna work with her. I have seen her come and go into this home 13, 14, 15 times. Drag the kids out. Drag the kids back. It's not that I'm not supportive of her, I just decided this was gonna stop. But he [the abuser] is not necessarily the whole problem. . . . You have to decide that these women do not have halos on. You'd know if you've ever seen them in action. . . . My biggest thing is that everyone is responsible. We make choices, as adults. And those women have to learn that. I don't think we are doing them a favor, whether we're the spouse abuse shelter or social services, if we pat them on the back and say, "honey, we know you went back because you really love him." It's not okay to do just because it's part of that cycle of violence. They have children, heck with it. They are gonna have to establish their home elsewhere and do what's right to protect those children, to get my support. I'm gonna support 'em as far as understanding the cycle, but I'm not gonna let that be an excuse for them.

In social worker Stern's words we witness some of the popular misconceptions about battered women. Somehow Stern expects the battered woman she is talking about to draw upon the same kinds of choices that Stern thinks "rational people" employ. Stern's logic is reminiscent of the police officer who could not understand why battered women "return their hand to the flame once they've been burned," or the judge who saw returning victims as "stupid."

For Stern, the family in this case was "dysfunctional." One of the reasons the husband battered the wife was because he was unemployed and stressed. In this particular case, the violence was essentially an expression of marital discord that has at its root multiple causes. Stern's approach to social work recalls Stark and Flitcraft's (1996) observation that often in cases of woman battering, "the social worker discovers what he or she has been trained to expect from the beginning, the multiproblem family" (p. 24). By definition, the violence in these families is part of a constellation of pathologies, and woman battering cannot therefore constitute the principal cause for intervention.

Tonya talked extensively of her negative experiences with social services. After leaving her abusive husband she later found out that their young daughter had contracted oral herpes as a result of being molested by her father. On contacting social services she ran into a number of roadblocks.

> *Tonya:* Social services took over. The woman that I dealt with completely amazed me with her attitude when I told her my suspicions toward my husband. I had reason to believe that he had abused her because of the way my daughter reacted to him at times. Things that were going on. I could attribute it to other things, but this just kept coming back. And her attitude was, before she even talked to him, was that, he didn't do it. Just plain out, he did not do this. You are doing this because you hate him.

Belinda reported that her father-in-law's hostility to government in general, but social services in particular, effectively stopped social workers from attending her residence.

> *Belinda:* Social Services has been down there. They're scared because he threatens 'em. My father-in-law, you know, it's his property. And he's like, "You don't step on this property or I'll blow your head off." And they won't come around.

This type of outright hostility to social services is probably more pronounced in rural communities. In Belinda's case we see almost a siege mentality on her father-in-law's part, or at least deeply felt residues of what Weber (1948) describes as the power of the master under traditional patriarchy to control and dispose of his property.

However, while more women I talked with reported being dissatisfied with social services, some women mentioned that they had very positive relationships with social workers. Elizabeth felt that her social worker showed genuine concern for her plight.

> *Elizabeth:* It was just me and Jason and I was gettin' $196 from AFDC and I was payin' $170 in rent. And that's all I had left.

And if it wasn't for a worker at Social Services helping me I don't know how I would have made it. She's been real nice to me, she always checked upon me. I felt that it wasn't just to be nosy or anything. I always felt that it was out of concern.

Margaret first reported her victimization to a social worker who hooked her up with the shelter. Margaret was pleased with the response of social services. She broke away from her violent husband, obtained AFDC and food stamps, and moved into subsidized Section 8 housing. With these meager but very meaningful provisions, Margaret felt empowered to the point that she could better survive with her children independently of her violent husband.

> *Websdale:* How did you find Social Services?
> *Margaret:* They was very helpful.

At a crucial moment in Anita's domestic violence hearing, her social worker supported her by raising her abuser's previous use of violence.

> *Anita:* Thank God the social worker spoke up for me and said, "Your Honor, Mr. Wilson has a previous history of domestic abuse."

I close this discussion of social services for rural battered women by reiterating perhaps the most important finding of all from the interviews: namely, that more than half of the women I talked with had no contact at all with social workers or social services in general. This lack of contact partially reflects the difficulties many rural women have in accessing these services. However, it also mirrors the failure of rural social service providers to get beyond seeing battered women as a "problem" and to identify male violence as a political issue. As part of a stinging critique of local social service providers, one spouse abuse shelter director observed,

> You try getting a social services worker after hours. They'll tell you it is because they are overburdened with cases. But the bottom line is those social service providers, and particularly the administrators, can't tolerate battered women making their own decisions. Kentucky is the only state that mandates that adult familial abuse be reported.

Yet very few social services workers actually work with battered
women. . . . Even although we at the shelter are mandated to report
women's victimization.

Lack of Child Care Services

Rural patriarchal ideology recommends that women live out a
biological destiny and not only bear, but also care for, children. This
ideology, stronger in some parts of rural Kentucky than others, makes
it more difficult for women to seek employment outside the home and
leave their children in child care. If rural battered women want to leave
violent relationships, then one thing they will often consider is the
possibility of surviving independent of a male's wage. One of the
things they must factor in here is the availability of suitable wage work
and the availability of child care. Even if rural women want to work
for wages from within a battering relationship, in order to gain some
degree of independence or to plan their escape child care is also
essential.

In Kentucky, there are fewer regulated day care facilities than in
any other state. In 1988, 15 of Kentucky's 120 counties had no
licensed day care facilities and 45 counties had no licensed family day
care homes (see Stewart & Payne, 1991, p. 32). Consequently, even
if battered women do leave their abusers and do have the chance to
engage in wage work, the lack of adequate day care facilities will
seriously limit their ability to take those jobs. Without the financial
contribution of the male's wage, women's prospects of surviving
independently are bleak in any economy that underpays them and
makes little provision for child care. As I have already pointed out,
rural battered women's "choices" often boil down to remaining with
abusers and enduring/resisting violence, leaving the abuser and enduring poverty under the welfare system, or leaving the abuser and
entering wage work in a hostile gendered capitalist economy. If
women elect the last "option," they must give up, often for the first
time, their everyday job of parenting their children. For some women,
this possibility pushes them more toward the welfare option.

Religion as Patriarchal Ideology

Sociologists have long debated the significance of religion in social
life. Emile Durkheim (1961) believed that religion contributed to the

maintenance of the collective conscience and therefore to social solidarity. Other theorists such as Marx saw a more sinister role for religion insofar as it acted as an opiate for the masses, a means of dulling the pain visited upon the growing working class by the rigors of capitalist production. The ascendant bourgeoisie also uses religion to justify its dominant position as ordained by God. However, neo-Marxists, among others, have also pointed to the relative autonomy of religion from the economic system and have highlighted the way in which religion can also be a source of revolutionary change (see Larrea Gayarre, 1994; Maduro, 1982).

Like some Marxist authors, some feminists also argue that religion acts as a mechanism of social control. Daly (1979) identifies religion as one of the dominant belief systems that authorizes diverse practices including foot binding in China, *suttee* or widow burning in India, clitoridectomy in Africa, and witch burning in medieval Europe. These practices are parlayed as being beneficial to women, but are ultimately of benefit to men and serve to reproduce patriarchy.[12] A number of other authors have also pointed to the role of the church and fundamentalist religion as disseminators of patriarchal ideology (see Kuczynski, 1981; Navin et al., 1993; Whipple, 1987). Several studies have highlighted how members of the clergy have failed to support battered women (see Alsdurf & Alsdurf, 1989; Bowker, 1983; Stacey & Shupe, 1983). Bowker (1983) found that battered women ranked clergy last on a list of those people they had turned to for help.

In my discussion of the judicial disposition of domestic cases and the availability of abortion services for rural women, I have already pointed to the significance of religious values in rural communities in Kentucky. As Miller (1994) notes, residents in Kentucky's most urban counties (Jefferson, Fayette, Kenton, Campbell, and Boone) were more likely than those from rural counties to report that the notion of maintaining a separation of church and state still applied (p. 73). She comments, "sentiment in Kentucky generally does not separate religion from the state's control of individual behavior" (p. 73).

Put simply, religious influences seem to be stronger in rural communities and appear to be more likely to work against battered women leaving violent men. These influences sometimes include local preachers who advise battered women to "weather the storm" with their abusers. The religious rationale behind discouraging women from leaving is often pitched in terms of maintaining the sanctity of the marital bond and also in terms of wives (not husbands) fulfilling their duty to stay in the marriage. In the "stay at all costs" imperative of rural religious doctrine we see parallels with the patriarchal legal code that has always recommended judges protect the marital bond.

Interviewees reported the strong influence of religion in social and cultural life in Kentucky. One rural police chief, Jones, who won a federal grant to work on the policing of rural domestic violence, used some of the money to print pamphlets for distribution to women. One of the key points he made in the pamphlet concerned the erroneousness of religious beliefs that argued that battered married women should remain with abusive men.[13] These beliefs, Jones noted, were more prevalent in remote rural areas.

Likewise, some battered women themselves reported the influence of religion on family values. Kindra saw her mother-in-law as being strongly influenced by religion and the family as a whole believing that marriages should last forever, whatever the problems.

Kindra: I think it has a lot to do with the religious beliefs of their mom.

Social worker Stern identified religious beliefs as being central to dilemmas faced by rural battered women. Note how the language of commitment, love, loyalty, and violence intersect with the demoralizing and debilitating effects of poverty and unemployment.

Stern: She's right there with the black eye. He's sitting right there, wringing his hands. State trooper standin' behind her. And she says, "nope, I fell." It's not acceptable to report spouse abuse. . . . It's, "you made your bed, you've got to lie in it." This is a religious/moral issue in Eastern Kentucky. "You took him for better or for worse and he's just goin' through a rough time." I've heard this a thousand times. "You know what it means to be a man, to be the breadwinner in the home. And it's very difficult during these times of unemployment. And it's very difficult when you're financially strained. You take it out on the people that you love the most. That's why he's beatin' her." This way of understanding domestic violence is a very important part of our culture. And it's not something that's just going to go away. Regardless of all the education regarding the reporting of abuse.

Stern's comments on the role of religion in the social control of rural battered women are important. From my ethnographic findings it is clear that religious influences can be a potent part of that constellation of patriarchal beliefs that make it more difficult for rural battered women to leave their abusers. That same patriarchal ideology also impacts the way women in general, and rural women in particular, infiltrate the ranks of formal political life. It is in the direction of the public sphere of formal politics that I now turn.

Formal Politics

Patricia Gagne (1996) shows how networks of feminists in state government in Ohio helped facilitate the granting of clemency to 26 women incarcerated for killing or assaulting abusive intimate partners or stepfathers. Using their careers and personal contacts, these feminists created new "democratic spaces" and allowed incarcerated women greater access to the authorities and the general public. Put simply, the activism of women in state government made a real difference to the lives of these 26 incarcerated women and their families. Gagne's research reminds us that the presence of feminist activists in state government can effect real changes in what may appear to be the iron cage of patriarchy. Indeed, the presence of women in positions of government may increase the likelihood that women's issues, particularly those relating to violence against women, will receive a more sympathetic or indeed empathetic ear.[14]

Attorney Shepherd identified a similar network of feminist women in Kentucky who work together on women's issues. Shepherd, who has been active in defending women who have killed their abusers, talked at length about the highly significant role of networking among Kentucky feminists to secure the release of 11 women incarcerated for killing their abusers.[15] My research indicates that, as it is in Ohio, such a feminist network is alive and well in Kentucky. In April 1995, Marsha Weinstein, then executive director of the Kentucky Commission on Women, contacted her predecessor Helen Howard Hughes, then head of the Kentucky Parole Board, to see if a number of women incarcerated for killing violent spouses or partners could be pardoned or have their sentences commuted.[16] During her time as executive director of the Kentucky Commission on Women, Helen Howard Hughes had received federal funding to conduct research on domestic violence and was familiar with the dynamics of domestic violence. At the same time as these developments were taking place, Chandra McElroy, a correctional counselor at the Kentucky Correctional Institution for Women (Pe Wee Valley), formed a support group for those incarcerated women who had been abused by their partners and had either killed or assaulted those partners. At the suggestion of Marsha Weinstein, this group of incarcerated women set about constructing a quilt depicting their life experiences, including their victimization. Weinstein saw the quilt as a traditional way in which "silenced" women had always communicated with each other and the world, and felt such a conjunction of art and politics would bode well for the incarcerated women. The finished product was a very moving and disturbing piece of folk art. Marsha Weinstein arranged for the public display of the quilt at the Kentucky State Fair, and also "arranged for" Governor Jones and his wife to pass by the display. According to a number of key informants, Governor Jones was deeply moved by the experience and said something to the effect that "we have to do something about the plight of these women." A number of informants commented that Governor Jones was not just engaging in political posturing, but was genuinely disturbed by what he saw. One informant, who met with Jones over the release of the women, commented,

> I thought I was going to meet a real dick of a politician. But Jones was deeply moved. In fact, before Jones appeared on the *Donahue Show* he had never met the women whose sentences he commuted and he was concerned that he would be so moved that he would cry on national television.

The female attorneys who acted on behalf of the incarcerated women are also part of this feminist advocacy network in Kentucky. Knowing that parole boards liked to see remorseful, humble inmates who acknowledge their own guilt but also ask for mercy, these attorneys worked behind the scenes to prepare their clients appropriately for their hearings. However, as a key informant at the KDVA put it,

> Much of the credit for the commutations must go to the incarcerated women themselves, who actively engaged Chandra and who brought a number of other [feminist] players onto the scene.

My point in citing this example, and its parallels with what Gagne found in Ohio, is that networks of women in professional positions and political office, together with the courage and resistance of the incarcerated women themselves, effected unprecedented social change in Kentucky.

We should not read into the above account that the formal political system in Kentucky is a haven of feminist activism. Women are heavily underrepresented among those holding political office. In 1992, Kentucky ranked last among the states, with only 6 women out of 138 legislators (5 in the house and only 1 in the state senate). Across the United States, nearly one fifth of legislators are women. In the U.S. Congress in 1992, the number of women senators rose from three to six, while women representatives in the House rose from 28 to 47. In Kentucky, both the proportion and number of women legislators actually decreased in 1992, from nine to six. At the time of writing there are two women in the State Senate and nine in House of Representatives. These women can hardly be described as feminist activists. The two women senators were both elected as pro-life, as opposed to pro-choice, candidates. For Senator Tori (Republican), the abortion issue is entirely distinct from domestic violence, which she sees as a bi-partisan issue. Senator Tori, who sat on the Legislative Task Force on Domestic Violence, supported all of the domestic violence legislation introduced during the 1996 legislative session.[17] Of the nine women currently serving in the House of Representatives, four were elected on what one key informant describes as a leftist (for Kentucky) /feminist or pro-feminist ticket. All of these women are from urban centers (one from Lexington and three from Louisville). The other five, like the two senators, are pro-life politicians.[18] According-ing to advocate Mellow, the underrepresentation of women, and particularly the dearth of a substantial feminist voice in formal politics, mirrors the much broader traditionalist condition of women in Ken-tucky. By *traditionalist,* Mellow is referring to men and women adhering to more stereotypical gender roles. Note how Mellow links this traditionalism with the rural nature of Kentucky.

Websdale: How do you see the condition of women in this state?
Mellow: I think this state is very traditional. We're very rural and
we've got a very poorly educated population. You know my
feeling. I would never say this publicly, but my feeling is that

the more traditional the state is, the more oppression you have. I think it's pretty appalling in parts of the state. You know, I spent eight years going to state legislatures around the country. And I have never seen this level of stereotyping. It's very paternalistic. Women in elected office in Kentucky are not taken seriously.

Advocate Mellow is also of the opinion that merely having women in positions of power in government or in the professions does not necessarily favor women. One woman senator that advocate Mellow had worked with over the years had herself been a battered woman. This senator initially opposed shelters for battered women, arguing that she herself had made it out of the relationship, so other women should also do so without shelters. Mellow feels that her concerns about women office holders not acting in the interests of women, particularly poor and minority women, are borne out by the case of women district judges. Of the 17 women district judges in Kentucky, Mellow feels that half are really in tune with women's issues and do a "fine job" of disposing of domestics. The other half, however, are "among the worst judges in the state when it comes to disposing of domestics."

Advocate Mellow did acknowledge the roll of women legislators in supporting the 1992 and 1996 domestic violence legislation. However, Mellow attributes the passage of the extensive 1992 legislation largely to battered and other women who called legislators to pressure them to pass the new laws. This telephone campaign was orchestrated through the shelters and relied upon a network of women contacting other women.

Mellow: The bottom line is, the reason we passed the 1992 legislation is because five thousand women made phone calls to their legislators in a three-day period. You know, we had the momentum going into it. The press has claimed credit for it. I have some concerns about that. I think there were lots of people involved. Lots of people did great. We did something pretty remarkable. I mean, when we went in to see legislators, they basically said, "you guys have the momentum, we have to pass something." I think the bottom line on all of this, is, as I'm sure you know, I think there is so much more domestic violence than we know of. There are too many women, too moved by it.

Mellow's observations and those of a number of other interviewees on the importance the 1992 telephone campaign, reminds us
that the state is not a monolithic entity that neatly and invariably
reproduces patriarchal interests. Amid the ol' boy latticework there
are spaces that disadvantaged women, in concert with feminist activists, can work to the advantage of all women.

Rural Spouse Abuse Shelters

Along with the KDVA and the Kentucky Commission on Women,
the spouse abuse shelters in Kentucky are agencies that work specifically
on behalf of women's interests. Borrowing from McBride-Stetson and
Mazur (1995), I describe these state and local-level organizations as
agencies of "state feminism." While these authors use the term to refer
specifically to those structures of government "that are formally charged
with furthering women's status and rights" (pp. 1-2), I extend its use to
encompass spouse abuse shelters and organizations such as the KDVA.
The former local agencies are not elements of governmental structure.
The latter engages in considerable lobbying work and is clearly influential
in the formulation of governmental policies, although it is funded by the
constituent shelters and not directly by the state of Kentucky.

Each year the state of Kentucky distributes roughly $4 million to
15 spouse abuse shelters. The level of funding per shelter differs
according to the number of clients served and various demographic
features of the region serviced by the shelter. The urban shelters were
formed first in Kentucky and took the lion's share of the funding until
the later 1980s. According to one key informant, nine of the rural shelters
got together and strategized about how to obtain a greater share of state
funds. Their voting power within the KDVA enabled them to effect a
significant redistribution of state funds in favor of rural shelters.[19]
Nevertheless, levels of funding for both rural and urban shelters in
Kentucky are pitifully low. As advocate Mellow puts it:

> *Mellow:* State funding for shelters in Kentucky amounts to next
> to nothing, especially when you compare it with what the state
> is spending on prisons.

Poorly paid shelter staff working in extremely difficult situations
in rural Kentucky complain bitterly about the funding priorities of the

state. For these workers, some funding is better than no funding. Most battered women I talked with saw the poorly provided shelters as highly beneficial to women residents. For example, Lisa told me that one shelter made all the difference in her life.

> *Lisa:* I got into public housing and the shelter helped me get set up on food stamps and AFDC. They told me about different programs around here like the jobs program and JTPA. And I've got signed up on all of them. Now I have an apartment, a home. I have a car now. I go to school and I'm taking very good care of my kids. I've got more stuff now than I have ever had.

A number of advocates informed me that the level of funding for shelters is such that politicians and state bureaucrats can point to it as if the problem of domestic violence is being addressed. The overwhelming majority of shelter directors and advocates for battered women argue that state funding is tokenistic. For director Johnson, who runs a rural spouse abuse shelter, the paucity of state funding is indicative of the differential life value attached to women and children:

> *Johnson:* Women and children have no value. You can always have more kids and get another wife. Wives and children are disposable commodities.

The closeting away of those traditionally devalued and victimized groups such as battered women, recalls those steps taken to secrete away slaves. Ann Jones (1994) compares the subterranean and covert traffic in battered women and their children to the underground railroad used to assist slaves in their escape from bondage. "In fact, the worst-case scenarios in both institutions, slavery and marriage, are grimly similar, right down to and including rape, torture, mutilation, and murder" (p. 10).

I traveled to all 15 shelters in Kentucky during the course of my ethnographic research, and it was clear that shelters in rural regions of the state were in the poorest physical condition. At one particularly ramshackle rural shelter, a shelter worker pointedly asked me, "Would you like to stay in a place like this, even for a short time?" Her question invites the obvious response: that these shelters are designed to "service" poor battered women who have no Visa card and few economic options. In other words, there is a social class, as well as a gender edge, to the provision of shelter services in rural Kentucky.[20]

While objecting to the inadequate levels of state funding, most rural shelter workers acknowledge that shelters do provide a temporary safe haven for battered women. In so doing, spouse abuse shelters symbolize a more generalized resistance to the patriarchal order. Women in shelter have a chance to reflect on their plight and strategize about their violent relationships, often with the informed support of shelter employees and other like-situated women. However, not all shelters are able to offer the same services. My ethnographic research findings are similar to those of Karen Tice (1990), who observes some of the difficulties organizing shelters in rural Appalachia. Among these difficulties she includes the general sociocultural climate that discourages women from leaving violent men, the lack of established feminist networks, and the lack of "alternative" service providers beyond those bureaucracies of state and local government. Although Kentucky shelters serve women from an average of eight counties, usually at least half of rural shelter residents are drawn from the counties in which the shelters are located. Outreach services to women in satellite counties are hindered by the geographical and sociocultural isolation of those communities and the general lack of state funding for rural shelters.

Divorce

The right of a woman to obtain a divorce and secure the custody of her children was a classic right fought for by 19th-century feminists. The long tradition of the English state refusing to grant divorces to any but a few wealthy women (by Act of Parliament) was added confirmation that marriage was a lifelong institution. The logic of the patriarchal state was that women "chose" to marry and should remain married regardless of how unbearable or brutal it was. The husband, as we have seen, had extensive rights over his wife and children. This legal tyranny continued in the United States, even in some of the more "progressive" states such as Oregon, which at least espoused a greater sensitivity to married women's legal rights (see Websdale, 1992).

The extension of divorce rights to married women is one of the most significant historical changes in the structure of patriarchal relations. However, as Carol Smart (1989) and numerous others[21] have warned, legal change is double edged and often ends up benefiting the institution of law itself more than those poised allegedly to benefit from the changes. Indeed, Smart argues that the

> law is so deaf to core concerns of feminism that feminists should be extremely cautious of how and whether they resort to law. . . . We need to be far more aware of the malevolence of law and the depth of its resistance to women's concerns. (p. 2)

These warnings about law and its patriarchal leanings are especially pertinent when it comes to the issue of divorce in Kentucky. It is one thing to enjoy a "right" and another thing entirely to be able to exercise it. In rural Kentucky it is possible for battered women to obtain a divorce if they have the financial and emotional resources to do so. I noted in Chapter 1 how dangerous it can be for a rural battered woman to assert her right to leave the marital relationship and seek divorce. The risk of lethal violence seems to be higher in rural communities, especially if the victim of violence is seeking divorce. It is more difficult for her to escape her influence completely and at the same time more difficult to survive independently in rural communities. With community pressure to stay together, combined with the more traditional view of men that women "belong" to them forever, leaving violent men is hazardous for rural women.

In small rural communities, there is a very long waiting list for legal aid. Many battered women complain about the time it takes the state to support women to leave violent marriages. Although attorneys are encouraged to do a certain amount of pro bono work, insufficient numbers work to secure divorces for battered women. As one advocate/ key informant put it to me,

> If you get a divorce, you can bet on being poor, and you can bet on him not paying child support, even if he is able to.

It is well documented that getting divorced usually results in a decline in the material living standards of women who go on to head up families (see Garfinkel & McLanahan, 1986; Hoffman & Duncan, 1988). As Paula Roberts (1994) explains,

> Today 40 percent of custodial mothers still don't have a child-support award. They don't even make it into the system because they can't get a lawyer to handle their cases. Of the remaining 60 percent who have managed to get an award, only half actually collect what is owed.

. . . Only about one-third of custodial mothers receive child support
as a regular source of income. (p. 78)

The provision of child support through court ordered payments
often depends upon the financial status of the father. Typically, the
custodial mother who receives the most support is white and college
educated. This class discrepancy also holds for more intangible forms
of support. For example, Jay Teachman (1991) found that fathers who
do contribute in various ways to their children's upbringing (especially
ways that involve direct participation; such as helping with
homework, attending school events) have more economic resources
in general and also enjoy a better relationship with their ex-wives.

All of these findings are consistent with my ethnographic data
which show that abusive husbands who live in impoverished rural
communities, especially in rural Eastern Kentucky, make very little
provision for their children once their wives and children have left
them. This lack of provision is one reason why many rural women in
Kentucky just leave their abusers without even bothering to file for
divorce. These women know of the difficulties of filing, the costs
involved, and the meager returns on the venture.

Women also know that if they live at home and their husbands
are out working for wages, attorneys are very reluctant to take
women's cases on a contingency basis for fear of not being paid. In
rural communities, those women who may be able to afford attorney's
fees sometimes find themselves competing for attorneys with their
husbands. One shelter director reported that "the best attorney in
town would not take a battered woman's divorce case because he was
personal friends with the abuser."

Given rural women's reluctance to seek divorce, the obtaining of
a Domestic Violence Order of Protection assumes much greater significance. The DVO in many ways serves the same functions as a
divorce decree, with the exception that it does not permit the woman
to marry again. While DVOs are no guarantee of protection, they do
remove some of the tension that attends the formal dissolution of rural
marriages. In some respects the DVO, in contrast to formal divorce,
may be less likely to enrage violent men toward acts of homicide or
homicide-suicide. For rural women and many other poor women in
Kentucky, divorce law is wholly out of touch with women's needs.
Given that one of the original reasons for seeking divorce was to allow
women to escape violent husbands, it is somewhat ironic that it is the

domestic violence laws that offer many rural women a more viable means of escaping violence than actual divorce itself.

Conclusion

I described some of the intricacies and idiosyncrasies of the state management of interpersonal violence against women. In spite of the fact that the concept of the modern state is predicated upon the structure of the patriarchal family, I emphasize the complex and contradictory workings of the state. My ethnography reveals that both battered women and activists have a key role to play in the formulation of some state policies that directly impact rural women. One of the defining qualities of rural patriarchy is the isolation that it visits upon battered women. Rural women's physical and sociocultural isolation is also embedded in the general impoverishment of some rural regions that experience a dearth of state supports such as public transportation, health care, and social services. When combined with the scarcity of licensed child care, the difficulties in obtaining affordable legal services in divorce cases, and the lack of representation of women through the machinery of formal politics, the picture looks pretty dismal for battered women who want to leave violent men. On the other hand, agents of state feminism clearly work for women's interests. A number of women reported receiving considerable support in their passage to a new life from spouse abuse shelters and, more indirectly, the KDVA. Although limited in number, some women did report that social workers helped them and acted to hook them up with a variety of state services. The problem with the provision of state services to rural battered women is twofold: First, services are wholly inadequate for the task at hand; second, they are often delivered in a manner that tends to revictimize battered women. In the next chapter, I will explore some of these problems and suggest some social policies that will address both the paucity and the patriarchal delivery of services.

Notes

1. Ralph Miliband (1969), in proposing an "instrumentalist" view of the capitalist state, sees the state acting directly as the tool or instrument of the bourgeoisie. In particular, Miliband emphasizes the role of the personnel who "man" the state apparatus.

These personnel come from the bourgeoisie or have been socialized to support the bourgeois class. Althusser (1966) and Poulantzas (1973) argue a "structuralist" model of the state, which recognizes the relative autonomy of the state from the bourgeoisie. Put simply, the capitalist state is somewhat distanced from the ruling class. This distancing is not sufficient to frustrate the long-term interests of capital, but works well to create the impression that the state does not act directly for capital. Gramscian "cultural" Marxists have developed the concept of hegemony, which describes the way in which the organization of social systems comes to be accepted or tolerated by large numbers of people (see Gramsci, 1971). Gramsci, unlike the structuralist Marxists, stresses the importance of divisions between groups within ruling blocs (e.g., financiers, wealthy landowners, and industrialists) and the way alliances are built up and compromises made with the machinery of the state. Under this model, subordinate classes make gains and their members both support and also see through the capitalist system at the same time. One of the advantages of the cultural Marxist model is that human beings do not appear to be wholly determined by their place in the capitalist mode of production (see also Thompson, 1968, 1975).

2. The first "states" appeared about 5,000 years ago in the Middle East and elsewhere. By *modern state,* sociologists and historians refer to the rise of the state in the post-Enlightenment period, circa post-1800.

3. The literature on the modern state is vast. For analyses that explore the patriarchal nature of the modern state, see Mimi Abramovitz (1988), Carol Brown (1981), Mary McKintosh (1978), Michelle Barrett (1980), Zillah Eisenstein (1984), Elizabeth Wilson (1983), Linda Gordon (1990), Wendy Brown (1992), Davina Cooper (1995), Seth Koven and Sonya Michel (1993), Roberts (1995), Deborah Rhode (1994), and a number of the contributors to the *Harvard Law Review's* symposium titled, "Changing Images of the State," *107*(6), April 1994. See also the contributions to the special edition of *Social Justice, 21*(1), Spring 1994, guest edited by Gwendolyn Mink, titled "Women and Welfare Reform." For an analysis of the way in which the welfare state engages in the cultural reproduction of gender in the Job Corps, see Quadangno and Fobes (1995).

4. See, for example, Bowker and Maurer (1987); Council on Ethical and Judicial Affairs, American Medical Association (1992); Council on Scientific Affairs, American Medical Association (1992); Currens (1991); Marzuk, Tardiff, and Hirsch (1992); Mercy and Saltzman (1989); and Sugg and Inui (1992).

5. This situation is not likely to improve in the future, especially not in impoverished rural communities such as those found in Kentucky. For a good discussion of the "industrial revolution" in health care provision in the United States and the rise of "for profit" health maintenance organizations, see Bodenheimer (1996).

6. Stark, Flitcraft, and Frazier (1979), using health data (trauma histories) from a sample of 481 women who requested assistance at a major urban emergency room during a period of one month, found that a quarter of the women could be identified as battered. In a later summary of their research, Stark and Flitcraft (1996) comment, "Of all injuries ever presented by the 481 women to the hospital, almost half (46.8%) were presented by victims of domestic violence" (p. 10). The fact that we know precious little about how rural battered women access emergency room services is a major social policy concern that I return to.

7. The most recent figures on abortion rates in Kentucky show that 10.4 abortions were performed per 1,000 women in 1987, compared to 26.7 per 1,000 nationally. For a discussion of public opinion on abortion in Kentucky see Miller (1994, pp. 73-75). One shelter director told me that she always kept an abortion fund readily available for her shelter clients. The fund was put together by private donations. This shelter director reported that to date no women have drawn upon those funds for an abortion.

8. As Mimi Abramovitz (1994) points out, 39 million people currently live in poverty in the United States, and 13 million receive AFDC (Aid to Families with Dependent Children). The typical AFDC family is composed of a mother with two children. Contrary to the research rhetoric of the Right, families do not remain on AFDC forever. The typical period of receipt is around 2 years. Likewise, the provision of state aid in general does not encourage increased out-of-wedlock births. Abramovitz estimates that the value of AFDC grants has declined by 40% over the past 20 years (p. 21). Amy Butler (1996), using event history analysis, finds that when all sources of income are considered, higher welfare guarantees increase the likelihood of families getting out of poverty. For an ethnographic appreciation of the way in which African American women negotiate the economic forces in their lives, see Jarrett (1994).

9. It is not only social services personnel who can give rural battered women the sense that it is shameful to be on welfare. Wanda told me that the county attorney who was handling her case of domestic violence chastised her for being on welfare.

Wanda: The County Attorney's like, "Well women like you, I work for women like you to raise your kids on welfare. I don't appreciate you being on welfare." And I told him, quit his damn job, that's what I told him.

10. Of the 50 women I interviewed, 28 had no significant contact with social workers or social services. Nine women described themselves as indifferent to the performance of social workers and social services in general. For a general look at the interaction between social workers and battered women, see Hamilton and Coates (1993).

11. I spent a lot of time in Simpson attempting to arrange an interview with a very reluctant county sheriff. A haircut and a sprinkling of information about marijuana growing and domestics could be had in Simpson for $3.50 in 1993.

12. Daly's work has been vehemently attacked as overly general and essentialist. See, for example, Segal (1987) and Grimshaw (1988). For a recent discussion of the relationship between feminist thought and religion, see Morny Joy (1996).

13. For more information on the complex role of rural religious values and battering, see McCullough (1993), Navin, Stockard, and Campbell-Ruggaard (1993), Peterson (1983), and Whipple (1987).

14. For a recent discussion of the links between violence against women and the incarceration of women, see Websdale and Chesney-Lind (in press).

15. Attorney Shepard and I had many discussions about domestic violence, criminal justice, and politics in Kentucky. Our conversation about Governor Jones's commutation of the sentences of 11 women took place on April 10, 1996. I also refer readers to the *Donahue Show* of March 14, 1996, during which several of the women appeared along with their respective attorneys and ex-Governor Jones.

16. Telephone conversation with Marsha Weinstein, April 10, 1996.

17. I am grateful to Senator Tori for discussing these matters with me. Telephone conversation, April 10, 1996.

18. While advocates clearly appreciate the support of pro-lifers like Senator Tori, when it comes to introducing domestic violence legislation, advocates also see the abortion issue as a litmus test of allegiance to women's interests.

19. I do not mean to imply that there is a rift between rural and urban shelters in Kentucky over the distribution of funds and resources. The KDVA is an organization composed of the constituent shelters in Kentucky. Directors and some staff meet at least quarterly to discuss common issues and concerns. Since it is an Association as opposed to a Domestic Violence Coalition, the KDVA does not allow members of the public or corporations or other organizations to join. According to a number of directors, the

"association" form of organization results in a more cohesive grassroots structure. This may be one of the reasons why the KDVA and battered women in Kentucky have been instrumental in introducing some of the most progressive domestic violence legislation in the country.

20. This intersection of poverty and woman battering is nothing new. As Dobash and Dobash (1992, p. 60, n. 1) point out, 18th-century Magdalen houses in Great Britain assisted poor women who had been forced into prostitution. Often these women were fleeing violent patriarchs or living destitute in a society that did not offer women a chance to survive economically without men. For an analysis of the history of prostitution in the United States, see Rosen (1982). Rosen notes that the prime reason women chose to enter prostitution was poverty. The situation is similar to the institutional response to female offenders. Meda Chesney-Lind (1997) discusses the way in which the intersection of gender, race, and class lie at the heart of the way female juveniles are treated by the juvenile justice system.

21. See, for example, Beth Schneider's (1990) analysis of the dialectical relationship between rights and politics. She argues that rights claims are not just part of a hierarchical and formal patriarchal legal code. Rather, she calls for a recognition of the way the language of rights and political struggle have become intertwined in ways that transcend individualistic rhetoric and enhance the development of collective identity.

7

Rural Battering and Social Policies

Introduction

The Role of Community Responses to Rural Woman Battering

In preceding chapters I drew attention to the fact that rural families are more privatized, isolated, and exhibit more traditional gender stereotyping. In these rural families, rates of marriage are higher than in their urban counterparts, and cohabitation appears to be less easily tolerated. Rural women are more closely tied to housework and child care. If rural women do work for wages outside of the home, they not only earn less than rural men in comparable paid labor, they also earn significantly less than their urban peers. Indeed, as I pointed out in Chapter 2, the earnings gap between men and women has been growing in rural communities while it has closed somewhat in urban communities. If we factor in the geographical and sociocultural isolation of rural battered women, a pattern of extreme disadvantage emerges that calls for careful policy analysis. This disadvantage clearly endangers battered women and can, as I highlighted in Chapter 1, have tragic consequences for women and their children. Consequently, social policies must, at their heart, have a commitment to instilling a cultural ethic that prioritizes the safety of women and children from the threat of male violence. Instilling this cultural ethic will undoubtedly come up against entrenched beliefs about the traditional place of women in a more privatized patriarchal order. However, given the relative homogeneity of rural communities, the inculcation of such an ethic is a distinct possibility.

Just as rural regions vary considerably, the battered women within those regions show marked differences that we ignore at our peril. While I have not focused very much on women of color in my ethnography, it is crucial that we factor race and ethnicity into our understanding of rural battering. If rural battered women are acutely isolated, then we must recognize the way in which the isolation of minority rural women is compounded by their race/ethnic background. In Chapter 4 I discussed the experiences of some African American women with local police. We cannot easily transpose their experiences to women of color in other rural regions of the country. For example, rural migrant women of color who live and work as illegal aliens in states such as Arizona and Florida, negotiate additional difficulties with their batterers. Batterers can use women's illegal status against them as a means of preventing them from calling the police in the first place. In addition to the standard plethora of control tactics, men who batter these women can threaten them with the possibility of deportation or of losing their children if they call the authorities about the violence. Put simply, when we formulate policies to help battered women, we must remember their idiosyncrasies and use these as a touchstone. This means asking these women about what they need and want.

As I showed in Chapter 3, social scientists have been reluctant to seek out the opinions of rural battered women, or indeed battered women in general. The reasons for this neglect are complex. One reason is the relative isolation of rural communities and the difficulty researchers may have in physically accessing people. Another is the reluctance, or perceived reluctance, of rural dwellers to submit their lives to the scrutiny of researchers or any outsiders. An important reason for this failure to study rural woman battering derives from the empiricism that dominates academic disciplines such as Sociology and Criminology. Learning about the firsthand experiences of battered women seems to lie beyond the epistemological vision of many of those who have conducted large-scale research into battering and the state response to it. If the "data" do not emerge in readily quantifiable forms, major funding agencies are less likely to consider research initiatives seriously. It is notable that the NIJ-funded "experimental" studies of the policing of domestic violence used large sums of money and left us in a state of malaise as to the efficacy of mandatory arrest (see Garner, Fagan, & Maxwell, 1995). If organizations such as the NIJ are not willing to take the subjective experiences of urban battered women seriously, then it is easy to see how accessing women's opinions in more remote rural settings would be seen by some funding agencies as an insurmountable problem.

Accessing the personal experiences of battered women is an absolutely crucial prerequisite to producing a culturally nuanced understanding of interpersonal violence against rural women and the "justice" system's response to that violence. We cannot simply take the things we have learned from urban studies of the same phenomenon and assume they hold true in what are often very different rural settings. We cannot just take the policies that appear to have worked in urban settings and assume they will be comparably effective for rural battered women. Given the relative homogeneity of rural communities compared with urban centers, we must critically assess our ideas and assumptions about how to reach and help rural women.

The sociocultural conditions that contribute to women's isolation in rural settings may also be a blessing in disguise when it comes to policy formulation. In those rural areas where people know each other well, where there is a homogeneity of values, it may be easier to develop community-based responses to woman battering. As Lori Heise (1996) puts it, "a community organizing approach to gender based abuse . . . would be especially appropriate for small towns and rural communities" (p. 26). Among the many tasks of those organizing, such a campaign would be to convene a coordinating council of local representatives from groups such as the police, courts, health care, shelters, religious organizations, and schools.

In regard to sexual violence, Liz Kelly (1996a) observes that victims draw as much, if not more, support from informal networks as formal ones (p. 69). Citing studies from Britain, she notes that informal networks can provide the kind of enduring support and resources to women that enable them to escape future victimization. According to Kelly, "Contrary to popular myth, most relatives and friends were helpful, offering emotional support and sanctuary" (1996a, p. 77). She acknowledges that more extensive examples of localized support systems for abused women come from countries in which the national and local state apparatus is poorly developed, and stresses that the community, and particularly networks of women in the community, can provide crucial support systems. The pistol-whipping of June that I discussed in Chapter 1, was met with disbelief by neighbors. Had the neighbors to whom June ran been alive to the significance of battering in rural communities, they might not have been so quick to disbelieve her report that she had been battered.

By highlighting the importance of higher levels of value consensus in rural communities we must not fall into the trap of seeing these communities as undivided or lacking in social conflict. My ethnography clearly identifies rural gender relations as highly conflictual. Though many people may know of a rural battered woman's family, be related to those family members, or be friends/neighbors to them, those people may not know of her interpersonal victimization. What community-oriented policy formation in rural areas must do is exploit the community ties in a way that facilitates getting women the kinds of support they need. Paradoxically, rural battered women can be extremely isolated within a relatively homogeneous community. Community-oriented policies must make use of the homogeneity in such a way as to funnel women into more formal supports that they might not have otherwise considered. Alternatively, if communities are sensitive to domestic violence it may be possible, often through the help of networks of women, to bring outreach programs, shelters, or both, to rural regions. This funneling process would do well to make use of the informal networks among women and also the weight that these networks can bring to the occupations dominated by men that women nevertheless need access to. Building tangible supports such as rural shelters is about much more than buying a house and furnishing it. In one rural community encountering problems in setting up a new shelter, advocates successfully utilized local networks of women to enlist the volunteer support of male firefighters in installing what would otherwise have been a prohibitively expensive sprinkler system, thus bringing the new building into line with the fire code.

Rural Battering and Recent Federal Legislation

The historically and culturally contingent phenomenon of domestic violence has moved to the foreground of political debate at times

when the feminist movement was strong (Gordon, 1988). As Pleck
(1987) argues, however, women's rights advocates have made the
most tangible gains when they have formed alliances with more
conservative politicians and particularly when they have refrained
from attacking the institution of the family.[1] This observation is
particularly important when formulating policies that impact rural
communities. These communities have what is often a healthy disrespect for central government. Consequently, the implementation of
social policies that are not mindful of this disrespect are less likely to
succeed.

Alliance building in a conservative political climate has at times
worked well for advocates of battered women under the Clinton
administration. The passage of the Violence Against Women Act
(VAWA) in 1994 introduced a number of important reforms challenging the criminal justice system to do more to offer protection to
women and families. It also set aside considerable amounts of federal
dollars for research, practical support, and policy development in
order to reduce violence against women. For example, under the
VAWA, hitherto unheard of amounts of funding have been made
available to confront rural battering. The VAWA also extends new
protections to alien spouses, who work in large numbers in rural parts
of states such as California and Arizona. For example, migrant spouses
now have the ability to petition for a reclassification of their immigration status. Prior to the VAWA, alien spouses had to rely upon their
abusers to apply on their behalf.[2]

It is important to note that the VAWA was passed with bipartisan
support and at a time when both Democrats and Republicans were
waxing lyrical about "family values." This passage of progressive
legislation designed to protect women recalls the campaign for women's
suffrage. As Pleck has so eloquently pointed out, those gains made by
the women's movement have often been the result of advocates for
women striking compromises with conservative politicians. These
kinds of compromises continue today across the country and were
clearly evident from my ethnographic research in Kentucky. As pro-
feminist and feminist politicians infiltrated the ranks of the formal
political system, women's issues have received a greater airing. My
ethnographic findings do not suggest that the sphere of formal politics
neatly and unproblematically reasserts the domination of men over
women. Women, and rural women in particular, are clearly underrepresented in formal politics at all levels. In Kentucky, the state

legislature, through its limited provision of funds for shelters, child care, women's health services, and social and legal services, ostensibly acts to keep many women in violent relationships. However, through the examples of the commutation of the sentences of the women who had killed their abusers, and the grassroots support of the progressive 1992 domestic violence legislation, I showed that the state does have a feminist lobby and a feminist network that creates democratic spaces through which the voices and interests of women can be heard.

In addition to the spaces worked by feminists, we must also note that political regimes, whatever their complexion, are not monolithic and insulated from the large numbers of people those systems attempt to manage. Any state that claims to be fair and credible has at times to be fair. In fact, the histories of liberal-democratic states are punctuated with progressive changes that have brought profound improvements to the lives of large numbers of people. E. P. Thompson (1975) once put it as follows:

> The rhetoric and rules of a society are something a great deal more than sham. In the same moment they may modify, in profound ways, the behavior of the powerful, and mystify the powerless. They may disguise the true realities of power, but, at the same time, they may curb that power and check its intrusions. And it is often from within that very rhetoric that a radical critique of the practice of the society is developed. (p. 265)

Social policies designed to strike at the heart of rural domestic violence have to be developed in a way that simultaneously strengthens women's position and power base in families vis-à-vis men without (paradoxically) appearing to attack the efficacy of the family as a social institution. Such artful formulation of rural policy initiatives does not stem simply from the broader lessons of the history of social reform in the battle against woman battering in general, although the need for accommodationist and consensus-building measures is essential. Rather, it also derives from the recognition that many rural citizens (among others, of course) display a healthy disrespect for central government initiatives.

We ought not take accommodationist approaches to policy formulation to the point that we lose sight of what it is that lies at the heart of rural battering. My ethnography clearly implicates rural patriarchy at the center of family violence. This means that strategies that fail to recognize the gendered nature of violence within families will end up reproducing ideologies that depict male and female intrafamilial violence to be essentially the same in character, although (perhaps) different in degree and consequences. Such ideologies are likely to recommend "conflict management" approaches, nonviolent conflict resolution, and psychological interventions. This may "feel good" in a "self-help" society that often prides itself on its individualism and the way its citizens have the "option" of traveling the road from the log cabin to the White House. However, astructural approaches will always be of limited use to rural battered women. Time and again, for example, rural women told me of the numerous economic obstacles to them leaving a violent relationship. Had the women I interviewed had the means to leave, they would not have endured the violence they did.

At a time in history when welfare provisions in the United States are shrinking and devolving to the individual states, and when lifetime limits are being placed on the receipt of welfare benefits, we must take care to see that the voices and concerns of rural battered women do not get lost in the bureaucratic shuffle of welfare provisions. Without concrete economic supports to put food, transportation, medical care, safe housing, and more rigorous legal/criminal justice protections in place for women and families, it is nothing short of insulting to keep asking battered women why they do not leave violent homes.

Extant Social Policies and the Need for Change

The patriarchal state regulates the options of rural battered women. However, it is also clear from my ethnography that "state feminism" or the "institutionalization of feminist interests" (Mazur & McBride-Stetson, 1995, p. 10) is also alive and well in Kentucky.[3] Recognizing the agency of battered women and the democratic spaces within the patriarchal state, I now build upon the ethnographic findings of Chapter 6 to suggest various social policy interventions with regard to the following law enforcement; the judiciary; criminal justice initiatives in general; shelters, health care, social and legal services, and child care; the role of the state in women's paid employment; and rural communications. Finally, I explore what I call a coordinated multiagency approach to the social problem of rural woman battering.

If we are to formulate viable social policies, we must recognize the unique difficulties faced by rural women in leaving battering relationships. As I have already discussed, these difficulties are many and include at their core a profoundly debilitating geographical and sociocultural isolation. This isolation impacts the extent and nature of the delivery of potentially beneficial state services. Consequently, any social policy initiatives must use the structure of rural patriarchy, in all its intricate manifestations, as an essential frame of reference. At the same time, policies must remain cognizant of those aspects of rural community life that may be used to orchestrate a multiagency intervention. All of the policy suggestions I introduce aim to improve the disadvantaged position of rural women and increase women's chances of surviving independently of violent partners.

Law Enforcement

More has to be done to confront the problem of local police officers being compromised around the enforcement of domestic violence laws. This involves much more than sensitizing and training police officers to handle domestics better. It seems clear that whatever changes in training were introduced in 1991, many have not translated into changes in officer performance. If rural officers are not receiving training in all aspects of enforcing the law at domestics, then they ought to. I think it is significant that not one rural officer complained to me that prosecutors were the reason that rural domestic cases did not end up in court. Only a few hinted that judges did little except slap abusers on the wrist and send them on their way. This glaring omission tells me that rural officers are often not cognizant of what it takes to prosecute a domestic criminal case. Much more attention needs to be paid to what rural officers observe at domestics and what they write in their reports. Particular attention needs to be paid to the communication between prosecutors and police over what the prosecutor needs to see in a police report in order to prosecute abusers. It is crucial that in rural areas, where abused women have a lot to lose in terms of extended family (either her own or the abuser's) and community contacts if the abuser is prosecuted, that police be trained to gather evidence at the scene that enables prosecutors to proceed against abusers without the help of victims themselves. This includes officers taking necessary photographs, capturing any subsequent bruising on film, describing the demeanor of perpetrators and victims at the scene, gathering comprehensive statements from victims and witnesses in such a way as to facilitate the subsequent prosecution of offenders (including listing names and dates of birth), and fully describing injuries. Likewise, 911 tapes can be powerful corroborating evidence and can be admitted into evidence under a number of different exceptions to the hearsay rule.[4]

It is not enough merely to alter the awareness of officers of their legal (and ethical) responsibilities to battered women. The training of officers must transcend the mechanics of dealing with the disturbance itself. Rather, rural police officers must receive information about the broader social condition of women so that the officers do not slide into the habit of victim blaming, however subtle that victim blaming may be. In other words, if we are to train police officers to deal better with domestics, we must access their attitudes about gender relations and not just improve their cognitive understanding of the technical aspects of their roles.

Changing officer attitudes is no easy task and care should be given as to who does the training. Ideally, a range of perspectives should be available to officers through multiagency involvement, in the hope that the crucial point about the disadvantaged social condition of rural women, and its link to violence, will sink in. This multiagency, multiperspective input into the training of police officers is sometimes referred to as "cross-training." At the presentation that I gave to the Legislative Task Force on Domestic Violence in August 1995 in Frankfort, Kentucky, the question of training police officers arose. In an exchange among Kentucky Police Commissioner Sayre, Marsha Weinstein, and myself, Commissioner Sayre made the point that the so-called cross-training of police officers in the handling of domestics has been in place in Kentucky since 1991. Marsha Weinstein, then executive director of the Kentucky Commission on Women, disagreed, saying that law enforcement agencies dominated the training of officers. In arguing against Sayre, I pointed out that in quantitative research conducted in Kentucky (see Websdale & Johnson, 1997a), battered women rated the performance of rural police at domestics significantly lower than that of urban police. Our research findings also revealed that battered women rated the performance of the state police at domestics to be superior to that of municipal police and sheriffs.[5] If cross-training had been in place and had really impacted rural police agencies, we would not have expected such a significant difference. In reality I think it is accurate to say that cross-training has not impacted rural police agencies very much. There are a number of reasons for this, including the fact that rural agencies do not have the funds to release officers for substantial training on domestic violence.

There is some evidence to show that women police officers perform more effectively at domestics than their male peers.[6] Out of the 120 county sheriffs in Kentucky, not one is a woman. In fact, the representation of women among the ranks of rural police officers who work domestics is extremely low. As of May 1996, there were 957 full-time and 75 part-time sheriff's deputies in Kentucky. In addition, there were another 400 to 415 special deputies available for emergency backup. Of all these deputies only 35 are women. This means that women make up only 2% to 3% of sheriff's departments' sworn personnel capable of attending domestics.[7] Given that roughly 9% of all sworn police officers are women, Kentucky's sheriff's departments are lagging well behind. Although not a panacea by any means, research suggests that the hiring of more women police officers to work domestics in rural communities may increase the level of sensitivity of law enforcement agencies to the plight of battered women.

Removing some of the other more deep-rooted social problems that either directly or indirectly impact policing might ease the degree to which some police officers are compromised in their handling of domestics. In Eastern Kentucky in particular, but also in many other rural counties, the levels of unemployment and poverty are very high. These levels encourage illegal activities such as marijuana growing operations, gambling, fencing stolen property, and more. In some instances, police officers actively engage in these activities, or at least acquiesce in them to the degree that it compromises their ability to arrest abusers who know of their involvement or acquiescence.

As we have seen in Chapter 4, interviewees are most disappointed with the performance of county sheriff's departments. In some regions the apathy of sheriffs or their open dismissal of domestic violence as a serious policing problem begs the question of whether specialized state police teams ought not to be used in their place. As noted in Chapter 4, some sheriff's departments do a sterling job, and rural battered women fully acknowledge this. However, for those found lacking, the state of Kentucky might consider using state police units specifically trained to respond to domestics in rural counties. These units might supplement existing units that perform routine patrol. The key here would be the relative autonomy of the state police units from the political milieu in the rural counties and particularly the detachment of those officers from the ol' boy networks in which abusers may be enmeshed.

The Judiciary

As we saw in Chapter 5, battered women often report being revictimized at the bench by rural judges. An important policy question arises, then, about how best to sensitize judges to the socially disadvantaged position of rural women and more specifically to the dynamics of domestic violence. At the time of writing, the issue of providing domestic violence training for Kentucky's judges is highly contentious. Judges excluded advocates for battered women from conducting training workshops at a training for judges (held in May 1996). At this training, the agendas for small group discussions specified those meetings as for "judges only." Advocates were not be permitted to attend. In many states, similar small group workshops are used to brainstorm the disposition of various domestic scenarios. Such groups are often cofacilitated by judges and advocates. It is most unfortunate that Kentucky's judges have chosen deliberately to exclude advocates from these important groups. According to a key informant, the judges' intent was deliberately to exclude KDVA Executive Director Sherrie Currens, who, according to my informant source, is perceived by at some of the judges to be a "flaming radical feminist and a real thorn in their side." A rural judge, whom I did not formally interview and who is finely attuned to domestic violence issues, simply remarked to me that "you cannot use advocates to train Kentucky's district judges in domestic violence." His observation, as a judge sensitive to violence against women, is instructive.

Without cross-training, judges, like law enforcement officers, will receive instruction only from their peers. The chances of them coming to appreciate domestic violence through the eyes of victims and advocates themselves are small. My research suggests that judges would benefit greatly from training conducted by persons from a range of agencies and also from selected battered women themselves. The idea here would be to offer judges different insights into the complexity of domestic violence. To the extent that the judges think they can solve the problems of disposing of domestic cases from largely within their own ranks, their myopia recalls the mentality of the patriarch who feels that his own family is beyond the intervention of the state. The entrenched position of judges regarding their own training on domestic violence may be even more important to overcome than that of police officers, because of the social class divide between the judiciary and the battered women who come before them.

Criminal Justice Foci: Illegal Drugs or Battering?

In Chapter 1, I discussed the 1991 case of Johnny Jacobs, who shot his wife in the face, killing her. Jacobs has been sentenced to 10 years for manslaughter but is currently out on appeal bond. His case took 4 years to come to trial. While in jail after the killing, Johnny Jacobs turned state's evidence against his dead wife's family and provided the FBI with grounds for obtaining a search warrant to look for illegal drugs. In contrast to the tardiness in bringing Jacobs to trial for murder, his dead wife's parents and brother were quickly tried and convicted in federal court, and received approximately 27 years each for marijuana growing and other related offenses. One might argue that the time taken to bring each of these cases to trial reflects the difference between the state and federal court systems, the former typically taking longer. However, the disparity in sentencing between these two cases also reflects the more profound enthusiasm of the criminal justice system to go after suspected marijuana dealers.

As I showed in Chapter 4, a number of law enforcement officers in Kentucky have protected marijuana growing and other illegal drug operations, or have turned a blind eye to them.[8] In a number of ways, this involvement or acquiescence can produce a compromised response to the policing of domestics. We must ask whether the diligent pursuit and punitive treatment of offenders such as marijuana growers is worthwhile. How do we expect people to make a living in profoundly impoverished rural communities? Is it not to be expected that people will resort to drug use to medicate their pain? or drug manufacture, sale, and distribution to make some much needed cash? Priscilla, who lives in a small town in a very depressed rural region of Eastern Kentucky, put it as follows:

> *Priscilla:* When there is nothing there is drugs and escapism. . . . Most of the businesses have gone and I would say that a good 75 percent of people in my county are on welfare or some kind of disability and food stamps. . . . There's a lot of marijuana grown and sold. Pills you can get anywhere. Any addict would love our county.

The moment is long overdue when the United States should seriously assess its approach to drug-related offenses. Chambliss (1995) informs us that in the Netherlands, a number of studies conclude that the "decriminalization of the use, possession and sale of small amounts of drugs has not led to any increase in usage and has decreased the amount of crime associated with drug use and dealing" (p. 102).

The subterranean economy in many parts of rural Kentucky is centered on illegal drug operations. The negotiated policing of these operations requires the use of informants and encourages corruption among often poorly paid police officers. The decriminalization of drugs would remove the need for excessively punitive measures. It would also reduce the number of times police officers are compromised when it comes to protecting battered women who are living with growers, dealers, informants, or other men hooked into the subterranean drug economy, or perhaps more commonly, those abusers who simply know of the officer's involvement or acquiescence. Although less significant, I would make the same argument about the sale of alcohol, which is banned in 77 of the 120 counties in Kentucky.

Shelters or Outreach?

I have noted how shelters themselves tend to serve those rural women who live nearby rather than in neighboring counties. Battered women who live in the peripheral rural regions served by the rural shelters (or even the urban shelters) are much less likely to utilize the shelters' residential services. Rural battered women may find it difficult to leave battering relationships and reside in shelters. The long distance to travel to shelter may be an obstacle too difficult for some women to overcome. Leaving may be even more troublesome if women have deep social roots in the community and a wide circle of family who are dear to them. We must therefore ask, "How might state funds be best utilized in rural regions?" It might be of more benefit to rural battered women if funds were spent on outreach programs rather than on in-shelter provisions. Ideally, state funding will increase as the social problem of rural woman battering is taken more seriously. If such an increase occurs, then we must look carefully at the deployment of funds, bearing in mind that it may be better to "reach" rural battered women in counties far removed from spouse abuse shelter networks, than to house a much smaller number of women as shelter residents.[9] This is a much more tricky issue than first meets the eye. If more "peripheral" rural battered women are accessed through outreach services, then contingency plans must be in place to accommodate the possible increase in requests for residential services. Put simply, the state cannot fund increased outreach services without making available more services based at shelters.[10]

Health Care

As Bodenheimer (1996) notes, the delivery of health care is far less important for lowering mortality and disability rates than is confronting the glaring social inequalities that often lie at the root of ill health (p. 27). As I have already pointed out, the delivery of health care to rural woman is inadequate to the point of being pathetic. Therefore, social policies that address rural battering must confront both the paucity and the lack of confidentiality of health care delivery to rural battered women. The lack of privacy and of respect for confidentiality is a particularly pressing difficulty for rural battered women. It is unreasonable and unsafe to expect a battered woman to go to an emergency room where the staff know her and are not prepared to protect her confidentiality diligently. The fact that this information may get back to her abuser, who may in turn beat her again for "going public," is a sufficiently strong deterrent for injured women. More specifically, the paucity of reproductive health services symbolizes a more generalized contempt for rural women.

In spite of the paucity of health services for rural women, far more rural battered women visit health services professionals than enter shelters. For this reason it would serve battered women well if health services professionals in rural areas were more finely attuned to the dynamics of domestic violence and especially women's need for confidentiality. In those remote areas of Kentucky where rural health care delivery has been acutely difficult to deliver, some grassroots health care providers have sprung up. Battered women need more of these grassroots services, and more services in general that cater specifically to the needs of women and children. In addition, health professionals serving rural communities need to be properly trained to recognize that symptoms such as depression, anxiety, substance abuse, and suicide attempts may be products of battering.[11] As such, these professionals need to work with women in a nonjudgmental supportive way, rather than attempting to medicate the pain or to diagnose women as mentally ill.

On a more general but related note, the United States must move toward the provision of socialized health care in order for primary care physicians to play any significant part in helping battered women. Many of the women I interviewed do not see physicians as a viable source of support because they do not have the money to develop relationships with them. In addition, those battered women and their advocates who have had dealings with physicians often find them insensitive to their plight as victims of violence.

Social Services

My ethnographic findings also mirror a large literature that points to the ways in which state social services are out of touch with the needs of poor women. While my findings do not support a conspiracy theory or any other theory that sees social service provision in monolithic terms, they do nevertheless show how patriarchal structures are consistently reproduced, either through the lack of support or the form that that support often takes. At the same time, many social workers, particularly those in the field rather than the bureaucrats who try to run the system, feel powerless when it comes to helping rural battered women. These frontline social workers have heavy caseloads. Whether we accept the heavy caseloads as a legitimate reason for not working with more battered women, or as an excuse, the fact remains that we need more social workers in rural regions to assist battered women. Since a number of women talked highly of their social workers, it would be folly to write social workers out of the loop of assistance. Rather, social workers in rural regions must be better prepared to work with battered women, and especially well trained to avoid falling into the trap of victim blaming. Any policy changes here will require a major escalation in funding by the state in order to put more and better trained social workers into the field to support, in a nonjudgmental way, rural battered women.

As the United States gears up to replace its AFDC system with the Temporary Assistance to Needy Families (TANF) program, states would do well to pay careful attention to the provision of aid to rural women. Rural welfare offices need to bear in mind the possibility that many of their clients are battered women. Offices ought to be designed to protect the confidentiality of these clients. This design should include architectural changes that protect the private information women provide, which, in rural communities in particular, can often be overheard by people in waiting areas or by people undergoing interviews of their own. The chances that people might overhear information about someone they know is much greater in smaller communities and therefore more likely to compromise the safety of women and children (Menard, 1997)

Legal Representation

As Sara Buel (1997) observes, it is possible for people charged with shoplifting bubble gum to receive legal aid for their defense. However, it is practically impossible for most battered women to obtain legal representation as they fight for divorce, custody of their children, or both.[12] A number of women I talked with expressed great frustration about their inability to dissolve their violent marriages and secure an equitable divorce settlement. Although I have noted the ways in which many rural battered women use DVOs as makeshift divorces, any comprehensive social policy on battering must make legal services for the purposes of marital dissolution more accessible to battered women. Women complained of having wait up to 2 years just to get some legal aid on their cases. While at this writing the Kentucky Bar Association strongly encourages attorneys to handle cases such as divorces for poor women on a pro bono basis, very few attorneys do. Rural battered women seeking divorce should become a priority target population for pro bono legal work.

Child Welfare

Given that abused and neglected children are often from homes in which women are battered, it is essential that child protective services agencies working with rural populations network more effectively with domestic violence agencies. On a number of occasions in my interviews women told me of the hostility of child protection workers toward them. As we saw in Chapter 6, social worker Stern was most keen to hold battered women accountable for the welfare of their children. It has long been known that serious injuries to children are more likely to be inflicted by fathers than mothers. Until child welfare workers are willing to recognize that the best way to protect most children at risk of abuse and neglect is to protect and support their mothers, we will be left with an intervention system that blames women who are often victims of battering for the abuse and or neglect of children.

Provision of Child Care

Another area that the patriarchal state appears not to attach very much importance to is the provision of child care services. The inability to find good child care is yet another factor that limits the options of rural women and children in their potential flight from violence. The United States has no nationally organized system for licensing child care, and the state of Kentucky is particularly poor when it comes to offering licensed child care facilities in rural communities. Any assault upon rural woman battering must include the provision of licensed child care facilities in all rural counties. Such provision is made all the more urgent by the fact that it is women of child-bearing age who seem more likely to be battered. If we add to this the rural patriarchal imperative that women be "barefoot and pregnant," we can see how offering the option of child care could offer new avenues for women when strategizing about how to leave violent relationships.

Churches

Though there is a formal separation of church and state, it is clear from Chapter 6 that the church can act as one of the ideological underpinnings of rural patriarchy. Those who run religious institutions in rural regions, be they churches, synagogues, or mosques, must be better trained about how to work with battered women. If nothing else, my conversations with rural women reveal that as a matter of urgent policy, pastors should not be telling battered women to go forth and endure, or to attend couples counseling. However, to argue that rural religious institutions only reproduce patriarchal relations is to ignore the words of some battered women who report receiving real help from their pastors. The fact that some pastors have great influence in the lives of the members of their rural congregations means that social policies addressing rural battering must confront the role of the churches. In particular, we must ask how churches can work with state agencies such as social services and shelters to intervene in ways that empower battered women.

The State and Women's Employment

Kentucky women require more and better jobs. The Homeless Job Training Initiative (HJTI; funded by the U.S. Department of Labor as a demonstration grant between 1991 and 1995) set out to train and then place Kentucky's homeless battered women in jobs and help them move toward economic independence. Preliminary findings suggest that those women who received job readiness skills, jobs, and independent housing experienced lowered levels of revictimization than women who did not receive these benefits (Websdale & Johnson, 1997b). While it may be argued that all "good" shelters offer these job readiness services, this cannot be said of underfunded shelters in rural Kentucky prior to the demonstration grants. Of the seven Kentucky shelters that participated in the HJTI, three (Hopkinsville, Mount Vernon, Elizabethtown) are based in rural regions. While the federal funds for job training have now dried up at the Kentucky shelters, the idea that women in rural shelters can be assisted toward the world of wage work is now firmly in place. It may be argued that these jobs are largely minimum wage and merely end up revictimizing women. However, many of the battered women I spoke with who had passed through this program reported feeling empowered by the experience of earning money and learning new skills. In tandem with the economic revitalization of rural regions, we also need to extend job training programs in rural shelters so that women can develop their resistive strategies from a broader array of options.

Improving Rural Communications

One of the defining characteristics of rural patriarchy is the physical and sociocultural isolation of rural women. This isolation can be addressed in a number of ways. Providing some means of public transportation to rural areas may be a starting point. Improving rural infrastructures and particularly the quality of roads might also help. Another possibility is increasing telephone subscription rates in rural counties through government aid. As noted, in some rural counties in Kentucky as many as 3 in 10 households are without phones. Increasing access to isolated households through telephones may increase battered women's ability to communicate with the outside world. Such increased access may also make it easier for shelter outreach programs to reach battered women. However, we must acknowledge that increasing telephone subscription rates will not prevent batterers from controlling access to the phone within their own households. For those battered women who live in rural areas but have left their abuser, we need to provide telephone communications that allow them to screen out calls from selected numbers, such as their ex-abuser, or to offer caller identification services.

The Media

In the small communities that I observed in Kentucky, one of the ingredients of the local social cement is the newspaper. In small towns the names of perpetrators of domestic violence are listed in the press under the police beat or other comparable section. When there is a domestic tragedy such as a homicide-suicide, the local press coverage is usually intense and detailed. However, from my reading of the many reports of domestic homicides and homicide-suicides in Kentucky, and indeed elsewhere, it is rare for journalists to get beyond what Alex Alvarez and I have called "forensic journalism" (Websdale & Alvarez, 1997). By forensic journalism we refer to that routinized style of crime reporting that focuses upon the forensic details of individual crimes and the immediate situational dynamics within which the crime takes place. This approach to the reporting of violent crime usually focuses upon individual offenders and virtually never on structural contexts (see also Barlow, Barlow, & Chiricos, 1995; Humphries, 1981). While we learn demographic details of the perpetrator and victim (ages, sex, race, etc.), whether they knew each other, and the gory details of the crime scene, we learn very little of the political nature of the offense or the gendered pattern of killings in tragedies such as domestic homicide-suicides. For example, although many homicide-suicides are preceded by a history of woman battering, we rarely learn this from the press accounts. Likewise, the press rarely tells readers that the typical perpetrator of homicide-suicides are men. These are simple details that are discernible from prior press reporting patterns. Such simple details inform the public about the gendered edge to these types of killings and could therefore serve as a powerful educational tool regarding violence against women. The force of a more "structurally oriented" style of newspaper reporting would be all the more powerful in rural areas where offenses such as domestic homicide and homicide-suicide seem more prevalent and where the participants are often known or known of by readers.

Education

If we recognize the potential of developing community-based responses to rural battering, then we must do more to involve schools in the process. Schoolteachers at all levels work with abused and neglected children. For this reason alone they should be better trained in the dynamics of domestic violence, but their knowledge ought to go beyond priming them to intervene in cases of abuse and neglect. Rather, information on domestic violence should become part of the curriculum from the earliest days a child attends school. In rural communities, students and parents alike should have the option of learning about parenting.

Fatality Review Teams

Given the number of domestic fatalities that occur in rural regions in states like Kentucky, there is an urgent need to set up domestic fatality review teams to explore fatalities to see if they were preventable. Child fatality reviews have been in operation for many years. When a child dies, a local team of people from multiple agencies convenes to scrutinize the events preceding the death. We will remember the victim blaming child fatality review in the aftermath of the homicide-suicide involving the Morrow family in Earlington, Western Kentucky, in which Leonard Morrow murdered his wife and two young children before taking his own life. There was no attempt in this case to explore the deaths of the adults. Indeed, adult domestic fatalities are only conducted in a limited number of jurisdictions, and then only in a very limited way. This tells us something about the dismissive way in which state agencies view the deaths of adults, particularly women, who have often borne the brunt of ongoing interpersonal violence. Again, funding agencies must take a lead here and begin the process of seriously reviewing what preceded these adult domestic fatalities with a view to understanding them better and, it is hoped, preventing future fatalities. We first need to know if there are any clear warning signs or identifiers with cases of woman battering that might escalate to lethal violence. The obvious candidates for red flags are things like (a) escalating violence, including threats to kill; (b) the use of weapons, especially firearms; (c) a history of hostage taking; (d) a history of the perpetrator committing violence against people other than his intimate partner; (e) the perpetrator being undeterred by standard criminal justice interventions, including a number of visits by police to the residence; (f) a history of being served with court orders restraining him from further abuse; (g) the perpetrator having a serious drug and/or alcohol problem; and (h) the perpetrator being suicidal. In cases where the risk of lethal violence seems high, we need to develop especially detailed safety plans for women and children. In the inevitable event that domestic fatalities occur, we need to convene fatality review teams, perhaps with some kind of enabling legislation, to conduct social postmortems on fatalities. These reviews should bring to the same table key players such as judges (not judges who sat in the case), police officers, prosecuting and defense attorneys, advocates for battered women, mental health professionals, other health professionals, and social service workers, depending upon the degree of involvement of these players prior to the fatal incident. The philosophy underpinning these inquiries should be one of discovering what happened, rather than attempting to attribute blame to various parties. These reviews could then provide a means for providing greater information to the public on domestic fatalities in their communities. Whether this dissemination of information would occur through the local or regional media would depend upon the nature of the case. Nevertheless, at some point the findings of these reviews should be made public. The publication would be just one more way of increasing awareness of the dangers posed by domestic violence and the failure to respond to it appropriately.

Conclusion: Battering, the Patriarchal State, and Rural Communities

The term *family values* is commonplace these days and its use is often underpinned by a longing to return the mythical good old days when women lived first and foremost as wives and mothers, duly nurtured by their husbands who sired their children. In many ways the use of the term family values recalls the older notion of the "Family

Ideal." Elizabeth Pleck (1987) reminds us that the Family Ideal has a long history dating back to antiquity (pp. 7-9). Its chief elements are: (a) a belief in the "privacy of the family" and the separation of the private and public spheres, and especially the celebration of the family as a respite from the incursions of the state; (b) a commitment to upholding conjugal and parental rights, including the rights of husbands to discipline wives, servants, and children; and (c) a conviction that the family be preserved and that marriage and the raising of children is a lifelong calling. As historians have pointed out, the Family Ideal has borne little resemblance to the diverse realities of family life (see Ryan, 1982). Modern-day talk of family values calls for a return to a nuclear family in which the husband is the principal or only breadwinner and "his" wife stays at home to have "quality time" with the children and look after the household. However, only a small proportion of modern families approximate this "ideal." Indeed, familial relations that come closer to the Family Ideal are more likely to be found in rural communities where marriage rates are higher, gender stereotypes more pronounced, and cohabitation less well tolerated.

The fact that rural communities exhibit more privatized forms of patriarchy than their urban counterparts may lead us to believe that policy initiatives designed to confront rural battering would be met with considerable resistance or doomed to failure. To some extent my ethnographic findings support such beliefs. However, rural communities also exhibit a homogeneity/cohesiveness that might be utilized to confront violence against women. Many men do not use violence against women. For some of these men the use of violence against women is cowardly or unmanly. Neither should we forget that many men do not need to use violence against women to benefit from the fruits of patriarchy. For still other groups of men, the use of violence against women in interpersonal relationships may even threaten the legitimacy of their patriarchal heritage. Betsy Stanko (1994) suggests "that how violence is invoked or provoked will differ widely among men" (p. 45, n. 1). Those rural men who do not resort to battering may be open to community-based education about the inappropriateness of this form of behavior. Given the closer ties in rural communities, it may be possible to enlist the support of these men in ways that would be more difficult to achieve in urban centers. If it were possible to enlist the support of rural men who eschew battering as a form of patriarchal control, then such a development might be the thin-end-of-the wedge toward a longer-term challenge to some of the nonviolent patriarchal

control mechanisms in families and elsewhere. None of these developments will be possible without a multitude of structural interventions
that elevate the social standing of rural women.

A central finding of my ethnography is that rural battered women
carve out opportunities to resist the violence of their abusers. Not all
of their interactions with state agencies are negative. A number of
women report that the interventions of police, judges, social workers,
and especially shelter providers, have been crucial to their survival.
This was as true for rural women who lived closer to shelters as it was
for women who lived in much more remote locations. We discount
the experiences of these women at our peril. If we write off these
apparently "good" experiences as mere "false consciousness," we
perpetuate that patriarchal style of reasoning that discounts the voices
of the subordinate. Rather, we would do well to integrate the voices
of those women who have had positive experiences with state agencies
and use them as a springboard to further action.

Mazur and McBride-Stetson (1995), in their comparative analysis
of the workings of state feminism, find that organizations set up by
the state to further women's interests have played a significant role in
improving the status of women. These authors usefully distinguish
between governmental agencies that act with a feminist agenda and
those that do not.[13] They observe,

> In contrast to the structures of the welfare state or of the liberal state,
> which have excluded feminist policy from political debate, those
> established with a mandate to focus directly on women's status have
> the capacity to turn leaders' attention, in some cases for the first time,
> to laws and regulations that can change the status of women in
> relation to men. (p. 272)

This distinction between feminist/pro-feminist state agencies and their
differential effectiveness in serving women is evident at the local level
in Kentucky. Rural shelter director Clay sees the state as a necessary
nuisance for the albeit paltry level of funding the shelters receive. She
resents the bureaucratizing tendencies of the state and sees the impersonal and formal face of state programs as antithetical to the interests
of battered women residing in rural shelters. Clay comments,

> *Clay:* Once they've funded us I want them to get the fuck out of
> the way. On our worst day we do a much better job of serving

and listening to women than the people at social services or mental health.

Her words clearly point to the disjuncture between the nonfeminist welfare agencies of the liberal state and the activist-type work performed on behalf of women in her spouse abuse shelter. For Clay, shelters have the potential to unleash powerful political forces that act with and for battered women. In this sense, shelters express the same feminist spirit as the KDVA itself and the Kentucky Commission on Women.[14] Given this divide between feminist and nonfeminist arms of the patriarchal state, a central policy issue is how to extend feminist influence to nonfeminist agencies that also have significant or potentially significant contact with rural battered women. I suggest this is a central issue because the patriarchal state is not going to go away. To ignore the state, or to dismiss it, is, I contend, of less use to rural battered women than to influence and infiltrate the nonfeminist state organizations. Put simply, my ethnographic findings suggest that extending the network of state feminism, rather than backing it into isolated pockets of resistance, is the way to proceed.

Other aspects of my ethnographic work support my argument for extending the net of state feminism. Although rural battered women are physically and socioculturally isolated, they are not completely cut off from the state. While there is clearly a rural antipathy toward government and outsiders in general, we cannot ignore the numerous links among battered women, rural police, the courts, social services, and shelter systems. My findings resonate with those of Linda Gordon's (1990) study of family violence in Boston. She comments,

> the condemnation of agency intervention into the family, and the condemnation of social control itself as something automatically evil, usually assumes that there can be, and once was, an autonomous family. On the contrary, no family relations have been immune from social regulation. (p. 191)

As I argued in Chapter 6, the patriarchal state does not act to reproduce neatly the structure of rural patriarchy. I highlighted what Patricia Gagne (1990) calls "democratic spaces," which battered women and advocates "work" to their own advantage. Again, Linda Gordon's (1990) critical analysis of the concept of "social control" as only oppressing women is helpful here. She comments, "the social control explanation sees the flow of initiative going in only one direction: from top to bottom, from professionals to clients, from elite to subordinate" (p. 192).

Increasing the role of the state in the handling of rural woman battering does not therefore have to work against the interests of battered women. If the state network is made more extensive through the expanding influence of state feminism, as articulated at state level in Kentucky through the Kentucky Commission on Women and the KDVA, and at local level through the spouse abuse shelters, then there is a much greater chance that the interests of battered women themselves will be represented. Indeed, the view of the state and social policy that emerge from my ethnography is consistent with other works that see the state as complex, contradictory, multifaceted, and relational (see Connell, 1987; Ehrenreich & Fox Piven, 1983; Fox Piven, 1990; Gagne, 1996; Walby, 1990).

Having said that the expansion of state feminism will benefit rural women, we must not fall into the trap of applying knowledge gained from urban settings to the politics of rural woman battering. Rural physical and sociocultural isolation make it more difficult for the services of the interventionist patriarchal state to infiltrate remote sites. For this reason we need much more research on the potential benefits of state intervention in the lives of rural battered women and their families. If we accept the potential of state involvement, then it is worth refining the delivery of these services.

In rural communities, the shelter and its attendant outreach capabilities ought to be considered the logical focal point from which to coordinate the delivery of a multitude of state services to battered women. For such focal points to emerge there has to be a dramatic increase in the level of state funding to rural shelters. Running a shelter is labor intensive and expensive. As it is, shelter staff are poorly paid and highly stressed. Rural shelters need more direct-contact personnel to work with battered women and orchestrate this multiagency offensive.

In so identifying shelters as the natural centers of coordinated state intervention into violent families, I conclude by reemphasizing the importance of having battered women and their advocates in the front line of service delivery. Rural shelters ought to be networked with law enforcement, the judiciary, social services, public health services, and job training agencies in a way that empowers battered women and educates nonfeminist state agencies.

If we are to move toward a solution to the social problem of rural woman battering, then we must operationalize those policies that women and their advocates report as beneficial. This means listening to rural battered women and recognizing their agency and resistance. It also means acknowledging the nuances of rural cultures and the differences among battered women within those cultures. As I have tried to show in the course of this ethnography, rural culture differs among regions in Kentucky. At the same time, rural culture differs in Oregon, Kentucky, and upstate New York. The idiosyncrasies of these cultural differences must be factored into the formulation of policy.

Notes

1. Pleck (1987) specifically notes, "The fate of proposed legislation against family violence has depended to a large extent on how reformers regarded the Family Ideal. Those who criticized it most directly and vehemently were defeated" (pp. 9-10).

2. VAWA s.5.32. Before VAWA, the alien spouse was able to blackmail the spouse he was abusing by threatening not to file on her behalf if she reported the abuse. This meant the abused alien spouse had to endure victimization or risk deportation.

VAWA makes it a federal crime to cross state lines "with the intent to injure, harass or intimidate a spouse or intimate partner and such an action involves a crime of violence by which the victim is injured" [Section 2261 (a) (1)]. This federal crime is punishable by up to 5 years in prison. The sentence is increased if the abuser uses a dangerous weapon (10 years), causes life-threatening injury (20 years), or kills the victim (life). The Act also makes it a federal crime for an abuser to cross state lines and violate a valid protection order (section 2262). VAWA extends "full faith and credit" to orders issued in states from which battered women have fled, thereby retaining the protective power of those orders in other states. This is an important provision. If a woman flees from Kentucky to West Virginia, with a protection order that is valid for 3 years, then authorities in West Virginia must honor that order regardless of the fact that in West Virginia protection orders are issued for only 90 days.

Given that firearms tend to be much more common in rural communities, the Federal Gun Control Laws (18 U.S.C.A s.922 [d] [8], 922 [g] [8], and 924 [d] [1]) all address the purchase, transportation, and possession of firearms and ammunition by persons against whom protection orders have been issued. Section (g) makes it unlawful for anyone who is subject to a protection order to ship, transport, or possess in interstate commerce any firearm or ammunition; or to receive said items through interstate commerce (note that for the purposes of this law, *firearm* refers to handguns but not rifles or shotguns).

3. For further discussion of the notion of state feminism see Eisenstein (1990), Outshoorn (1992), Sawer (1990, 1993), and Siim (1991). For a different approach to the use of the term *state feminism*, see Hatem (1992), who uses the term to refer to welfare state policies in general.

4. Specifically: (a) the "excited utterance exception," see Federal Rule of Evidence 803 (2). An "excited utterance" is a statement relating to a startling event or condition made while the declarant was under the stress of excitement caused by the event or condition. These statements can be offered to prove the existence of an event, the fact the declarant witnessed the event, or the identity of the perpetrator; (b) the "present sense impression exception," which deems that if a statement describing or

explaining an event or condition is made while the declarant was in the process of perceiving the event, or immediately subsequent to the event, then that statement is not covered by the hearsay rule, see Federal Rule of Evidence 803 (1); (c) the "business record exception," see Federal Rule of Evidence 803 (6). This exception is especially useful when there are no witnesses to identify voices on 911 tapes.

5. This project involved conducting 510 structured interviews with a random sample of battered women residing in spouse abuse shelters in Kentucky. Findings indicate that when battered women present visible injuries to police officers, rural and urban women report few differences in the immediate provision of police services such as transporting women to shelters and arresting the abuser. In terms of rating police handling of domestics in their areas, urban battered women consistently evaluate police more highly. Both urban and rural women rate the overall performance of state police to be superior to that of local police. See Websdale and Johnson (1997a).

6. See, for example, Jeanne McDowell (1992). Nationally, roughly 9% of sworn police officers are women. In some urban centers such as Madison, Wisconsin, fully a quarter of the urban police force is composed of women. The numbers in Kentucky are much lower, however, especially in rural areas.

7. I am indebted to Helen Barter, Secretary of the Kentucky Sheriffs Boys and Girls Ranch, for providing me with these numbers. Telephone conversation, May 7, 1996.

8. For a recent analysis of the corrupt involvement of law enforcement agencies with illegal drug operations, see Chambliss (1995, pp. 108-111).

9. It is not my argument that existing shelters should be disbanded and the money plowed into outreach. Rather, we should build more shelters and dramatically increase the outreach services from both existing and new shelters.

10. The overall effect of increasing networking through shelters and their outreach services will be to bring women together. In farming areas in Kentucky the Homemaker Clubs traditionally served the purpose of bringing women together.

11. For an analysis of the social context of women's nervous complaints in Eastern Kentucky, see Van Schaik (1988). In particular, Van Schaik observes that the women she interviewed with "the nerves" had daily lives characterized by family problems, poverty, restricted employment opportunities, and limited emotional and social support. She comments, "The widespread use of psychotropic drugs, readily identified by these women as nerve pills, supports the belief that the nervous system, not the social system, is at fault" (p. 96).

12. Sara Buel, giving the keynote address at the Florida Coalition Against Domestic Violence Annual Meeting, January 29-31, 1997, Melbourne, Florida. Buel noted how some shelters had developed their own legal aid programs. For example, the House of Ruth in Baltimore now has its own attorneys. The American Bar Association also offers some pro bono services to battered women.

13. Mazur and McBride-Stetson conclude that women's policy machineries in Australia, Holland, Norway, and Denmark offer the greatest influence in the formulation of state policies and provide the greatest access to feminist groups, interests, and activists.

14. In other states we find a similar feminist or pro-feminist philosophy in the various Governor's Offices for Women. In Kentucky, the role of the Governor's Office for Women is filled by the Kentucky Commission on Women.

Appendix 1

Methodological Considerations

The Ethnographer as Invader

Whatever culture an ethnographer studies, there will always be limits to his or her understanding of that culture. Unfamiliar cultures have regularly sabotaged those of us who purport to understand social life. Classic ethnographic research (Malinowski, 1926, 1944, 1948; Mead, 1935; Radcliffe-Brown, 1948) involved cultural anthropologists immersing themselves in "strange" cultures in an attempt to describe and explain those cultures. These anthropologists described "primitive" peoples living in small-scale, preindustrial societies. Many of these classic studies provided an ideological justification for colonialism. Through long periods of fieldwork and by getting as close as possible to native culture, the cultural anthropologist aimed to produce an objective and scientific account of that culture. Denzin and Lincoln (1994) characterize the work of the classic ethnographer in the following terms: "The field-worker, during this period, was lionized, made into a larger-than-life figure who went into and then returned from the field with stories about strange people" (p. 7).

Borrowing from the logic of the early cultural anthropologists, a number of sociologists also engaged in ethnographic research. In a number of influential studies, sociologists did not seek out the "native" or "primitive" of preindustrial societies, but instead trained their gaze upon certain deviantized inhabitants of the burgeoning American city. The Chicago School sociologists developed rich descriptions of urban life through extensive observation and interviewing. The "other" in urban life was written into the tapestry of modern sociology through these research projects. These projects focused on the ecological distribution of social phenomena in different zones of the city. We learn in rich detail about "natural areas" such as the Jewish ghetto (Wirth, 1928/1956), Little Germany (Park, 1922/1971), Chinatown (Wu, 1926), hobo jungles (Anderson, 1923/1961), and places where the suicidal (Cavan, 1928/1965), the drug addicted (Dai, 1937/1970), and the mentally ill (Faris & Dunham, 1939/1965) congregate.

According to the Chicago School theorists, the distribution of urban deviance was governed by the degree of social disorganization in an area. Behaviors were deviant and certain urban zones socially disorganized if they departed from the middle-class norms of small town America and the wealthier suburbs of the cities. In the Chicago School analysis, the "primitive" studied by the cultural anthropologist was replaced by the "underclass deviant" constructed through the value judgments of the middle-class sociologists of the Chicago School. As with the cultural anthropologists, the Chicago School theorists constructed the "other" out of their own constellation of values and particularly their sense of what was normal and deviant. That labeling an urban zone "socially disorganized" was somewhat arbitrary is evidenced in William Foot Whyte's (1943) research into similar zones in the North End of Boston. Through his use of participant observation in the Italian American communities, Whyte argued that slum neighborhoods display high levels of social organization and cohesion. However, this cohesion may not be immediately apparent if sociologists enter the scene with a preconceived grid of ideas and questions based on their own (different) life experiences.

One of the strengths of Whyte's work was his keen appreciation of just how he differed from those he was studying. This appreciation allowed him partial entrance to the world of the Cornerville boys. In this sense, Whyte's appreciation of his own "otherness" as researcher is echoed in the work of a number of postmodernist ethnographers who openly acknowledge their limited ability to "tell it like it is." Michelle Fine (1994) discusses how qualitative researchers have created the "other" through their texts, which in some cases speak for and therefore simultaneously silence the "researched." She recommends that researchers acknowledge their own political role in the research and "position ourselves as no longer transparent, but as classed, gendered, raced, and sexual subjects who construct our own locations, narrate these locations, and negotiate our stances with relations of domination" (p. 76).

Fine also warns of recreating the exploitative colonial relation between cultural anthropologist and native through qualitative researchers purporting to "help" the researched. Instead, Fine alerts us to the dangers of speaking for the researched "other," at the same time remembering that valuable insights can emerge from outsiders studying insiders. She rejects the essentialist argument that only people of color can and should do race work, and only women can and should do gender work. However, the problem of what she calls "imperial translation" remains.

There are a number of parallels between the desire of ethnographers to acknowledge the role of their own political stance and the work of feminist criminologists in pointing out the political basis of traditional positivist criminology. Feminist criminologists have called for methodologies that debunk the objectivist posturing of the social scientific paradigm. Gelsthorpe and Morris (1990) call for an enrichment of criminology through the utilization of feminist approaches that accentuate "engaging with the 'researched,' . . . and using sensitive research methods which maximize opportunities to reflect more accurately the experiences of 'the researched' " (p. 88).

Feminist criminologies have moved away from what has sometimes been called "malestream" criminology (see Gelsthorpe & Morris, 1990) and have broadened the research agenda to include topics hitherto ignored or marginalized by traditional criminology and the crime statistics and official (impersonal) data it feeds off of. These topics include studies of domestic violence, rape, and sexual assault. Feminist criminologists have also accessed the experiences of women and in so doing have contributed to an ongoing critique of empiricism in criminology. Their critique is not confined to epistemologies informed by feminist ways of knowing, but is embedded in the well-established tradition of ethnographic research.

Research Concerning Men Interviewing Women

There are few studies on the impact of gender incongruence between interviewer and interviewee. Among the few, most have studied structured interviews. For example, Hyman (1954) found that women were more likely to give conventional responses to male survey interviewers. Benney, Reisman, and Star (1956) found that male survey interviewers elicited fewer responses during interviews than women interviewers. Solicitation was lowest of all when men interviewed men. Landis, Sullivan, and Sheley (1973) report on 45 structured interviews of women by male interviewers and 45 by female interviewers. The interviews supposedly accessed interviewees' attitudes to feminist statements such as: "Women are definitely discriminated against." In comparing the outcomes of the interviews, Landis et al. note, "For eleven of the thirteen items, the response to the male interviewer was more 'feminist' than was the response to the female interviewer" (p. 309). This finding confounded their original hypothesis that women would present themselves as more feminist in the presence of female interviewers. Landis et al. suggest that their sample of women interviewees, drawn from college women, were at pains to assert themselves more in the presence of male interviewers.

Carol Warren (1988, p. 44) notes that women researchers may be better able to access to the inner world of feelings. A number of writers have suggested this might be because the "researched" open up more to women because they see women as less threatening (Codere [1986], Golde [1986], and Whitehead & Conaway [1986], all cited by Warren, 1988, p. 44). It may not always be desirable that women interviewers and ethnographers in general are perceived as less threatening. A number of researchers point out that in some field situations "anonymous, tense and even conflictual interactions may best elicit information" (Hondagneu-Sotelo, 1988, p. 617; see also Warren, 1988).

Notwithstanding the virtues of woman-to-woman research, there is evidence that sometimes women may not be able to interview other women successfully. Catherine Riessman (1987) reminds us that gender congruence may not be a sufficient condition for ensuring an empathetic exchange between interviewer and interviewee. She cites the discordance between a middle-class Anglo female interviewer and a working-class Hispanic woman (Marta). In particular, the interviewer attempted to control the interview process by trying to solicit a chronologically ordered narrative from Marta. Such solicitation was incongruous with Marta's ethnic background and life experiences. The middle-class Anglo interviewer was more successful when interviewing a white middle-class divorcee (Susan) who offered up her life as a "temporally ordered narrative" (p. 176). The lesson from Marta's interview was that, "Gender congruity is not enough . . . to overcome the ethnic incongruity" (p. 188). There have been a number of other examples in which gender congruence is not enough. These examples raise the question, just how much of an insider does one have to be to gain rich insights into the lives of interviewees? Nancie Gonzalez (1984) found that married Guatamalan women with children found it discourteous and embarrassing to discuss issues such as childbirth and pregnancy with women who were unmarried, childless, or both.

In their study of the effects of interviewer gender in in-depth interviews, Williams and Heikes (1993) found that "people used the interviewer's gender as a cue to gauge the interviewer's orientations and opinions, and they developed their responses within that gendered context" (p. 288). Williams and Heikes found a number of subtle differences in the way male nurses responded to male and female interviewers. Male nurses were more direct and forceful with male interviewers about expressing stereotypical views of women and the occupational place of women in nursing. Likewise, male nurses, in talking with female but not male interviewers, did not interject comments about their own sexual orientation. The nurses, when talking with female interviewers, were quicker to criticize the sexism directed at women. According to Williams and Heikes, the more "open" response to male interviewers may in part be a product of the "social desirability effect," whereby interviewees want to "look good" in front of the interviewer. For example, male nurses, not wanting to offend female interviewers, may have toned down their expression of stereotypical beliefs about the (gendered) place of women.

In spite of the profound influence of the gender of the interviewer upon the outcome of the interview, Williams and Heikes (1993) conclude that "the gender of the interviewer is not an insurmountable barrier to establishing rapport and achieving reliable results in in-depth interviewing" (p. 289).

However, they caution that,

> Men who study women using qualitative interviews may confront more formidable obstacles to rapport. Members of a subordinate group may be more wary and careful about what they say—as well as how they say it—to someone who represents the interests of powerful groups in society. (p. 289)

Other studies of the interview medium attacked the structured interview itself as being too impersonal and "objective" and especially unsuited for interviewing women about their life experiences (see Finch, 1984; Oakley, 1981). Ann Oakley (1981) identifies the traditional social scientific interview as masculinist. She argues the traditional interviewer is ideally objective; a mere conduit who elicits information from "respondents." The term *respondent* is a telling one for Oakley because it conveys the reality that interviewees are nonparticipating objects who essentially reply to questions. According to the textbook model, interviewers are ideally "friendly but not too friendly" (p. 33). Since the interviewer remains emotionally detached, he or she is less likely to contaminate the "yield" from the interviewee. Interviewers must strike the difficult balance between establishing enough rapport so that the respondent is sufficiently forthcoming, and yet remaining suitably detached so as not to contaminate the "data."

The traditional interview is designed to elicit a certain type and amount of information. According to Oakley, the traditional interview takes one of two forms. In the first, the interviewer assumes the role of phonograph and recording system. Here, the interviewer and interviewee are depersonalized. In the second, the interviewer assumes the role of psychotherapist. As an all-knowing listener, the interviewer makes nonjudgmental statements in order to build a permissive atmosphere that encourages openness on the part of interviewees. In both forms of traditional social science interviewing, the interviewer remains objective and the "yield" more scientific if the interviewee is objectified. Such interviewing assumes that "truth" awaits discovery and that only through the appropriately detached and clinical method can the interviewer approach that truth. This truth takes two forms. First, the interviewer elicits "the (little) truth" from the interviewee. Second, because the approach of the interviewer was standard in any number of interviews, the multiple truths can be compared to see if there is some "overriding (big) Truth" about the social phenomenon in question. By remaining detached, clinical, friendly, and professional, and by building suitable rapport, the interviewer ensures that little or no bias creeps into the interview exchange. Interview outcomes directed at the same topic can then be compared.

For Oakley, traditional interviewing styles will be particularly problematic for feminists who are interviewing other women, who may or may not be feminist. Here the hierarchical mode will be counterproductive because it is the experiences that women share that can be accessed through mutual and empathetic exchange that will tell us the most about women's lives. Rather than building rapport, the feminist interviewer already enjoys a certain level of rapport with women participants. This type of exchange is the antithesis of the traditional textbook interview. The nonhierarchical interview makes no pretense at being objective or unbiased.

If, according to Oakley, the traditional interview is masculinist, then do all men who interview women end up reproducing this hierarchical relationship? Is the interview exchange between men and women always doomed by wider structural constraints to be of a certain (exploitative) nature? or, can the adoption of subjective, qualitative methods by male, especially pro-feminist, interviewers sufficiently compensate for the political/emotional/experiential divide between men and women? While Oakley's pathbreaking analysis argues the masculinist interviewing mode is poorly suited to feminists interviewing women about their personal lives, she does not fall into the trap of essentialism by explicitly stating or, in my opinion implying, that when men interview women the result inevitably reproduces the masculinist paradigm of traditional textbook interviewing.

The interviewing work of both Oakley and Finch has been criticized for its insensitivity to the racial and class dynamics of the interview exchanges between women. Oakley (1980) withdrew minority women from her sample of interviewees to ensure "cultural homogeneity" (p. 99). She then proceeded to talk about "women" in general as a result of her findings. There are at least two problems here.

First, if feminism is concerned with inclusion rather than exclusion, the marginalization of minority women is deeply problematic. bell hooks (1982) sees the absence of black women from white feminist's accounts of women's lives as follows:

> The force that allows white feminist authors to make no reference to racial identity in their books about "women" that are in actuality about white women, is the same one that would compel any writer writing exclusively on black women to refer explicitly to their racial identity. That force is racism. (p. 138).

Edwards's (1990) interviews with black women in London found that these women were much less willing than white women to share information with her. She reports that the building of trust was not based on gender congruence alone. In fact, Edwards reports that

> rapport was easier after I had signaled not a non hierarchical, non exploitative, shared-sex relationship, but rather an acknowledgment that I was in a different structural position to them with regard to race and did not hold shared assumptions on that basis. (p. 486)

Second, Oakley interviewed both middle-class and working-class women in her culturally "homogeneous" sample. To suggest that the experiences of women from different classes can be conflated is to deny social class biography, or at least subsume it to the lived realities of gender oppression.

Rather than ruling out the possibility of men "successfully" interviewing women, some feminists have pointed to the experiential congruence between women as women that assists female interviewers and interviewees to explore hitherto marginalized areas of women's lives. Janet Finch (1984) observes,

> there are grounds for expecting that where a woman researcher is interviewing other women, this is a situation with special characteristics conducive to the easy flow of information . . . the structural position of women, and in particular their consignment to the privatized, domestic sphere makes it particularly likely that they will welcome the opportunity to talk to a sympathetic listener. (p. 74)

Importantly, Finch also states that while woman-to-woman interviewing constitutes a special situation, "This is not to say that men can never make good interviewers. . . . Men . . . can be very effective in getting both women and men to talk about intimate aspects of their lives" (p. 75).

As a pro-feminist man, I readily acknowledge that feminism has enlivened academic discourse and forced sociologists to reassess their ontological, epistemological, and methodological axioms. By *pro-feminist men,* I refer to those men who are sympathetic to the broad aims of feminist perspectives and recognize the systemic and historically enduring oppression of women, but who have not felt the weight of that oppression firsthand. I emphasize pro-feminist men here, not in the sense of privileging them vis-à-vis research on gender issues, but because I think pro-feminist men might be among those most interested in and knowledgeable about the oppression of women. Part of the reason for my stressing pro-feminist men is that I am working from the assumption that good ethnographic research and interviewing is best achieved by establishing some rapport with researched subjects.

Rapport building requires a familiarity on the part of the interviewer with the life "issues" of researched subjects.

However, few men conduct personal interviewing with women from a pro-feminist stance. Male researchers' lack of interest in women's issues is probably one reason why they have not interviewed women. In addition, the job of interviewing requires listening skills and empathy. These qualities have stereotypically been associated with women. Employers have therefore been more likely to hire women as interviewers. Moreover, interviewing work has been traditionally poorly paid and often part-time. These factors have also reduced the willingness of men to be interviewers.

My Conversations With Battered Women

By setting up a situation in which many women came to the interview as "battered" women (and many other kinds of women, be they "religious," "working-class," "Caucasian," etc.) wanting to tell their stories, I hoped to break down some of the obvious barriers to sharing. The battered women I talked with were living in the shelter because they had been battered. They came to the interviews knowing that I wanted to talk to them about some of the offenses committed against them. It might be objected that battered women on their way out of abusive relationships, or at least strategizing about how to change them, would resist/be incensed by an interviewer reminding them of their victimization. I have no easy way of knowing how this resistive effect played out. It is likely that women resisted my questions in ways that I was not (and still am not) aware of. Suffice it to say that overt and covert resistance in interviewing is probably an ever-present aspect of the negotiated encounter between researcher and researched.

I conducted focused or in-depth interviews with women. The types of questions varied considerably among interviews and similar questions were not asked in the same order or the same way. Interviews were taped and transcripts made available to interviewees. Only one woman objected to taping (in this case I took notes with her consent) although a number asked questions about my reasons for taping and how the tapes would be used. Many interviews took the form of partial life histories because I was interested in exploring the familial and cultural backgrounds of women. Usually, life history themes opened our conversations. Although I followed a "key words" card that reminded me of certain themes to raise, the directions taken by the interviews were heavily influenced by the women themselves. Usually we moved from a discussion of life history into conversations about her relationship with her abuser. This led into conversations about the interviewee's experiences of abuse. Having learned of her place in the community, her background, and her experience of abuse, I raised issues related to the state response to her victimization. Unlike Oakley (1981), who was able to engage in longitudinal interviewing and build personal friendships with some of her interviewees, my interviews were "one-offs." There were a number of reasons for this, most important of which was the personal safety of women. To "track" women once they had left the shelter would not have been safe for them (or myself).

Raised as a Caucasian male in a working-class British community, I had many things in common with interviewees around the axis of social class. In addition, all but five of the women I interviewed were Caucasian. As well as experiential incongruence based on gender, the cultural incongruence between us was marked. I, a college professor with a British accent, and they, women immersed in an impoverished rural cultural setting that, according to several women, dictated that women be "barefoot and pregnant."

It is important to note that during my conversations with women (battered and nonbattered) I did not directly ask questions like: "How do you feel about being interviewed by a man?" or "Are there things you might not feel comfortable talking with me about because I am a man?" To ask such a question early on may have primed the interviewee that there are things that should be withheld from a male interviewer. I did not want to set up a self-fulfilling prophecy. Neither did I later ask the question: "During the interview would you have given different answers if the interviewer was female?" I did not want to embarrass or indeed potentially harass women by asking them if they had not covered certain topics because I was male. Perhaps mistakenly, I felt that questions about the possibility of my maleness taking the conversations in different directions might be construed by women as insensitive or pushy.

It is possible that the effects of gender incongruence work themselves out in unforeseen and rather discrete ways. While women may not have openly refused to divulge sensitive information, the gender incongruence between us may have impacted the interview exchange in other ways. In talking about her dealings with a woman judge, Deanna comments:

> *Deanna:* She was nice. I thought she would be more understanding toward women because she was a woman judge [Belson] herself.

However, later in the interview Deanna reports Judge Belson failed to live up to her potential as a sensitive ear.

> *Websdale:* So what did you think of Judge Belson's decision in the case?
>
> *Deanna:* I thought it was unfair [The judge slapped a restraining order on Deanna based on the fact that Deanna had assaulted her husband].

Our discussion about the gender of Judge Belson did not seem to be hindered by gender incongruence. Deanna was not shy about expressing her initial thoughts that a woman might make a more sympathetic judge. Consequently I did not get the sense that the social desirability bias was at work at this stage of the interview. Had it been, Deanna may have been reluctant to tell me that she thought female judges had the potential to be more understanding. It was not until a good bit later in the interview that Deanna reported she was unhappy with Judge Belson's handling of the case.

Mimi also went before a female judge to obtain a restraining order against her abusive husband. She reported that the judge was overly sympathetic in a manner bordering bias. The conversation developed as follows:

> *Websdale:* How did you find the judge?
>
> *Mimi:* I found her extremely sympathetic to me. I would say she was biased in favor of me. . . . I'm not sure what word I'm looking for. It's not "hostile." She just seemed extremely biased. If, if I have any criticism of the handling of the case (and I'm not sure that I want to think of it as a criticism) it was Judge Cole's attitude toward my husband.

Here we might be seeing the operation of the social desirability bias, as Mimi tells me that she may have been favored because she was a woman. In deference to my status as a man, she may have been telling me that her abuser was unfairly treated because he was a man.

However, this is a difficult judgment call because Mimi also says that even if the judge did have a bias against her husband solely because he was a man, Mimi is not sure if she wants to criticize that bias.

In the final analysis, I concluded it was impossible to tell how the mixed-sex conversations between us were shaped by gender incongruence. In my interviews with African American women, my (uncertain) sense is that race trumped sex as the key point of difference between us. Then again, it is difficult to tell how the role of local rural culture and my position as outsider affected exchanges.

Conversations With Other "Others"

In addition to the 50 battered women, I also interviewed 46 people including police officers who worked "domestics," judges who deliberated over domestics, social workers who worked with families in which domestic violence was occurring, shelter personnel who worked with women and families in shelters, attorneys who worked domestic cases, leaders of the spouse abuse shelter movement in Kentucky, and journalists. Many of the points I have made above about experiential incongruence would also apply to these interviews as well. However, none of the 46 professionals I talked with occupied the same social position as the battered women. Put simply, the professionals are other "others," insofar as the power differential between myself and them tended to be much less than it was between myself and battered women. In many of my interviews with professionals, the interviewees not only knew a lot more about certain aspects of "domestics" than I did, but they also occupied positions of high social standing in the community. Among those of high social standing I include judges, attorneys, and some local sheriffs. Often, I had to ask favors of people to arrange these interviews for me.[1]

Academic knowledge is seen by many people as somehow abstracted from the real world. In these hard times, college professors are often regarded as privileged people who live in an insulated ivory tower of books and obscure knowledge. This perception is not without foundation. In my interviews with professionals I was aware of this rift between myself and them. Some interviewees directly reminded me of the worth of their practical everyday experience versus "book knowledge." I tried to use this rift to my advantage wherever I could by telling interviewees up front that I had no firsthand experience that could compare to their own and that that was why I wanted to interview them.

I interviewed 17 police officers of varied rank and from various rural jurisdictions.[2] The idea was to tap the experiences of those officers who dealt firsthand with rural domestics. I was introduced to these officers in a variety of ways and by a number of different people, some of whom were involved in the spouse abuse shelter movement in Kentucky. My conversations with police officers, as with battered women, were open ended and covered a wide range of topics. Although they knew I wanted to address the topic of domestic violence, they talked freely about a variety of issues. Conversations normally began with a brief life history and career sketch and then moved on to a general discussion of policing issues in the particular locale where they worked. Only then did we move on to talk about violence within families and the criminal justice response to it. In particular, the officers shared their perceptions of how they and other officers dealt with rural domestics. They also addressed diverse topics such as the role of training in improving police responses, the role of liability issues and the officers' legal responsibilities at the scene, and the problems associated with patrolling in difficult rural terrain.

Nearly all of the officers had lived in their rural communities all their lives and knew those communities very well. They were virtually unanimous in their perception that rural policing is very different from big city or even small city policing. In particular, they stressed their connectedness to the public. Having talked of the technicalities of policing domestics and their broader role in the community, we discussed some of the thornier issues with regard to their response to rural battering. These issues included discussing the patriarchal attitudes of police; and the compromised nature of rural policing, especially when officers know batterers personally, or, on rarer occasions, when batterers may know that attending officers sometimes engage in illegal activities.

I also interviewed 11 judges, all of whom had considerable experience dealing with domestic cases.[3] These included one state Supreme Court Justice, whom I interviewed face to face; 4 circuit court judges; and 6 district judges. My conversations with these judges covered a vast amount of ground and did not dwell too long on the legal technicalities of disposing of domestic cases. I was much more interested in their perceptions of the communities in which they worked and their general feelings about violence against women in rural communities. We talked a lot about politics in Kentucky and legal change. Since 3 of the judges were women, our conversations also explored the position of women in Kentucky. With all judges I delved into their understanding of the gendered dynamics of violence within families.

The nine advocates for battered women I interviewed worked in shelters or for what I call in the text "agencies of state feminism." These nine women were incredibly knowledgeable about rural domestic violence and also had a fine read of local and statewide politics, particularly as those politics impact the battered women's movement in Kentucky. It was during these interviews that I was able to glean information that allowed me to construct a number of bridging links between acts of battering, the local patriarchal milieu, and the specific elements of the state response or lack of response to violence within families, between intimate partners, or both.

I also interviewed four attorneys who all had experience working domestic cases. Two of the attorneys had served on advisory boards and task forces on domestic violence and had worked with poor clients in rural communities. Both had worked domestic cases involving severe violence. One had worked a recent and well-publicized rural domestic homicide case, successfully prosecuting a batterer who had murdered his wife. These interviews provided yet another lens through which to visualize the phenomenon of rural battering and the criminal justice response to it. My intent in interviewing these attorneys was not to gain any "representative" insights into how lawyers worked rural domestics, but rather to gain a general sense of how the law applied to various aspects of domestic cases. In addition to these four interviews, I talked with a dozen attorneys to clarify smaller points about specific cases I was interested in. Some of these attorneys I talked with on a number of occasions. These became more like key informants, often providing helpful leads to sources of information (and controversy).

As with the four attorneys, I interviewed two social workers to gain an entrée into the world of social work and rural domestic violence. Spouse abuse shelter employees provided the names of both social workers. One social worker was supportive of battered women and worked well with them. The other had a reputation for wanting battered women to "pull themselves up by their own bootstraps," and was not liked by spouse abuse shelter employees. The two represented opposite ends of a continuum of social worker involvement in domestics from supportive/understanding to dismissive/unsympathetic.

Observation

Direct and overt observation of police behavior is a well-established ethnographic method in criminology and sociology (see Bittner, 1967; Black, 1971; Black & Reiss, 1967; Chambliss, 1994; Ferraro, 1989a; Piliavin & Briar, 1964). Different researchers have immersed themselves to different degrees in police subculture in order to observe behavior. Some have ridden with police officers and otherwise observed interactions between the police and the public. Other researchers have immersed themselves in police culture for much longer periods of time and engaged in what is more aptly called participant observation (see Punch, 1979). Regardless of the degree of immersion in police subculture, there are a number of problems and limitations with observation or participant observation work with police. Most important perhaps is that police may alter their behavior because of the presence of the observer. Punch (1979) spent 6 months observing the same group of police officers to produce only a partial account of their behavior. He notes the limitations of his own method by documenting what happened at a social event with police officers after he had ceased his field observations of them:

> One evening I went to Ivan's flat for a celebration and several policemen began talking excitedly about corruption. I learnt more in that evening, thanks to the liberating effects of alcohol, than in all my fieldwork. It was not so much a series of shocking personal revelations ... but more a subterranean police culture which had largely escaped me. (Punch, 1979, p. 13, cited in Brogden, Jefferson, & Walklate, 1988, pp. 45-46)

As Punch found, secrecy is a key component of police subculture, and as one officer told him at the social event referred to above, "We only let you see what we wanted you to see. You only saw about fifty per cent" (Punch, 1979, p. 13, cited in Brogden et al., 1988, pp. 45-46).

For the purposes of learning more about the policing of rural woman battering, I made limited use of direct observation of police intervention. In total, I spent 24 hours riding with and observing officers in rural locations. Some of this time, officers worked domestic cases. It became clear to me that officers were understandably reluctant to allow a member of the public access to a heated domestic scene. Officers communicated this danger to me in different ways. Before our ride commenced, one officer opened the trunk of the vehicle and showed me how to use the shotgun, just in case "we" got into trouble and I was left on my own. I clearly did not engage domestics in the same way officers did. In one incident, we rode to a domestic at a remote house several miles up a hollow in Eastern Kentucky. Two officers approached the premises where a suspect was believed to be armed and dangerous. I was told to remain behind the vehicle while officers intervened and apprehended the offender, who had assaulted a woman he was living with. It was not my desire to approach the residence and observe while officers handled the situation. In fact this incident, among many, reminded me of my cushy number in the academic ivory tower.

It also became clear to me that I would not be able to observe many of the behaviors that battered women had complained about police officers engaging in. While I had no way of knowing whether officers I rode with concealed their true beliefs about domestics, my sense is that my presence limited how they behaved and what they revealed. Knowing that I was interested in the policing of domestic violence, and knowing that the press had been very critical of some police action at domestics in rural Kentucky, it is reasonable to assume officers would have been wary of me. Consequently, I chose to use the observation time to talk more with officers and scout out the communities officers policed. These observations of rural policing were, in many ways, more helpful than many of things I heard from officers about domestics.

Participant Observation

In addition to my interviewing and limited observation work, I also participated in a number of activities that increased my understanding of rural woman battering. For a year, I served on the advisory board of a rural spouse abuse shelter and became familiar with a number of different aspects of running a shelter, including building maintenance and security, the relationship between the shelter and the criminal justice system and the shelter and the community, fund-raising, the transportation of women, the networking between the shelter and the courts and social services, and the hiring of shelter personnel.

For 2 consecutive years (Websdale & Johnson, 1993, 1994) I acted as the evaluator of a U.S. Department of Labor demonstration grant in 7 of the 15 spouse abuse shelters in Kentucky. This demonstration grant provided approximately $500,000 per annum to provide homeless battered women with job training, job leads, and independent housing in an attempt to empower them. In the space of 2 years I conducted more than 100 in-depth interviews with spouse abuse shelter staff, battered women who were participating or had participated in the program, job trainers, social service providers in the community, and teachers. Three of these seven shelter sites are located in rural areas, and the other four, although located in urban areas, serve large numbers of women from the rural hinterland. The findings from these two evaluations form the subject of other research and, for the most part, are not reported in this book. However, the problems of rural women who entered the job training program are similar to those of other rural women who have not had the choice to participate in such a program. Consequently, although I do not report excerpts from these interviews with rural women who participated in the job training programs, the general themes from those interviews consistently blend with the themes from my conversations with battered women noted above. Most important, the job training interviews added to my beliefs that the rural sociocultural context is profoundly constricting for battered women.

Finally, in my role as a researcher, I presented a number of findings on woman battering and the criminal justice system response to it, to the Kentucky Legislative Task Force on Domestic Violence.[4] My interaction with members of the Task Force is discussed in Chapter 6. Suffice it to say at this point that the preparation, presentation, and discussion of these research findings provided rich insights into the mechanics of formal political processes.

Notes

1. My interview with Kentucky Supreme Court Justice Stumbo took a couple of months to arrange. This was not because of the judge's reluctance to talk, but because of the problem of going through intermediaries who had very busy schedules and who trod very delicately in the political arena. When I finally did talk with this judge, the conversation was long, cordial, and extremely valuable.

2. These included one police chief, three sheriffs, seven municipal officers, three state troopers, and three sheriff's deputies.

3. In addition to these 11, I also contacted a number of other judges who disposed of some of the cases I discuss in Chapter 5. Given the negative press a number of these judges received, I wanted to give them a chance to respond. While conversations were often long, I do not include these judges among the ranks of interviewees because they explicitly stated they did not want to be cited in the book. One of these judges told me he could not "take on the press."

4. This presentation was given with a coresearcher on some later research, Dr. Byron Johnson. I presented material on urban and rural violence against women and rural and urban policing. Dr. Johnson presented findings from a needs assessment survey funded by the Jewish Women's League. The hearing took place in Frankfort, Kentucky on August 22, 1995. See *Lexington Herald-Leader,* August 23, 1995 for a brief summary of the hearing.

Appendix 2
Regional Map of Kentucky

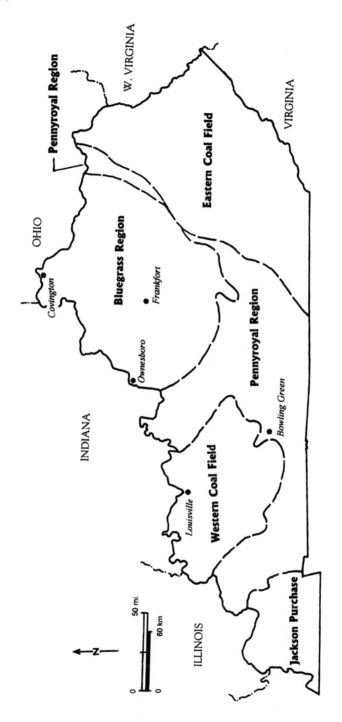

References

Abramovitz, M. (1988). *Regulating the lives of women: Social welfare policy from colonial times to the present.* Boston: South End.

Abramovitz, M. (1994). Challenging the myths of welfare reform from a woman's perspective. *Social Justice, 21*(1), 17-21.

Allen, N. H. (1983). Homicide followed by suicide: Los Angeles, 1970-1979. *Suicide and Life Threatening Behavior, 13*(3), 155-165.

Alsdurf, J., & Alsdurf, P. (1989). *Battered into submission.* Downers Grove, IL: InterVarsity Press.

Althusser, L. (1966). *For Marx.* London: Allen Lane.

Anderson, N. (1961). The hobo: The sociology of the homeless man. Chicago: University of Chicago Press. (Original work published 1923)

Aries, P. (1962). *Centuries of childhood: A social history of family life.* New York: Random House.

Attorney General's Task Force on Domestic Violence Crime. (1993). *Domestic violence fatalities, a statistical report, October 1993.* Frankfort: Kentucky Cabinet on Human Resources.

Austin, T. L. (1981). The influence of court location on type of criminal sentence: The rural-urban factor. *Journal of Criminal Justice, 9,* 305-316.

Avila, M. (1969). *Tradition and growth.* Chicago: University of Chicago Press.

Bachman, R. (1992). Crime in nonmetropolitan America: A national accounting of trends, incidence rates and idiosyncratic vulnerabilities. *Rural Sociology, 57*(4), 546-560.

Bachman, R. (1994). *Violence against women: A National Crime Victimization Survey report.* Washington, DC: Bureau of Justice Statistics.

Bachman, R., & Saltzman, L. (June, 1995). *Violence against women: Estimates from the redesigned survey.* Washington, DC: Bureau of Justice Statistics.

Bankston, W., & Allen, H. (1980). Rural social areas and patterns of homicide: An analysis of lethal violence in Louisiana. *Rural Sociology, 45,* 223-237.

234

Barlow, M., Barlow, D. E., & Chiricos, T. (1995). Economic conditions and ideologies of crime in the media: A content analysis of crime news. *Crime and Delinquency, 41*, 3-19.

Barrett, M. (1980). *Women's oppression today: Problems in Marxist feminist analysis.* London: Verso.

Bartol, A. (1996). Structures and roles of rural courts. In F. D. McDonald, B. Wood, & M. Pflug (Eds.), *Rural criminal justice: Conditions, constraints and challenges* (pp. 79-92). Salem, WI: Sheffield.

Baumer, T. (1978). Research on fear of crime in the U.S. *Victimology, 3*(3-4), 254-264.

Bealer, R. C., Willits, F. K., & Kuvlesky, W. P. (1965). The meaning of rurality in American society: Some implications of alternative definitions. *Rural Sociology, 30*(3), 255-266.

Becker, H. (1963). *Outsiders: Studies in the sociology of deviance.* New York: Free Press.

Bell, D., & Klein, R. (Eds.). (1996). *Radically speaking: Feminism reclaimed.* North Melbourne, Australia: Spinifex.

Bell, D. J. (1984a). The police response to domestic violence: An exploratory study. *Police Studies, 7*, 23-30.

Bell, D. J. (1984b). The police response to domestic violence: A replication study. *Police Studies, 7*, 136-143.

Bell, D. J. (1985). A multiyear study of Ohio urban, suburban, and rural police dispositions of domestic disputes. *Victimology, 10*, 301-310.

Bell, D. J. (1986). Domestic violence in small cities and towns: A pilot study. *Journal of Crime and Justice, 9*, 163-181.

Bell, D. J. (1989). Family violence in small cities: An exploratory study. *Police Studies, 12*(1), 25-31.

Benney, M., Reisman, D., & Star, S. (September, 1956). Age and sex in the interview. *American Journal of Sociology, 62*, 143-152.

Berk, R. A., Campbell, A., Klap, R., & Western, B. (1992). A Bayesian analysis of the Colorado Springs Spouse Abuse Experiment. *Journal of Criminal Law and Criminology, 83*(1), 170-200.

Berman, A. L. (1979). Dyadic death: Murder-suicide. *Suicide and Life Threatening Behavior, 9*(1), 15-23.

Bergen, R. K. (1996). *Wife rape: Understanding the response of survivors and service providers.* Thousand Oaks, CA: Sage.

Bescher-Donnelly, L., & Whitener-Smith, L. (1981). The changing roles and status of rural women. In R. T. Coward & W. M. Smith, Jr. (Eds.), *The family in rural society* (Westview Special Studies in Contemporary Social Issues, pp. 169-185). Boulder, CO: Westview.

Bishop, B. (1993, June 6). Rural America strangles in grip of lasting poverty. *Lexington Herald-Leader,* pp. D1, D4.

Bittner, E. (1967). The police on death row: A study in peacekeeping. *American Sociological Review, 32*, 699-715.

Black, D. (1971, June). The social organization of arrest. *Stanford Law Review, 23*, 1087-1111.

Black, D. (1989). *Sociological justice.* New York: Oxford University Press.

Black, D., & Reiss, A. (1967). *Studies of crime and law enforcement in major metropolitan areas* (Vol. 2). Washington, DC: Government Printing Office.

Bodenheimer, T. (1996). The industrial revolution in health care. *Social Justice, 22*(4), 26-42.

Bogal-Allbritten, R., & Daughaday, L. R. (1990). Spouse abuse program services: A rural-urban comparison. *Human Services in the Rural Environment, 14*(2), 6-10.

Boggs, S. L. (1971). Formal and informal crime control: An exploratory study of urban, suburban, and rural orientations. *Sociological Quarterly, 12*(Summer), 319-327.

Bordua, D. J., & Lizotte, A. J. (1979). Patterns of illegal firearms ownership. *Law and Policy Quarterly, 1*(2), 147-175.

Bowker, L. H. (1983). *Beating wife beating.* Lexington, MA: Lexington Books.

Bowker, L. H. (1997). A criminological perspective: Redefining "battered women" for use in legal proceedings. *Domestic Violence Report, 2*(2), 17-18, 29.

Bowker, L. H., Arbitell, M., & McFerron, J. R. (1988). On the relationship between wife beating and child abuse. In K. Yllo & M. Bograd (Eds.), *Feminist perspectives on wife abuse* (pp. 158-174). Newbury Park, CA: Sage.

Bowker L. H., & Maurer, L. (1987). The medical treatment of battered wives. *Women's Health, 12,* 25-45.

Bowman, C. G. (1992). The arrest experiments: A feminist critique. *Journal of Criminal Law and Criminology, 83*(1), 201-208.

Breines, W., & Gordon, L. (1983). The new scholarship on family violence. *Signs: Journal of Women in Culture and Society, 8,* 490-531.

Brogden, M., Jefferson, T., & Walklate, S. (1988). *Introducing policework.* London: Unwin Hyman.

Brown, C. (1981). Mothers, fathers, and children: From private to public patriarchy. In L. Sargent (Ed.), *Women and revolution: A discussion of the unhappy marriage of Marxism and feminism* (pp. 239-267). Boston: South End.

Brown, S. E. (1984). Police responses to wife beating: Neglect of a crime of violence. *Journal of Criminal Justice, 12,* 277-288.

Brown, W. (1992). Finding the man in the state. *Feminist Studies, 18*(1), 7-34.

Browne, A. (1987). *When battered women kill.* New York: Free Press.

Bureau of Justice Statistics. (1990). *Handgun crime victims* (Special Report for the U.S. Department of Justice). Washington, DC: U.S. Department of Justice.

Bureau of Justice Statistics. (1990). Law enforcement management and administrative statistics (LEMAS) [Computer file]. Washington, DC: U.S. Department of Justice.

Bushy, A. (1993). Rural women: Lifestyle and health status. *Rural Nursing, 28*(1), 187-197.

Butler, A. (1996). The effect of welfare benefit levels on poverty among single-parent families. *Social Problems, 43*(1), 94-115.

Butler, J. (1990). *Gender trouble: Feminism and the subversion of identity.* New York: Routledge.

Buzawa, E. S., & Buzawa, K. (1990). *Domestic violence: The criminal justice response.* Newbury Park, CA: Sage.

Byles, J. A. (1978). Family violence: Some facts and gaps. A statistical overview. In V. D'Oyley (Ed.), *Domestic violence: Issues and dynamic* (pp. 53-83). Toronto: Ontario Institute for Studies in Education.

Cain, M. (1973). *Society and the policeman's role.* London: Routledge & Kegan Paul.

Carby, H. (1982). White woman listen! Black feminism and the boundaries of sisterhood. In Centre for Contemporary Cultural Studies (Ed.), *The empire strikes back: Race and racism in 70s Britain* (pp. 212-235). London: Hutchinson.

Carter, T. J. (1982). The extent and nature of rural crime in America. In T. J. Carter, G. H. Phillips, J. F. Donnermeyer, & T. N. Wurcsmidt (Eds.), *Rural crime: Integrating research and prevention* (pp. 20-33). Totowa, NJ: Allanheld, Osmun.

Caudill, H. (1963). *Night comes to the Cumberlands: A biography of a depressed area.* Boston: Little, Brown.

Cavan, R. S. (1965). *Suicide.* New York: Russell and Russell. (Original work published 1928)

Chamberlain, M. (1975). *Fenwomen.* London: Virago.

Chambliss, W. (1994). Policing the ghetto underclass: The politics of law and law enforcement. *Social Problems, 41*(2), 177-194.

Chambliss, W. (1995). Another lost war: The costs and consequences of drug prohibition. *Social Justice, 22*(2), 101-124.

Chan, W. (1994). A feminist critique of self-defense and provocation in battered women's cases in England and Wales. *Women and Criminal Justice, 6*(1), 39-65.

Chesney-Lind, M. (1997). *The female offender.* Thousand Oaks, CA: Sage.

Chester, R., & Streather, J. (1972). Cruelty in English divorce: Some empirical findings. *Journal of Marriage and the Family, 34,* 706-710.

Christie, N. (1993). *Crime control as industry.* London: Routledge & Kegan Paul.

Chused, R. H. (1984). The Oregon Donation Act of 1850 and 19th century federal married women's property law. *Law and History Review, 2*(1), 44-78.

Clough, P. (1993). On the brink of deconstructing sociology: Critical reading of Dorothy Smith's standpoint epistemology. *The Sociological Quarterly, 34*(1), 169-182.

Cloward, R. (1959). Illegitimate means, anomie, and deviant behavior. *American Sociological Review, 24,* 164-176.

Codere, H. (1986). Field work in Rwanda, 1959-1960. In P. Golde (Ed.), *Women in the field: Anthropological experiences* (pp. 143-164). Berkeley: University of California Press.

Coles, R. (1971). *Children of crisis: Vol. 2. Migrants, sharecroppers, mountaineers.* Boston: Little, Brown.

Conklin, J. E. (1971). Dimensions of community response to the crime problem. *Social Problems, 18*(Winter), 373-385.

Conklin, J. E. (1976). Robbery, the elderly and fear: An urban problem in search of a solution. In J. Goldsmith & S. S. Goldsmith (Eds.), *Crime and the elderly* (pp. 99-110). Lexington, MA: Lexington Books.

Connell, J. (1978). *The end of tradition.* London: Routledge & Kegan Paul.

Connell, R. W. (1987). *Gender and power: Society, the person and sexual politics.* Palo Alto, CA: Stanford University Press.

Cooper, D. (1995). *Power in struggle: Feminism, sexuality and the state.* New York: New York University Press.

Council on Ethical and Judicial Affairs, American Medical Association. (1992). Physicians and domestic violence: Ethical considerations. *Journal of the American Medical Association, 267,* 3190-3193.

Council on Scientific Affairs, American Medical Association. (1992). Violence against women: Relevance for medical practitioners. *Journal of the American Medical Association, 267,* 3184-3189.

Currens, S. (1991). Homicide followed by suicide—Kentucky, 1985-1990. *Journal of the American Medical Association, 266,* 2062-2063.

Dai, B. (1970). *Opium addiction in Chicago.* Montclair, NJ: Patterson Smith. (Original work published 1937)

Daly, M. (1979). *Gyn/ecology: The metaethics of radical feminism.* London: Women's Press.

Davis, R. S., & Potter, G. W. (1991). Bootlegging and rural entrepreneurship. *Journal of Crime and Justice, 14*(1), 145-159.

Dawson, J. M., & Langan, P. A. (1994). *Murder in families* (U.S. Department of Justice, Bureau of Justice Statistics Special Report). Washington, DC: Government Printing Office.

Deavers, K. (1992). What is rural? *Policy Studies Journal, 20*(2), 184-189.

Decker, S. (1979). The rural county sheriff: An issue in social control. *Criminal Justice Review, 4*(2), 97-111.

Delphy, C. (1977). *The main enemy.* London: WRRC.

Denzin, N., & Lincoln, Y. (1994). Introduction: Entering the field of qualitative research. In N. Denzin & Y. Lincoln (Eds.), *Handbook of qualitative research* (pp. 1-17). Thousand Oaks, CA: Sage.

DeVault, M. (1990). Talking and listening from women's standpoint: Feminist strategies for interviewing and analysis. *Social Problems, 37*(1), 701-721.

Dewey, R. (1960). The rural-urban continuum: Real but relatively unimportant. *American Journal of Sociology, 66,* 60-66.

Dinitz, S. (1973). Progress, crime, and the folk ethic: Portrait of a small town. *Criminology, 112,* 3-21.

Dobash, R. E., & Dobash, R. (1977/1978). Wives: The "appropriate" victims of marital violence. *Victimiology, 2,* 426-442.

Dobash, R. E., & Dobash, R. (1979). *Violence against wives.* New York: Free Press.

Dobash, R. E., & Dobash, R. (1992). *Women, violence and social change.* New York: Routledge.

Dobash, R. E., Dobash, R., Wilson, M., & Daly, M. (1992). The myth of sexual symmetry in marital violence. *Social Problems, 39*(1), 71-91.

Dorpat, T. L. (1966). Suicide in murderers. *Psychiatry Digest, 7,* 51-55.

Duncan, C. (1992). Persistent poverty in Appalachia: Scarce work and rigid stratification. In C. Duncan (Ed.), *Rural poverty in America* (pp. 111-133). Westport, CT: Auburn House.

Dunford, F., Huizinga, D., & Elliot, D. S. (1990). The role of arrest in domestic assault: The Omaha police experiment. *Criminology, 28*(2), 183-206.

Durkheim, E. (1961). *The elementary forms of the religious life.* New York: Collier Books.

Durkheim, E. (1964). *The division of labor in society.* New York: Free Press.

Dutton, D. G. (1987). The outcome of court-mandated treatment for wife assault: A quasi-experimental evaluation. *Violence and Victims 1*(3), 163-175.

Dworkin, A. (1981). *Pornography: Men possessing women.* London: Women's Press.

Eaton, M. (1994). Abuse by any other name: Feminism, difference, and intralesbian violence. In M. A. Fineman & R. Mykitiuk (Eds.), *The public nature of private violence: The discovery of domestic abuse* (pp. 195-223). New York: Routledge.

Edwards, R. (1990). Connecting method and epistemology: A white woman interviewing black women. *Women's Studies International Forum, 13,* 477-490.

Edwards, S. (1989). *Policing domestic violence: Women, the law and the state.* Newbury Park, CA: Sage.

Ehrenreich, B., & Fox Piven, F. (1983). Women and the welfare state. In I. Howe (Ed.), *Alternatives: Proposals for America from the Democratic Left* (pp. 41-60). New York: Pantheon.

Eigenberg, H. (1990). The National Crime Survey and rape: The case of the missing question. *Justice Quarterly, 7,* 655-673.

Eisenstein, H. (1990). Femocrats, official feminism, and the uses of power. In S. Watson (Ed.), *Playing the state: Australian feminist interventions* (pp. 87-103). London: Verso.

Eisenstein, Z. (1984). *Feminism and sexual equality: Crisis in liberal America.* New York: Monthly Review Press.

Engels, F. (1970). The origin of the family, private property and the state. In K. Marx & F. Engels, *Selected works* (pp. 455-593). Moscow: Progress Publishers.

Engels, F. (1984). *The condition of the working class in England.* Chicago: Academy Publishers.

Esselstyn, T. C. (1953). Social role of the county sheriff. *Journal of Criminal Law and Criminology, 44*(2), 177-184.

Esterle, J. (1986). Crime and the media. *Jericho, 41*(5), 7.

Fagan, J. (1996). *the criminalization of domestic violence: Promises and limits.* Washington, DC: National Institute of Justice.

Fahnestock, K. (1992, Summer). Not in my county: Excerpts from a report on rural courts and victims of domestic violence. *The Judges Journal, 3,* p. 10.

Fahnestock, K., & Geiger, M. D. (1993). We all get along here: Case flow in rural courts. *Judicature, 76(5),* 258-263.

Faris, R. E. L., & Dunham, H. W. (1965). *Mental disorders in urban areas: An ecological study of schizophrenia and other psychoses.* Chicago: University of Chicago Press. (Original work published 1939)

Fassinger, P. A., & Schwartzweller, H. K. (1984). The work of farm women: A midwestern study. In H. K. Schwartzweller (Ed.), *Research in rural sociology and development* (pp. 37-60). Greenwich, CT: JAI.

Federal Bureau of Investigation. (1993). *Uniform crime reports: Crime in the United States.* Washington, DC: Government Printing Office.

Ferraro, K. J. (1989a). The legal response to woman battering in the U.S. In J. Hanmer, J. Radford, & E. Stanko (Eds.), *Women, policing, and male violence: International perspectives* (pp. 155-184). New York: Routledge.

Ferraro, K. J. (1989b). Policing woman battering. *Social Problems, 36,* 61-74.

Ferraro, K. J. (1993). Cops, courts and woman battering. In P. Bart & E. G. Moran (Eds.), *Violence against women: The bloody footprints* (pp. 165-176). Newbury Park, CA: Sage.

Field, M., & Field, H. (1973). Marital violence and criminal process: Neither justice nor peace. *Social Service Review, 47(2),* 221-240.

Finch, J. (1984). It's great to have someone to talk to: The ethics and politics of interviewing women. In C. Bell & H. Roberts (Eds.), *Social researching: Politics, problems, practice* (pp. 70-87). London: Routledge & Kegan Paul.

Fine, M. (1994). Working the hyphens: Reinventing self and other in qualitative research. In N. Denzin & Y. Lincoln (Eds.), *Handbook of qualitative research* (pp. 70-81). Thousand Oaks, CA: Sage.

Fink, D. (1986). *Open country, Iowa: Rural women, tradition and change.* Albany: State University of New York Press.

Fink, D. (1992). *Agrarian women: Wives and mothers in rural Nebraska 1880-1940.* Chapel Hill: University of North Carolina Press.

Finkelhor, D., & Yllo, K. (1985). *License to rape: Sexual abuse of wives.* New York: Holt, Rinehart & Winston.

Finn, P. (1989). Statutory authority in the use and enforcement of civil protection orders against domestic abuse. *Family Law Quarterly, 24(1),* 43-73.

Fischer, C. (1981). The public and private worlds of city life. *American Sociological Review, 46,* 306-316.

Fishman, P. (1978). Interaction: The work women do. *Social Problems, 25,* 397-406.

Fleming, J. B. (1979). *Stopping wife abuse.* Garden City, NY: Anchor.

Ford, D. A. (1991). Prosecution as a victim power resource: A note on empowering women in violent conjugal relationships. *Law and Society Review, 25,* 313-334.

Foucault, M. (1977). *Discipline and punish: The birth of the prison.* London: Tavistock.

Fox Piven, F. (1990). Ideology and the state: Women, power and the welfare state. In L. Gordon (Ed.), *Women, the state and welfare* (pp. 250-264). Madison: University of Wisconsin Press.

Frankenberg, R. (1957). *Village on the border.* London: Cohen and West.

Friedland, W. H. (1982). The end of rural society and the future of rural sociology. *Rural Sociology, 47,* 589-608.

Gagne, P. L. (1992). Appalachian women: Violence and social control. *Journal of Contemporary Ethnography, 20,* 387-415.

Gagne, P. (1996). Identity, strategy, and feminist politics: Clemency for battered women who kill. *Social Problems, 43*(1), 77-93.

Galliher, J. F., Donavan, L. P., & Adams, D. L. (1975). Small town police—Trouble, tasks and publics. *Journal of Police Science and Administration, 3*(1), 19-28.

Gans, H. (1962). Urbanism and suburbanism as ways of life. In A. Rose (Ed.), *Human behavior and social processes* (pp. 625-648). London: Routledge & Kegan Paul.

Gaquin, D. A. (1977/1978). Spouse abuse: Data from the National Crime Survey. *Victimology, 2,* 632-643.

Gardner, L., & Shoemaker, D. J. (1989). Social bonding and delinquency: A comparative analysis. *The Sociological Quarterly, 30,* 481-500.

Garfinkel, H. (1956). The conditions of successful degradation ceremonies. *American Journal of Sociology, 61,* 420-424.

Garfinkel, I., & McLanahan, S. (1986). *Single mothers and their children.* Washington, DC: Urban Institute.

Garkovich, L. (1991). Governing the countryside: Linking politics and administrative resources. In K. E. Pigg (Ed.), *The future of rural America: Anticipating policies for constructive change* (pp. 173-193). Boulder, CO: Westview.

Garner, J., Fagan, J., & Maxwell, C. (1995). Published findings from the Spouse Assault Replication Program: A critical review. *Journal of Quantitative Criminology, 11*(1), 3-28.

Gelles, R. (1974). *The violent home: A study of physical aggression between husbands and wives.* Beverly Hills, CA: Sage.

Gelles, R. (1979, October 7). The truth about husband abuse. *Ms.,* pp. 65-66.

Gelles, R. (1985). *Intimate violence in families.* Beverly Hills, CA: Sage.

Gelles, R., & Straus, M. (1988). *Intimate violence.* New York: Simon & Schuster.

Gelsthorpe, L., & Morris, A. (1990). *Feminist perspectives in criminology.* Philadelphia: Open University Press.

Gibbons, D. (1972). Crime in the hinterland. *Criminology, 10*(August), 177-190.

Giles-Sims, J. (1983). *Wife battering: A systems theory approach.* New York: Guilford.

Goffman, E. (1961). *Asylums: Essays on the social situation of mental patients and other inmates.* Harmondsworth, UK: Penguin.

Golde, P. (1986). Odessey of encounter. In P. Golde (Ed.), *Women in the field: Anthropological experiences* (pp. 67-93). Berkeley: University of California Press.

Gonzalez, N. (1984). The anthropologist as female head of household. *Feminist Studies, 10,* 97-114.

Gordon, L. (1988). *Heroes of their own lives: The politics and history of family violence.* New York: Penguin.

Gordon, L. (1990). Family violence, feminism, and social control. In L. Gordon (Ed.), *Women, the state and welfare* (pp. 178-198). Madison: University of Wisconsin Press.

Gorham, L. (1992). The growing problem of low earnings in rural areas. In C. Duncan (Ed.), *Rural poverty in America* (pp. 21-39). Westport, CT: Auburn House.

Graber, D. (1980). *Crime news and the public.* New York: Praeger.

Gramsci, A. (1971). *Selections from the prison notebooks.* London: Lawrence & Wishart.

Greven, P. (1991). *Spare the child: The religious roots of punishment and the psychological impact of physical abuse.* New York: Knopf.

Grimshaw, J. (1988). Pure lust: The elemental feminist philosophy of Mary Daly. *Radical Philosophy, 49,* 24-30.

Hagan, J. (1977). Criminal justice in rural and urban communities: A study of the bureaucratization of justice. *Social Forces, 55,* 597-612.

Hall, S. (1984). The state in question. In G. McLennan, D. Held, & S. Hall (Eds.), *The idea of the modern state* (pp. 1-28). Milton Keynes, UK: Open University Press.

Hamilton, B., & Coates, J. (1993). Perceived helpfulness and use of professional services by abused women. *Journal of Family Violence, 8,* 313-324.

Hanmer, J. (1978). Violence and the social control of women. In G. Littlejohn, B. Smart, J. Wakefield, & N. Yuval-Davis (Eds.), *Power and the state* (pp. 217-238). London: Croom Helm.

Hanmer, J. (1996). Women and violence: Commonalities and diversities. In B. Fawcett, B. Featherstone, J. Hearn, & C. Toft (Eds.), *Violence and gender relations: Theories and interventions* (pp. 7-21). Thousand Oaks, CA: Sage.

Hanmer, J., Radford, J., & Stanko, E. (Eds.). (1989). *Women, policing, and male violence: International perspectives.* New York: Routledge.

Hanmer, J., & Saunders, S. (1984). *Well-founded fear: A community study of violence to women.* London: Hutchinson.

Haraway, D. (1991). *Simians, cyborgs and women: The reinvention of nature.* New York: Routledge.

Harrell, A. (1991). *Evaluation of court-ordered treatment for domestic violence offenders* (Final report). Washington, DC: Urban Institute.

Hart, B. (1988). Beyond the duty to warn: A therapist's duty to protect battered women and children. In K. Yllo & M. Bograd (Eds.), *Feminist perspectives on wife abuse* (pp. 234-247). Newbury Park, CA: Sage.

Hart, B. (1993). Battered women and the criminal justice system. *American Behavioral Scientist, 36,* 624-638.

Hartmann, H. (1981). The family as the locus of gender, class, and political struggle: The example of housework. *Signs: Journal of Women in Culture and Society, 6,* 366-394.

Hatem, M. F. (1992). Economic and political liberation in Egypt and the demise of state feminism. *International Journal of Middle East Studies, 24,* 231-251.

Heidensohn, F. (1992). *Women in control? The role of women in law enforcement.* Oxford, UK: Clarendon.

Heise, L. I. (1996). Violence against women: Global organizing for change. In J. Edleson & Z. Eisikovits (Eds.), *Future interventions with battered women and their families* (pp. 7-33). Thousand Oaks, CA: Sage.

Hirschel, J. D., & Hutchinson, I. (1992). Female spouse abuse and the police response: The Charlotte, North Carolina experiment. *Journal of Criminal Law and Criminology, 83,*(1), 73-119.

Hirschel, J. D., Hutchinson, I., Dean, C., Kelley, J., & Pesackis, C. E. (1990). *Charlotte Spouse Assault Replication Project: Final report.* Washington, DC: National Institute of Justice.

Hoffman, S., & Duncan, G. (1988). What are the economic consequences of divorce? *Demography, 25,* 641-645.

Hondagneu-Sotelo, P. (1988). Gender and fieldwork. *Women's Studies International Forum, 11,* 611-618.

hooks, b. (1982). *Ain't I a woman: Black women and feminism.* London: Pluto.

hooks, b. (1984). *Feminist theory: From margin to center.* Boston: South End.

Hopkins County Joint Child Fatality Task Force report. (1993, December). (Contact Joel T. Griffith, Department of Social Services, 275 East Main Street 6W, Frankfort, KY 40621. Fax: 502-564-3096; phone: 502-564-2136.)

Humphries, D. (1981). Serious crime, news coverage, and ideology: A content analysis of crime coverage in a metropolitan paper. *Crime and Delinquency, 27*(2), 191-205.

Hyman, H. (1954). *Interviewing in social research.* Chicago: University of Chicago.

Jarrett, R. (1994). Living poor: Family life among single parent, African-American women. *Social Problems, 41*(1), 30-49.

Jones, A. (1994). *Next time she'll be dead: Battering and how to stop it.* Boston: Beacon.

Joy, M. (1996). Looking for God in all the wrong places: Feminists seeking the radical questions in religion. In D. Bell & R. Klein (Eds.), *Radically speaking: Feminism reclaimed* (pp. 111-125). North Melbourne, Australia: Spinifex.

Kalmuss, D., & Straus, M. (1982). Wife's marital dependency and wife abuse. *Journal of Marriage and Family, 44,* 277-286.

Karp, D., Yoels, W. C., & Stone, G. P. (1989). *Being urban: A sociology of city life* (2nd ed.). New York: Praeger.

Kelly, D. (Ed.). (1990). *Criminal behavior* (2nd ed.). New York: St. Martin's.

Kelly, L. (1996a). Tensions and possibilities: Enhancing informal responses to domestic violence. In J. Edleson & Z. Eisikovits (Eds.), *Future interventions with battered women and their families* (pp. 67-86). Thousand Oaks, CA: Sage.

Kelly, L. (1996b). When does the speaking profit us? In M. Hester, L. Kelly, & J. Radford (Eds.), *Women, violence and male power: Feminist activism, research and practice* (pp. 34-49). Philadelphia: Open University Press.

Kessler-Harris, A. (1982). *Out to work: A history of wage-earning women in the United States.* Oxford, UK: Oxford University Press.

Koven, S., & Michel, S. (Eds.). (1993). *Mothers of a new world: Maternalist politics and the origins of welfare states.* New York: Routledge.

Kowalski, G. S., & Duffield, D. (1990). The impact of the rural population component on homicide rates in the United States: A county-level analysis. *Rural Sociology, 55,* 76-90.

Kuczynski, K. (1981). New tensions in rural families. *Human Services in the Rural Environment, 6*(3), 54-56.

Kurz, D. (1987). Responses to battered women: Resistance to medicalization. *Social Problems, 34,* 501-513.

Kurz, D. (1993). Social science perspectives on wife abuse: Current debates and future directions. In P. Bart & E. G. Moran (Eds.), *Violence against women: The bloody footprints* (pp. 252-269). Newbury Park, CA: Sage.

Landis, J. R., Sullivan, D., & Sheley, J. (1973). Feminist attitudes as related to sex of the interviewer. *Pacific Sociological Review, 16,* 305-314.

Langan, P., & Innes, C. (1986). *Preventing domestic violence against wives.* Washington, DC: U.S. Department of Justice, Bureau of Justice Statistics.

Larrea Gayarre, J. (1994). Liberation theology's challenge to neoliberal economic theory. *Social Justice, 21*(4), 34-45.

Laub, J. H. (1983). Patterns of offending in urban and rural areas. *Journal of Criminal Justice, 11*(2), 129-142.

Lemert, E. M. (1972). *Human deviance, social problems, and social control* (2nd ed.). Englewood Cliffs, NJ: Prentice Hall.

Lerman, L. G. (1992). The decontexualization of domestic violence. *Journal of Criminal Law and Criminology, 83*(1), 217-240.

Levinger, G. (1966). Sources of marital dissatisfaction among applicants for divorce. *American Journal of Orthopsychiatry, 36,* 803-806.

Littlejohn, J. (1964). *Westrigg.* London: Routledge & Kegan Paul.

Lockley, F. (1971). *Conversations with pioneer women.* Eugene, OR: Rainy Day Press.

Lucal, B. (1995). The problem with battered husbands. *Deviant Behavior, 16*(2), 95-112.

Lyerly, R. R., & Skipper, J. K. (1981). Differential rates of rural-urban delinquency. *Criminology, 19,* 385-399.

Lystad, M. H. (1975). Violence at home: A review of literature. *American Journal of Orthopsychiatry, 45,* 328-345.

MacKinnon, C. (1979). *The sexual harassment of working women: A case of sex discrimination.* New Haven, CT: Yale University Press.

MacKinnon, C. (1987). Feminism, Marxism, method and the state: Toward a feminist jurisprudence. In S. Harding (Ed.), *Feminism and methodology* (pp. 135-156). Indianapolis: Indiana University Press.

Maduro, O. (1982). *Religion and social conflicts*. New York: Orbis.

Mahoney, M. R. (1991). Legal images of battered women: Redefining the issue of separation. *90 Michigan Law Review, 1,* 43-49.

Malinowski, B. (1926). *Crime and custom in savage society*. London: Kegan Paul.

Malinowski, B. (1944). *A scientific theory of culture and other essays*. New York: Oxford University Press.

Malinowski, B. (1948). *Magic, science and religion*. Boston: Beacon.

Maran, R. (1996). After the Beijing Women's Conference: What will be done? *Social Justice, 23*(1-2), 352-367.

Marenin, O., & Copus, G. (1991). Policing rural Alaska: The Village Public Safety Officer (VPSO) program. *American Journal of Police, 10*(4), 1-26.

Martin, D. (1976). *Battered wives*. San Francisco: Glide Publications.

Marx, K., & Engels, F. (1970). Manifesto of the Communist Party. In K. Marx & F. Engels, *Selected works* (pp. 35-63). Moscow: Progress Publishers.

Marzuk P. M., Tardiff, K., & Hirsch, C. S. (1992). The epidemiology of murder-suicide. *Journal of the American Medical Association, 267,* 3179-3183.

Maxfield, M. G. (1989). Circumstances in supplementary homicide reports: Variety and validity. *Criminology, 27,* 671-695.

Mazur, A. G., & McBride-Stetson, D. (1995). Conclusion: The case for state feminism. In A. G. Mazur & D. McBride-Stetson (Eds.), *Comparative state feminism* (pp. 272-291). London: Sage.

McBride-Stetson, D., & Mazur, A. G. (1995). Introduction. In A. G. Mazur & D. McBride-Stetson (Eds.), *Comparative state feminism*. London: Sage.

McCullough, L. (1993). Study reveals that few counselor education programs address religious and spiritual issues. *Guidepost, 35*(9), 28.

McDowell, J. (1992, February 17). Are women better cops? *Time,* pp. 70-72.

McFarland, C. K. (1984). *Bethenia Owens-Adair. Oregon pioneer, physician, feminist and reformer*. Unpublished master's thesis, University of Oregon, Eugene.

McKintosh, M. (1978). The state and the oppression of women. In A. Kuhn & A. M. Wolpe (Eds.), *Feminism and materialism: Women and modes of production* (pp. 254-289). London: Routledge & Kegan Paul.

McLeer, S., & Anwar, R. (1989). A study of battered women presenting in an emergency department. *American Journal of Public Health, 79,* 65-66.

McNelly, R. L., & Mann, C. R. (1990). Domestic violence is a human issue. *Journal of Interpersonal Violence, 5,* 129-132.

McNelly, R. L., & Robinson-Simpson, G. (1987). The truth about domestic violence: A falsely framed issue. *Social Work, 32,* 485-490.

McRobbie, A. (1978). Working class girls and the culture of femininity. In Women's Studies Group, Centre for Contemporary Cultural Studies (Eds.), *Women take issue* (pp. 96-108). London: Hutchinson.

Mead, M. (1935). *Sex and temperament in three primitive societies*. New York: William Morrow.

Menard, A. (1997, January). *Welfare reform: Implications for battered women and their children*. Paper presented at the annual meeting of the Florida Coalition Against Domestic Violence, Melbourne, FL.

Mercy, J. A., & Saltzman, L. (1989). Fatal violence among spouses in the United States, 1976-1985. *American Journal of Public Health, 79,* 595-599.

Merton, R. (1938). Social structure and anomie. *American Sociological Review, 3,* 672-682.

Merton, R. (1972). Insiders and outsiders: A chapter in the sociology of knowledge. *American Journal of Sociology, 78*(1), 9-47.

Michalowski, R. (1985). *Order, law and crime: An introduction to criminology.* New York: Random House.

Michalowski, R. (1996). Ethnography and anxiety: Field work and reflexivity in the vortex of U.S.-Cuban relations. *Qualitative Sociology, 19*(1), 59-82.

Miliband, R. (1969). *The state in capitalist society.* London: Weidenfeld & Nicolson.

Miller, P. (1994). *Kentucky politics and government.* Lincoln: University of Nebraska Press.

Millett, K. (1977). *Sexual politics.* London: Virago.

Morgan, R. (1996). Light bulbs, radishes, and the politics of the 21st century. In D. Bell & R. Klein (Eds.), *Radically speaking: Feminism reclaimed* (pp. 5-8). North Melbourne, Australia: Spinifex.

Moynihan, R. B. (1983). *Rebel for rights: Abigail Scott Duniway.* New Haven, CT: Yale University Press.

Murray, C. (1984). *Losing ground: American social policy, 1950-1980.* New York: Basic Books.

Myers, M. A., & Talarico, S. M. (1986). Urban justice, rural injustice? Urbanization and its effect on sentencing. *Criminology, 24*(2), 367-391.

National Center for Health Statistics. (1990). *Vital statistics of the United States.* Washington, DC: Government Printing Office.

Navin, S., Stockum, R., & Campbell-Ruggaard, J. (1993). Battered women in rural America. *Journal of Humanistic Education and Development, 32,* 9-16.

O'Brien, J. (1971). Violence in divorce-prone families. *Journal of Marriage and the Family, 33,* 692-698.

Oakley, A. (1980). *Women confined: Towards a sociology of childbirth.* Oxford, UK: Martin Robertson.

Oakley, A. (1981). Interviewing women: A contradiction in terms. In H. Roberts (Ed.), *Doing feminist research* (pp. 30-61). London: Routledge & Kegan Paul.

Okun, L. (1986). *Women abuse: Facts replacing myths.* Albany: State University of New York Press.

Olsen, C. S. (1988). Blue Ridge blues: The problems and strengths of rural women. *Affilia, 3*(1), 5-17.

Outshoorn, J. (1992). *Femocrats in the Netherlands: Mission or career?* Paper presented at the European Consortium for Political Research Joint Sessions of Workshops, Limerick, Eire.

Pahl, J. (Ed.). (1985). *Private violence and public policy: The needs of battered women and the responses of the public services.* London: Routledge & Kegan Paul.

Pahl, R. E. (1965). *Urbs in rure.* London: London School of Economics and Political Science, Geographical Papers No. 2.

Pahl, R. E. (1966). The rural-urban continuum. *Sociologia Ruralis, 6,* 299-329.

Palmer, S., & Humphrey, J. A. (1980). Offender-victim relationships in criminal homicide followed by offender's suicide, North Carolina, 1972-1977. *Suicide and Life-Threatening Behavior, 10*(2), 106-118.

Park, R. E. (1971). *The immigrant press and its control: The acculturation of immigrant groups into American society.* Montclair, NJ: Patterson Smith. (Original work published 1922)

Parnas, R. (1967). The police response of the domestic disturbance. *Wisconsin Law Review, 2,* 914-916.

Peterson, K. (1983, November 25). Wife abuse: The silent crime, the silent church. *Christianity Today, 27*(18), 22-26.

Piliavin, I., & Briar, S. (1964). Police encounters with juveniles. *American Journal of Sociology, 70*(September), 206-214.

Pleck, E. (1987). *Domestic tyranny.* New York: Oxford University Press.

Police Foundation. (1976). *Domestic violence and the police response: Studies in Detroit and Kansas City.* Washington, DC: Wilt Bunnoy.

Pope, C. E. (1976). The influence of social and legal factors on sentencing dispositions: A preliminary analysis of offender based transaction statistics. *Journal of Criminal Justice, 4,* 203-221.

Potter, G. W., & Gaines, L. K. (1992). Country comfort: Vice and corruption in rural settings. *Journal of Contemporary Criminal Justice, 8*(1), 36-61.

Poulantzas, N. (1973). The problem of the capitalist state. In J. Urry & J. Wakeford (Eds.), *Power in Britain.* London: Heinemann.

Prejean, H. (1993). *Dead man walking.* New York: Random House.

Punch, M. (1979). *Policing the inner city: A study of Amsterdam's Warmoesstraat.* London: Macmillan.

Quadangno, J., & Fobes, C. (1995). The welfare state and the cultural reproduction of gender. *Social Problems, 42*(2), 171-190.

Radcliffe-Brown, A. R. (1948). *A natural science of society.* New York: Free Press.

Radford, J. (1987). Policing male violence—Policing women. In J. Hanmer & M. Maynard (Eds.), *Women, violence and social control* (pp. 30-45). Atlantic Heights, NJ: Humanities Press.

Ragsdale, K. H. (1995). The role of religious institutions in responding to the domestic violence crisis. *58 Albany Law Review,* 1149.

Redfield, R. (1947). The folk society. *American Journal of Sociology, 52,* 293-308.

Reid, J. N., & Whitehead, E. (1982). *Federal funds in nonmetro areas: Patterns and trends* (SRS-678). Washington, DC: U.S. Department of Agriculture, Economic Research Service.

Renzetti, C. (1992). *Violent betrayal.* New York: Russell Sage.

Rhode, D. (1994). Feminism and the state. *Harvard Law Review, 107,* 1181-1208.

Rich, A. (1980). Compulsory heterosexuality and lesbian existence. *Signs: Journal of Women in Culture and Society, 5,* 631-660.

Riessman, C. (1987). When gender is not enough: Women interviewing women. *Gender and Society, 1,* 172-207.

Roberts, M. J. D. (1995). Feminism and the state in later Victorian England. *The Historical Journal, 38*(1), 85-110.

Roberts, P. (1994). Child support enforcement and assurance: One part of an anti-poverty strategy for women. *Social Justice, 21*(1), 76-79.

Rosen, R. (1982). *The lost sisterhood.* Baltimore, MD: Johns Hopkins University Press.

Rosenbaum, M. (1990). The role of depression in couples involved in murder-suicide and homicide. *American Journal of Psychiatry, 147,* 1036-1039.

Rural Justice Center. (1991). *Not in my county: Rural courts and victims of domestic violence.* Montpelier, VT: Author.

Rural Justice Center. (1993). *Domestic violence: A curriculum for rural courts.* Montpelier, VT: Rural Justice Center/National Council of Juvenile and Family Court Judges.

Russell, D. E. H. (1981). *Sexual exploitation: Rape, child abuse and sexual harassment.* Beverly Hills, CA: Sage.

Russell, D. E. H. (1990). *Rape in marriage.* Bloomington: Indiana University Press.

Ryan, M. (1982). The explosion of family history. *Reviews in American History, 10*(4), 181-195.

Sampson, R. J. (1986). The effects of urbanization and neighborhood characteristics on criminal victimization. In R. M. Figlio, S. Hakim, & G. F. Rengert (Eds.), *Metropolitan crime patterns* (pp. 3-25). Monsey, NY: Willow Tree.

Sawer, M. (1990). *Sisters in suits: Women and public policy in Australia.* Sydney: Allen and Unwin.

Sawer, M. (1993). Reclaiming social liberalism: The women's movement and the state. *Journal of Australian Studies, 37,* 1-21.

Schecter, S. (1996). The battered women's movement in the United States: New directions for institutional reform. In J. Edleson & Z. Eisikovits (Eds.), *Future interventions with battered women and their families* (pp. 53-66). Thousand Oaks, CA: Sage.

Schneider, E. (1990). The dialectic of rights and politics: Perspectives from the women's movement. In L. Gordon (Ed.), *Women, the state and welfare* (pp. 226-249). Madison: University of Wisconsin Press.

Schuller, R. A. (1994). Applications of battered woman syndrome evidence in the courtroom. In M. Costanzo & S. Oskamp (Eds.), *Violence and the law* (pp. 113-134). Thousand Oaks, CA: Sage.

Schulman, M. A. (1979). *A survey of spousal violence against women in Kentucky* (U.S. Department of Justice). Washington, DC: Government Printing Office.

Segal, L. (1987). *Is the future female? Troubled thoughts on contemporary feminism.* London: Virago.

Seroka, J. (1986). (Ed.). *Rural public administration.* New York: Greenwood.

Sherman, L. (1992). *Policing domestic violence: Experiments and dilemmas.* New York: Free Press.

Sherman, L. W., & Berk, R. A. (1984a). *The Minneapolis domestic violence experiment.* Washington, DC: Police Foundation Reports 1.

Sherman, L. W., & Berk, R. A. (1984b). The specific deterrent effects of arrest for domestic assaults. *American Sociological Review, 49,* 261-272.

Siim, B. (1991). Welfare state, gender politics, and equality policies: Women's citizenship in the Scandinavian welfare states. In E. Meehan & S. S. Huijsen (Eds.), *Equality, politics, and gender* (pp. 175-193). London: Sage.

Simmel, G. (1950). The metropolis and mental life. In *The sociology of George Simmel* (K. Wolff, ed.) (pp. 409-424). Glencoe, IL: Free Press.

Sitomer, C. J. (1985, May 28). Rural justice affects many, but may serve few. *Christian Science Monitor,* p. 23.

Smart, C. (1989). *Feminism and the power of law.* London: Routledge & Kegan Paul.

Smart, C., & Smart, B. (Eds.). (1978). *Women, sexuality and social control.* London: Routledge & Kegan Paul.

Smith, B. L. (1980). Criminal victimization in rural areas. In B. R. Price & P. J. Baunach (Eds.), *Criminal justice research: New models and findings.* Beverly Hills, CA: Sage.

Smith, D. (1987). *The everyday world as problematic: A feminist sociology.* Boston: Northeastern University Press.

Smith, D. (1990). *Tests, facts and femininity, exploring the relations of ruling.* New York: Routledge.

Smith, D. (1993). High noon in textland: A critique of Clough. *The Sociological Quarterly, 34*(1), 183-192.

Smith, M. D. (1990). Patriarchal ideology and wife beating: A test of a feminist hypothesis. *Violence and Victims, 5*(4), 257-273.

Sorokin, P., & Zimmerman, C. C. (1929). *Principles of rural-urban sociology.* New York: Henry Holt.

Spender, D. (1985). *Man made language* (2nd ed.). London: Routledge & Kegan Paul.

Spitzer, S. (1975). Toward a Marxian theory of deviance. *Social Problems, 22,* 638-651.

Stacey, W., & Shupe, A. (1983). *The family secret.* Boston: Beacon.

Stanko, E. A. (1982). Would you believe this woman? In N. H. Rafter & E. A. Stanko (Eds.), *Judge, lawyer, victim, thief: Women, gender roles and criminal justice.* Boston: Northeastern University Press.

Stanko, E. A. (1989). Missing the mark? Policing battering. In J. Hanmer, J. Radford, & E. Stanko (Eds.), *Women, policing, and male violence: International perspectives* (pp. 46-69). New York: Routledge.

Stanko, E. A. (1994). Challenging the problem of men's individual violence. In T. Newburn & E. A. Stanko (Eds.), *Just boys doing business? Men, masculinities and crime* (pp. 32-45). London: Routledge & Kegan Paul.

Stanko, E. A. (1995). Women, crime and fear. *Annals of the American Academy of Political and Social Science, 539*(May), 46-58.

Stark, E. (1993a). Mandatory arrest of batterers: A reply to its critics. *American Behavioral Scientist, 36*(5), 651-680.

Stark, E. (1993b). The myth of black violence. *Social Work, 38*, 485-490.

Stark, E. (1994, September). Should police officers be required to arrest abusive husbands? *Health,* p. 32.

Stark, E., & Flitcraft, A. (1996). *Women at risk: Domestic violence and women's health.* London: Sage.

Stark, E., Flitcraft, A., & Frazier, W. (1979). Medicine and patriarchal violence: The construction of a "private" event. *International Journal of Health Services, 9,* 461-493.

Steinmetz, S. (1977). *The cycle of violence: Assertive, aggressive and abusive family interaction.* New York: Praeger.

Steinmetz, S. (1977-1978). The battered husband syndrome. *Victimology, 2,* 499-509.

Stephens, R. (1990, January/February). Merit: A better way to select our judges. *The Kentucky Journal,* p. 3.

Stewart, H. R., & Payne, J. S. (1991). *Women in Kentucky: A documented profile* (Report). Frankfort, KY: Cabinet for Workforce Development.

Stone, L. (1977). *The family, sex and marriage in England 1500-1800.* London: Penguin.

Straus, M. (1973). A general systems theory approach to a theory of violence between family members. *Social Science Information, 12,* 105-125.

Straus, M. (1976). Sexual inequality, cultural norms and wife-beating. *Victimology, 1,* 54-76.

Straus, M. (1979). Measuring intrafamily conflict and violence: The Conflict Tactics (CT) Scales. *Journal of Marriage and the Family, 41,* 75-88.

Straus, M. (1980a). The marriage license as a hitting license: Evidence from popular culture, law and social science. In M. Straus & G. Hotaling (Eds.), *The social causes of husband-wife violence* (pp. 39-50). Minneapolis: University of Minnesota Press.

Straus, M. (1980b). A sociological perspective on the prevention of wife beating. In M. Straus & G. Hotaling (Eds.), *The social causes of husband-wife violence* (pp. 211-234). Minneapolis: University of Minnesota Press.

Straus, M. (1980c). Victims and aggressors in marital violence. *American Behavioral Scientist, 23,* 681-704.

Straus, M., & Gelles, R. (1990). Societal change and change in family violence from 1975 to 1985 as revealed by two national surveys. In D. Kelly (Ed.), *Criminal behavior* (2nd ed., pp. 114-136). New York: St. Martin's.

Straus, M., & Gelles, R. (1995). *Physical violence in American families: Risk factors and adaptations to violence in 8,145 families.* New Brunswick, NJ: Transaction Books.

Straus, M., Gelles, R. J., & Steinmetz, S. (1980). *Behind closed doors.* Garden City, NY: Doubleday.

Sugg, N. K., & Inui, T. (1992). Primary care physicians' response to domestic violence: Opening Pandora's box. *Journal of the American Medical Association, 267,* 3157-3160.

Taves, A. (Ed.). (1989). *Religion and domestic violence in early New England: The memoirs of Abigail Abbott Bailey.* Bloomington: Indiana University Press.

Taylor, L., Walton, P., & Young, J. (1973). *The new criminology.* London: Routledge & Kegan Paul.

Taylor, L., Walton, P., & Young, J. (Eds.). (1975). *Critical criminology.* London: Routledge & Kegan Paul.

Teachman, J. (1991). Contributions to children by divorced fathers. *Social Problems, 38,* 358-371.

Thompson, E. P. (1968). *The making of the English working class.* London: Pelican.

Thompson, E. P. (1975). *Whigs and hunters.* Harmondsworth, UK: Penguin.

Tice, K. (1990). A case study of battered women's shelters in Appalachia. *Affilia, 5*(3), 83-100.

Tifft, L. L. (1993). *Battering of women: The failure of intervention and the case for prevention.* Boulder, CO: Westview.

Tolbert, C. M., & Lyson, T. A. (1992). Earnings inequality in the nonmetropolitan United States: 1967-1990. *Rural Sociology, 57,* 494-511.

Tong, R. (1984). *Women, sex, and the law.* Totowa, NJ: Rowman & Allenheld.

Tonnies, F. (1940). *Fundamental principles of sociology (Gemeinschaft and Gesellschaft).* New York: American Book.

U.S. National Conference of Catholic Bishops Committee on Women in Society and in the Church and the Committee on Marriage and Family Life. (1992). *Origins, 22,* 21 (November 5, 1992) under the title "When I call for help: Domestic violence against women."

Vanfossen, B. E. (1979). Intersexual violence in Monroe County, New York. *Victimology, 4,* 299-305.

Van Schaik, E. (1988). The social context of "nerves" in Eastern Kentucky. In S. Emley Keefe (Ed.), *Appalachian mental health* (pp. 81-100). Lexington: University of Kentucky Press.

Vidich, A., & Bensman, J. (1968). *Small town in mass society.* Princeton, NJ: Princeton University Press.

Vidich, A., & Lyman, S. (1994). Qualitative methods: Their history in sociology and anthropology. In N. Denzin & Y. Lincoln (Eds.), *Handbook of qualitative research* (pp. 23-59). Thousand Oaks, CA: Sage.

Walby, S. (1990). *Theorizing patriarchy.* Oxford, UK: Basil Blackwell.

Walby, S. (1992). Post-post-modernism? Theorizing social complexity. In M. Barrett & A. Phillips (Eds.), *Destabilizing theory: Contemporary feminist debates* (pp. 31-52). Palo Alto, CA: Stanford University Press.

Walker, L. (1984). *The battered woman syndrome.* New York: Springer.

Waller, A. L. (1988). *Feud: Hatfields, McCoys, and social change in Appalachia, 1860-1900.* Chapel Hill: University of North Carolina Press.

Warren, C. (1988). *Gender issues in field research.* Newbury Park, CA: Sage.

Warshaw, C. (1989). Limitations of the medical model in the care of battered women. *Gender and Society, 3,* 506-517.

Weber, M. (1948). *From Max Weber: Essays in sociology* (H. H. Gerth & C. Wright Mills, Eds.). London: Routledge & Kegan Paul.

Websdale, N. (1991). *I spy with my little eye: A history of the policing of class and gender relations in Eugene, Oregon.* Unpublished doctoral thesis, University of London.

Websdale, N. (1992). Female suffrage, male violence and law enforcement. *Social Justice, 19*(3), 82-106.

Websdale, N. (1995a). An ethnographic assessment of the policing of domestic violence in rural Eastern Kentucky. *Social Justice, 22*(1), 82-102.

Websdale, N. (1995b). Police history and the question of gender: The case of Eugene, Oregon in the post World War Two period. *Policing and Society, 5*, 313-338.

Websdale, N. (1995c). Rural woman abuse: The voices of Kentucky women. *Violence Against Women, 1*, 309-339.

Websdale, N. (1996). Predators: The social construction of "stranger-danger" in Washington state as a form of patriarchal ideology. *Women and Criminal Justice, 7*(2), 43-68.

Websdale, N., & Alvarez, A. (1997). Forensic journalism as patriarchal ideology: The media construction of domestic homicide-suicide events. In D. Hale & F. Bailey (Eds.), *Popular culture, crime and justice*. Belmont, CA: Wadsworth.

Websdale, N., & Chesney-Lind, M. (in press). Doing violence to women. In L. Bowker (Ed.), *Masculinities and violence*. Thousand Oaks, CA: Sage.

Websdale, N., & Johnson, B. (1993). *Final evaluation, Homeless Job Training Initiative: Kentucky Domestic Violence Association*. Report submitted to the U.S. Department of Labor.

Websdale, N., & Johnson, B. (1994). *Final evaluation, Homeless Job Training Initiative: Kentucky Domestic Violence Association*. Report submitted to the U.S. Department of Labor.

Websdale, N., & Johnson, B. (1995, August). *A comparison of the forms and levels of domestic violence in urban and rural areas of Kentucky*. Paper presented at the annual conference of the Society for the Study of Social Problems, Washington, D.C.

Websdale, N., & Johnson, B. (1997a). The policing of domestic violence in rural and urban areas: The voices of battered women in Kentucky. *Policing and Society, 6,* 297-317.

Websdale, N., & Johnson, B. (1997b). Reducing woman battering: The role of structural approaches. *Social Justice, 24*(1), 54-81.

Weisheit, R., Falcone, D., & Wells, E. (1994a). Community policing in small town and rural America. *Crime and Delinquency, 40,* 549-567.

Weisheit, R., Falcone, D., & Wells, E. (1994b). Crime and policing an rural and small town America: An overview of the issues. Draft of National Institute of Justice "Issues and Practice" Monograph.

Weisheit, R., Falcone, D., & Wells, E. (1994c). *Rural crime and rural policing.* Washington, DC: National Institute of Justice: Research in Action, October 1994.

Weisheit, R., Falcone, D., & Wells, E. (1996). *Crime and policing in rural and small-town America*. Prospect Heights, IL: Waveland.

Weller, J. E. (1966). *Yesterday's people: Life in contemporary Appalachia*. Lexington: University of Kentucky Press.

West, C., & Zimmerman, D. H. (1983). Small insults: A study of interruptions in cross-sex conversations between unacquainted persons. In B. Thorne, C. Kramarae, & N. Henley (Eds.), *Language, gender and society* (pp. 86-111). Rowley, MA: Newbury House.

West, D. (1967). *Murder followed by suicide*. Cambridge, MA: Harvard University Press.

Whipple, V. (1987). Counseling battered women from fundamentalist churches. *Journal of Marital and Family Therapy, 13,* 251-258.

Whitehead, T. L., & Conaway, M. E. (1986). In T. L. Whitehead & M. E. Conaway (Eds.), *Self, sex and gender in cross-cultural fieldwork* (pp. 1-14). Urbana: University of Illinois Press.

Whyte, W. F. (1943). *Street corner society: The social structure of an Italian slum.* Chicago: University of Chicago Press.

Williams, C., & Heikes, E. J. (1993). The importance of researcher's gender in the in-depth interview: Evidence from two case studies of male nurses. *Gender and Society, 7,* 280-291.

Williams, W. M. (1956). *The sociology of an English village.* London: Routledge & Kegan Paul.

Willits, F. K., Bealer, R. C., & Timbers, V. (1990). Popular images of rurality: Data from a Pennsylvania survey. *Rural Sociology, 55,* 559-578.

Wilson, E. (1983). *What is to be done about violence against women?* Harmondsworth, UK: Penguin.

Wilson, M., & Daly, M. (1992). Who kills whom in spouse killings? On the exceptional sex ratio of spousal homicides in the United States. *Criminology, 30,* 189-215.

Wirth, L. (1938). Urbanism as a way of life. *American Journal of Sociology,* pp. 1-24.

Wirth, L. (1956). *The ghetto.* Chicago: University of Chicago Press. (Original work published 1928)

Wolfgang, M. E. (1958). An analysis of homicide-suicide. *Journal of Clinical and Experimental Psychopathology and Quarterly Review of Psychiatry and Neurology, 19,* 208-218.

Wright, J. D., Rossi, P., & Daly, K. (1983). *Under the gun: Weapons, crime and violence.* New York: Aldine.

Wu, C. C. (1926). *Chinese immigration in the Pacific area.* Unpublished doctoral dissertation, University of Chicago.

Yllo, K., & Bograd, M. (Eds.). (1988). *Feminist perspectives on wife abuse.* Newbury Park, CA: Sage.

Yoder, D. R. (1980). Spouse assault: A community approach. *Human Services in the Rural Environment, 5*(2), 25-28.

Zorza, J. (1992). The criminal law of misdemeanor domestic violence, 1970-1990. *The Journal of Criminal Law & Criminology, 83*(1), 46-72.

Index

About the Author

Neil Websdale is Associate Professor in the Department of Criminal Justice at Northern Arizona University. He has published work on violence against women, the policing of class and gender relations, and the discursive representation/construction of intimate partner violence. He has presented his research findings to the Kentucky Legislative Task Force on Domestic Violence, and is currently working on a study of domestic fatalities for the Florida  Governor's Task Force on Domestic and Sexual Violence. He is also engaged in writing a book based on case studies of intimate partner homicide, titled *Death by Intimacy*. In addition, he is coediting two anthologies: one with Jeff Ferrell, tentatively titled *Cultural Constructions of Crime and Deviance*, and the other with Byron Johnson, concerning the implementation of Full Faith and Credit under the Violence Against Women Act.

CPSIA information can be obtained at www.ICGtesting.com
Printed in the USA
LVOW12s0231050814

397570LV00001B/104/P